FM 22

Narration in Nineteenth-Century French Short Fiction:
Prosper Mérimée to Marcel Schwob

Copyright © Peter Cogman 2002

The right of Peter Cogman to be identified as the author of this work has been asserted by him in accordance with the Copyright, Designs and Patents Act 1988.

Published by Manchester University Press
Oxford Road, Manchester M13 9NR, UK
and Room 400, 175 Fifth Avenue, New York, NY 10010, USA
www.manchesteruniversitypress.co.uk

Distributed exclusively in the USA by
Palgrave, 175 Fifth Avenue, New York NY 10010, USA

Distributed exclusively in Canada by
UBC Press, University of British Columbia, 2029 West Mall, Vancouver, BC, Canada V6T 1Z2

British Library Cataloguing-in-Publication Data
A catalogue record for this book is available from the British Library

Library of Congress Cataloging-in-Publication Data
A catalog record for this book is available from the Library of Congress

ISBN 978 0 7190 8592 5 *paperback*

First published 2002 by Durham Modern Languages Series

This edition first published 2011 by Manchester University Press

Printed by Lightning Source

Narration in Nineteenth-Century French Short Fiction:

Prosper Mérimée to Marcel Schwob

Peter Cogman

Durham Modern Languages Series

University of Durham 2002

Contents

Acknowledgements		vi
Preface		vii
Introduction. Getting to Grips with Short Fiction: Maupassant, 'Le Garde'; the periodical context and the difficulty of definition; storytelling and the possibility of analysis		1
1.	Tellers and Listeners: 'making the frame part of the story' Mérimée, 'Carmen'; Maupassant, 'Les Bécasses'; Villiers, 'Sombre récit, conteur plus sombre'	21
2.	Hesitant Tellers, Reluctant Listeners Maupassant, 'Un cas de divorce'; Barbey, 'Le Rideau cramoisi'	51
3.	Singular Things: prompting and focusing Mérimée, 'Le Vase étrusque', 'La Partie de trictrac'; Barbey, 'La Vengeance d'une femme'	75
4.	Structure, Patterning and Point Maupassant, 'Marroca', 'Promenade'; Villiers, 'Les Brigands', 'A s'y méprendre'; Schwob, 'Arachné'; Mérimée, 'Djoûmane'	97
5.	Playing with the Kaleidoscope: repetition and patterning Gautier, 'Le Roi Candaule', 'Avatar', 'Jettatura'	121
6.	Closed Worlds Maupassant, 'Le Signe'; Balzac, 'La Grande Bretèche'; Barbey, 'A un dîner d'athées'	147
Conclusion Villiers, 'Le Convive des dernières fêtes'		173
Glossary		185
Bibliography		189
Index of Main Stories Discussed		201

Acknowledgements

I should particularly like to thank Michael Kelly, Peter Whyte, and the Reader of the Durham Modern Language Series for their advice and encouragement. I am grateful to the editors and publishers of the following journals for permission to rework material already published: *Bulletin de la Société Théophile Gautier* for a section of Chapter 5 which appeared as 'Le Triangle de la mort' (no. 18 (1996), 239-54); *Essays in French Literature* for a section of Chapter 4 (*'Nudité de l'intrigue* or *intrigue de nus'* (30 (1993), 16-29); Oxford University Press and *French Studies* for a section of Chapter 3 ('Criminal Conversation', 51 (1997), 30-42); Oxford University Press and *Forum for Modern Language Studies* for a section of Chapter 2 ('Not the Whole Truth', 30 (1994), 124-34); the MHRA and *Modern Language Review* for a section of Chapter 1 ('Subversion of the Reader', 83 (1988), 30-39); *Neophilologus* for a section of Chapter 2 ('Maupassant's Inhibited Narrators', 81 (1997), 35-47); *Nineteenth-Century French Studies* for sections of Chapter 3 and Conclusion ('Masks and Madness', 21 (1992-1993), 102-13, and 'Cheating at narrating', 26 (1997-1998), 80-90); and *Nottingham French Studies* for a section of Chapter 1 ('The Narrators of Mérimée's *Carmen*', 27 (1988), 1-12). I am indebted to Janet Starkey, of Durham Modern Languages Series, for her editorial assistance. I am grateful to the University of Southampton for financial assistance towards publication. My thanks are also owed to Barbara, Genevieve, David and Susannah for their patience at hearing tales retold.

Preface

The short fiction that flourished in nineteenth-century France has attracted relatively little critical attention compared with its big brother the novel. This study focuses on some key stories by major authors of *contes* and *nouvelles* from the late 1820s to the 1890s, taking as a starting-point aspects of narrative technique as a way of exploring not just characteristic strategies of short fiction, but also the ends to which they were put: recurrent themes, and the vision of mankind. My aim is to indicate what questions one can usefully ask when confronted with short fiction. The choice of stories has not been determined by any attempt at a comprehensive historical survey, which remains to be written, though works by Albert J. George, David Bryant, and Florence Goyet have filled in part of the picture.[1] Nor am I attempting to give an exhaustive typology of narrative techniques. Rather I have chosen authors who use shorter fiction and its necessary constraints to do what cannot be done elsewhere as effectively, or who exploit techniques recurrent in *conte* and *nouvelle*. I have moreover concentrated on authors and texts that are readily accessible.[2] Mérimée and Maupassant remain the outstanding writers of short fiction in the period; with *Contes cruels* and *Les Diaboliques* Villiers de l'Isle-Adam and Barbey d'Aurevilly provide the two most provocative single collections. They consequently figure more prominently than writers who turned to short

1. Albert J. George, *Short Fiction in France 1800-1850* (New York: Syracuse University Press, 1964); David Bryant, *Short Fiction and the Press in France 1829-1841* (Lewiston: Mellon, 1995); Florence Goyet, *La Nouvelle 1870-1925: histoire d'un genre à son apogée* (Paris: Presses Universitaires de France, 1993).
2. René Godenne has brought out the diversity of authors seldom or never reprinted ('Un premier inventaire de la nouvelle française au xixe siècle', in Johnnie Gratton and Jean-Philippe Imbert (eds), *La Nouvelle hier et aujourd'hui* (Paris: L'Harmattan, 1997), 323-73. See notably, in the same volume, Richard Hobbs, 'L'Esthétique excentrique des premiers contes de Champfleury', 41-51.

fiction on occasion, but whose major achievement lies elsewhere: Balzac, for whom the short story was a stage in his career, but who found it difficult to sacrifice to the constraints on length and subject imposed by reviews; Flaubert, who wrote unpublished stories before his major novels, then returned to the genre largely by chance at the end of his career, with the *Trois contes* which stand apart from the short fiction of the period; or Stendhal, who was more at ease the more leisurely the form he used. Edgar Allan Poe features frequently as, like E.T.A. Hoffmann, a key presence in nineteenth-century French short fiction, and an honorary Frenchman through Baudelaire's translations and essays. The Introduction and Chapter 1 establish my approach and the terms used. Each chapter looks in some detail at three or four stories, referring briefly to other tales for illustration. As the reader may not be familiar with all of these, I have included summaries: the nineteenth-century tale, destined originally for periodical publication and rapid consumption, permits a summary of 'what happened' — even though this will often be a simplification or distortion. And the underlying point that should emerge from this study is that the interest of a tale lies in the telling, not the events.

A note on terminology

French writers in the nineteenth century, apart from Baudelaire's rather misleading paraphrase of some remarks of Poe, and Marcel Schwob's attempt to define his own practice, theorised little about short fiction. Above all they tended not to distinguish between *conte* and *nouvelle*, even though these terms had generally distinct uses before then. Mérimée uses both terms about 'La Vénus d'Ille' in a single letter,[3] and again about 'Federigo' in his introduction to that tale. There have been subsequent attempts to distinguish the two, but these have been bedevilled by mixing differently based criteria. Criteria based on form see the *conte* as imitating or representing an oral performance, the

3. *Correspondance générale*, edited by Maurice Parturier, 17 vols (Paris: Divan, 1942–1947 (Vols I–VI); Toulouse: Privat, 1953–1964 (Vols VII–XVII)), V, 200.

nouvelle as a self-consciously literary prose form, or the *conte* as briefer, the *nouvelle* longer. Those based on prestige see the *conte* as popular or journalistic, the *nouvelle* as more literary and so more serious. Those based on content see the *conte* as humorous or not aiming at realism, the *nouvelle* as realistic. A complicating factor is that some sub-categories, notably the *conte fantastique*, are associated almost exclusively with one term. Mérimée's 'Lokis', in spite of its length, its series of episodes, its development of character, all of which would make it a *nouvelle*, is nevertheless a *conte fantastique* because of the nature of the events portrayed and its clear echo of fairy-tale elements: could a man be the son of a bear? It is also a cross between the pseudo-oral story, in that the frame presents a narrator who delivers his tale aloud to a group of friends, and the literary, in that he is reading a manuscript... Clear distinctions between *conte* and *nouvelle* tend not to stand up to scrutiny, at least in the nineteenth century. Arguably, the key feature of all the works to be discussed, whether relatively long like 'Carmen', or short like most of Maupassant's, whether *fantastique* and exotic like 'Jettatura' or representing the everyday world realistically like Maupassant's 'Le Garde', is that they are very different from the novel of the period. Imposing on them current and disputed distinctions would not help to clarify either their technique or their continuing effectiveness; consequently I have preferred the terms short fiction or tale to refer to them.

Introduction

Getting to Grips with Short Fiction

Maupassant, 'Le Garde'

The nineteenth century is the golden age of short fiction in France, when it established itself as a major literary genre. Various forms of short fiction had preceded it — the medieval *fabliau*, the tales told to each other by a group of narrators as in Marguerite de Navarre's *Heptaméron*, modelled on Boccaccio's *Decameron*, the fairy tales of Perrault, various types of short story in the eighteenth century: the oriental tale with its debt to the 'Thousand and One Nights', the philosophical tale as practised by Voltaire, the libertine tale.[1] But what appeared suddenly in the nineteenth century — the publication of Mérimée's 'Mateo Falcone' in the *Revue de Paris* in May 1829 is generally seen as the founding moment — is something immediately recognisable as a short story as we understand it: a work of prose fiction more structured than an anecdote, more focused and coherent than a short novel, challenging and not overtly moralising or didactic. It derived in part from literary models. Experiments had been made in short fiction since the Revolution by writers such as Chateaubriand, Madame de Staël, Nodier, and Benjamin Constant. Above all, the enormous success that greeted, from 1828, the first translations into French of the *contes fantastiques* of E.T.A. Hoffmann led many writers to imitate his brief and bizarre tales. But from the start of the explosion of the publication of short fiction in the late 1820s, *contes* and *nouvelles* were essentially a phenomenon of the periodical press; this conditions their length, subject and themes, and their appeal to the reader.

---

1. For a useful survey of these origins, see notably René Godenne, *La Nouvelle* (Paris: Champion, 1995); Ian Reid, *The Short Story*, The Critical Idiom, 37 (London: Methuen, 1977).

The periodical context and the difficulty of definition

A combination of factors contributed to a growth of newspapers and reviews, and led their editors to seek out short fiction for material, and writers to turn to periodicals rather than publication in book form as outlets. Among these were technological advances which enabled the cheaper production of periodicals and newspapers in greater volume,[2] to feed the appetites of a reading public that was increasing in size thanks to the spread of literacy, and the growth of Paris and an urban middle-class. In addition a phase of commercial difficulty between 1827 and 1830 kept book prices up and production down, leaving badly paid writers to seek refuge in journalism. The bulk of Balzac's short fiction, some 24 of 37 works,[3] dates from 1830-1833; from 1835 to 1845 in contrast he produced at most one or two short works in any one year. Such financial considerations have their parallel in the United States, where the absence of copyright led to pirated editions of European novels and to local authors producing short stories for gift annuals and periodicals; and again in Germany after World War II, where the paper shortage favoured short fiction.[4] Together technology, literacy and commerce lay behind the creation by the enterprising Dr Louis Véron, later director of the Paris Opera, of *La Revue des Deux Mondes* in 1829 (taken over in 1831 by the journalist François Buloz), and of *La Revue de Paris*. These two heavyweights of the monthly and bi-monthly reviews of the time both relied on short fiction, amidst other 'œuvres rapides, d'un agrément varié, et accessibles à tous',[5] as a staple ingredient.

2. See Claude Bellenger and others, *Histoire générale de la presse française*, 5 vols (Paris: Presses Universitaires de France, 1969-1976), II (1969), 15-26, and George, *Short Fiction*, 55.
3. In the survey by Diana Festa McCormick, *Les Nouvelles de Balzac* (Paris: Nizet, 1973), though Balzac's reworking of stories makes such counting problematic.
4. Reid, *Short Story*, 28; Etiemble, 'Problématique de la nouvelle', in *Essais de littérature (vraiment) générale* (Paris: Gallimard, 1974), 192-208 (207).
5. Louis Véron, *Mémoires d'un bourgeois de Paris*, 6 vols (Paris: Gonet, 1853-1855), III (1853), 103.

Véron was well aware of the need to entertain, to target a wider readership than the more serious *Globe* and *Revue française*, and to 'aider les muses à faire des prisonniers parmi les intelligences vulgaires et parmi les ignorants':

> En fondant la *Revue de Paris*, je voulus ouvrir [...] les deux battants d'une grande publicité à tous les jeunes talents encore obscurs, comme à tous les écrivains déjà célèbres, et en même temps assurer une certaine rémunération aux compositions littéraires qui demandaient trop de développement pour être réduits aux proportions d'un journal, mais qui n'en pourraient point fournir assez pour défrayer un livre.[6]

As Véron's remark suggests, reviews like his offered a home for longer short fiction (Mérimée's 'Colomba', about 50,000 words, was first published in a single number of *La Revue des Deux Mondes*), and newspapers one for briefer tales of 2,500 to 3,000 words. In 1836 Emile de Girardin founded *La Presse*, the first of the cheaper popular daily newspapers relying on advertising and a wider readership, though the annual subscription of 40 francs still restricted it to the fairly well-to-do.[7] Followed by *Le Siècle* in the same year, these dailies also offered an outlet to writers of short stories, at least until 1841, when the vogue for the serialised *roman-feuilleton* briefly eclipsed shorter fiction.

Later in the century it was again the periodical press that was to drive a second boom in short fiction. New technology allowed *Le Petit Journal*, launched in 1863 and the first newspaper aimed at a genuinely mass audience (selling at 5 centimes and offering crime reporting and low-grade *romans-feuilletons*) to produce 250,000 copies by the late 1860s, five times the circulation of the major Parisian dailies ten years earlier.[8] Another key factor contributing to this 'apogée de la presse française' between 1880 to 1914[9] was its liberation from the constraints

6. *Ibid.*, III, 109; I, 14.
7. At 40 francs, as opposed to the 80 francs of previous newspapers, they were beyond the reach of the working class and much of the bourgeoisie, but they could be consulted for a modest price in *cabinets de lecture*. See Henri-Jean Martin and Roger Chartier (eds), *Histoire de l'édition française*, 4 vols (Paris: Promodis, 1983–1986), III (1985), 457.
8. *Histoire générale de la presse*, II, 24.
9. *Ibid.*, III (1972), 235.

of censorship after the liberalisation of the press laws in 1881. *Gil Blas*, founded in 1879, was the first of the big dailies habitually to substitute short fiction for the *roman-feuilleton* usual in papers by then; other papers followed, opening up a vast market in which Maupassant was to thrive. The two main newspapers in which he published between 1880 and 1891, the conservative *Gaulois* where 'le bon ton et la pudeur [...] étaient de règle', and the overtly licentious *Gil Blas* (both selling at 15 centimes, so appealing to the comfortably off), were printing respectively 15,000 and nearly 30,000 copies a day in the early 1880s.[10] For the late nineteenth-century writer, periodical publication provided both a source of money and a wider readership than obtainable by publication in volume. At the same time small reviews with a limited circulation and often an equally limited life, such as *La Revue des Lettres et des Arts* founded by Villiers de l'Isle-Adam and the music critic Armand Gouzian, which survived only from October 1867 to March 1868, offered an outlet for writers like Villiers with less immediate public appeal. Although he also published in *Le Figaro* and *Gil Blas*, at least half the *Contes cruels* first appeared in such highly literary reviews.

In this commercial world, the writer had to adapt to the dictates of the publishers and the requirements of the readers. As *La Revue des Deux Mondes* noted in 1836,

> L'instinct commercial de l'éditeur est devenu la principale règle de l'écrivain, et la littérature, rabaissée à un rôle subalterne, reçoit l'impulsion au lieu de la donner.[11]

The short story typically appears amidst other, often unrelated, texts, whether in a periodical, surrounded by news items or essays, or subsequently in a collection of short fiction. Its publication, as Bruno Monfort has put it, was polytextual, not monotextual.[12] Several

---

10. *Ibid.*, III, 322, 234, 380.
11. 1 April 1836; quoted by Bryant, *Short Fiction*, 17.
12. Bruno Monfort, 'La Nouvelle et son mode de publication: le cas américain', *Poétique*, 23 (1992), 153–71 (157). For the effects of this 'contextualising' in periodical publications of short fiction in the nineteenth century, see Goyet, *La Nouvelle*, 91–130; on the vanity of the quest for essences, see also Mary Louise Pratt, 'The Short Story: the long and the short of it', *Poetics*, 10

characteristics result from external constraints, notably its brevity, and to some extent its subject-matter. The *conte fantastique*, the exotic story, the story with a nautical setting were all favoured by the public of the 1830s. Moreover, it has to be immediately accessible to the reader. At the same time periodical publication could prohibit certain themes: in the early 1830s, both explicitly sexual and political themes were taboo. Both critics and practitioners have been tempted to seek the elusive 'essence' of the short story, ever since Edgar Allan Poe defended the 'brief prose tale' in a review of Nathaniel Hawthorne's *Twice Told Tales* and made several bold but unhelpful assertions about it: that it should be read in one sitting in order to avail itself of 'the immense benefit of *totality*', that it should be constructed to achieve 'a certain *single effect*', that its features should contribute to 'the one pre-established design', that the conclusion should be 'climactic'.[13] These cryptic assertions were later misleadingly paraphrased by Baudelaire in his 'Notes Nouvelles sur Edgar Poe' and rigidly codified by Brander Matthews as 'The Philosophy of the Short-Story' (1884).[14] But Poe's argument here for the creative autonomy of the writer of the short prose tale, where, 'during the hour of perusal, the soul of the reader is at the writer's control', the emphasis on construction — 'in the whole composition there should be no word written of which the tendency, direct or indirect, is not to the one pre-established design' — can best be understood, as Daniel Grojnowski has argued, not so much as a definition of a new genre, as a protest against commercialisation. Poe

(1981), 175-94 (176).
13. In his article 'Nathaniel Hawthorne', in *The Complete Works of Edgar Allan Poe*, ed. by John H. Ingram, 4 vols (Edinburgh: Black, 1874-1875), IV (1975), 213-27; it is an expanded version of a review of Hawthorne's *Twice Told Tales* (*Selected Writings*, ed. by David Galloway (Harmondsworth: Penguin, 1967), 437-47). For accounts of the sense of the essay in context and how it was later misinterpreted as a 'theory' of the *nouvelle* or the short story, see the important correctives by Monfort, 'La Nouvelle et son mode de publication', and Daniel Grojnowski, 'De Baudelaire à Poe: l'"effet de totalité"', *Poétique*, 27 (1996), 101-109; Andrew Levy, *The Culture and the Commerce of the American Short Story* (Cambridge University Press, 1993), 23: 'Critics, audience, and publishers all disappear from the loop of creation, publication, dissemination and canonization.'
14. Partially reprinted in Charles E. May (ed.), *Short Story Theories* (Athens: Ohio University Press, 1976), 52-59.

may claim that the writer is in control; in fact it was largely publisher and public who dictated themes and form.

It might be safer to abandon prescriptive definitions of the 'essence' of the short story (or *conte*, or *nouvelle*), while accepting that those who sought to define it have pointed to what *some* short fiction *sometimes* does: that it can be read at one sitting as Poe argued (but so can some short novels, and how long is a sitting?), or typically represents lonely figures on the fringes of society, as Frank O'Connor claimed (but so does *Robinson Crusoe*), or again that it deals with revelation and exposure,[15] or with unique perceptions, such as a fleeting moment of mythic experience (the epiphany:[16] but does not *A la recherche du temps perdu*?). The circumstances of initial publication remain its only unproblematic defining feature: 'a complete narrative usually too short to be published by itself'.[17] But although brevity may be imposed as an external constraint, successful authors turn to their advantage this limitation. To take an example from another genre: in the theatre there is a single stage, although it can be made to represent different scenes, the cast is restricted in number compared to that of *War and Peace*, the actors are not 'really' the characters they are portraying, and their actions have no real effect. Sartre turns these 'problems' to his advantage in *Huis clos*, setting it in Hell, in a single claustrophobic room from which the characters cannot escape, exploiting the intolerable tensions between three unchanging individuals, preoccupied with the effect they have on each other, and frustrated by their inability to carry out any real act. Seen in this way, Mérimée and Maupassant stand out as writers who were able to find formulae for short fiction that dovetailed with the requirements of the publishing environment and exploit them to produce works more formally satisfying and with more

---

15. Murray Sachs, 'The Emergence of a Poetics', in *The French Short Story*, ed. by Philip Crant, French Literature Series, II (Columbia: University of South Carolina, 1975), 139-51 (149).
16. Charles May; and for a sceptical review of these attempts, see Norman Friedman, 'Recent Short Story Theories,' in *Short Story Theory at the Crossroads*, ed. by Susan Lohafer and Jo Ellyn Clarey (Baton Rouge: Lousiana State University Press, 1989), 13-31.
17. Helmut Bonheim, *The Narrative Modes: Techniques of the Short Story* (Cambridge: Brewer, 1982), 166.

challenging implications than the vast amount of largely unmemorable work produced in these circumstances. Short fiction obviously shares many features with the novel (plot, characters, prose narrative...) and exists in a continuum with it: a short story does not suddenly become a novel after a certain number of pages, nor by tackling a particular theme or using a certain type of character. It is only the problematic issue of brevity and the polytextual mode of publication that make it 'not the novel'. This is perhaps why, if it seeks to establish a separate identity, the short story defines itself in terms of and in opposition to the more powerful genre. Hence the contrasts to which writers defining it are so frequently drawn: the novel deals with life, the short story deals with a fragment of life; the novel deals with many things, the short story with a single thing; the novel is linked to the written, to books, the short story to orality; the novel is an art, short fiction a craft.[18] But for such oppositions to be useful, they need to be situated in a historical context. As Marcel Raymond notes, both the novel and the modern *nouvelle* reach adulthood and become clearly defined genres only in the nineteenth century.[19] Against an increasingly assertive novel, shorter fiction retains an inferiority complex.

In the 'Avant-propos' to *La Comédie humaine*, Balzac claimed to 'écrire l'histoire oubliée par tant d'historiens, celle des mœurs':[20] those of French society in the Restoration and July Monarchy. In their subtitles, *Le Rouge et le Noir* is a 'Chronique de 1830', and Zola's Rougon-Macquart cycle the 'Histoire naturelle et sociale d'une famille sous le Second Empire'. If the serious novel was becoming, as the Goncourt brothers self-importantly put it in the Preface to *Germinie Lacerteux*, 'la grande forme sérieuse, passionnée, vivante, de l'étude littéraire et de l'enquête sociale', and even 'par l'analyse et la recherche psychologique, l'Histoire morale contemporaine' (leaving escapism and violence to the popular novel of Dumas *père* or Eugène Sue), short fiction can be seen as shifting to the position of what has been termed a

---

18. Pratt, 'The Short Story', 182-92.
19. Marcel Raymond, 'Histoire et poétique de la nouvelle,' in *Vérité et poésie* (Neuchâtel: La Baconnière, 1964), 131-74 (132).
20. Balzac, *La Comédie humaine*, ed. by Pierre-Georges Castex and others, Bibliothèque de la Pléiade, 12 vols (Paris: Gallimard, 1976-1981), I (1976), 11.

'countergenre'.[21] It takes contrasting preoccupations as recurrent themes: the *fantastique* as opposed to everyday reality; the exotic and the regional as opposed to the 'large-scale social patterns [...] of urban life' portrayed in the novel;[22] extremes and violence rather than normality. Rather than explaining (Balzac's 'Voici pourquoi...'), it seizes on the irrational and the inexplicable,[23] from Mérimée's 'Vision de Charles XI' in 1829 to Maupassant's 'Le Horla' in 1887 and the tales of Barbey d'Aurevilly. The phrases 'une singulière aventure' or 'un drame assez singulier' often introduce a tale by Maupassant.[24] Mérimée remarked when writing 'Lokis': 'J'ai pris le sujet le plus extrême et le plus atroce que j'ai pu.'[25]

What is true of theme is also true of form. Novels from Balzac and Stendhal to Zola rely overwhelmingly on the omniscient extradiegetic narrator, and in the case of Flaubert especially, one who seeks to disguise his presence; for Barbey, the true novelist was 'un conteur qui montre les choses vivantes en cachant la main qui les montre'.[26] In contrast, the narrator of short fiction is more visible; we find, as Peter

21. The term, from Claudio Guillén, is used by Pratt, 'The Short Story', 182.
22. Reid, *Short Story*, 24. A standard explanation for the predominance of the *Novelle* in nineteenth-century Germany over the novel has been that 'the novel is a product of the city, the Novelle of the province' (Roger Paulin, *The Brief Compass: the Nineteenth-Century German Novelle* (Oxford: Clarendon Press, 1985), 5). Florence Goyet (*La Nouvelle*, 91–130) has stressed the 'exotic' aspect of short fiction in the periodical press: readers would almost always be different in class, region, wealth, from the characters portrayed.
23. Nadine Gordimer has noted: 'Short story writers see by the light of the flash. Ideally they have learned to do without explanation of what went before, or what happens beyond this point'. Clare Hanson comments: 'The form of the short story has lent itself to the representation of the partial, the incomplete, that which cannot be [...] entirely satisfactorily organised or "explained"', Clare Hanson (ed.), *Re-reading the Short Story* (New York: St Martin's Press, 1989), 2.
24. In tales as varied as 'Châli', 'Rose', 'Les Tombales', 'Le Garde', and 'En voyage': see Guy de Maupassant, *Contes et nouvelles*, ed. by Louis Forestier, 2 vols, Bibliothèque de la Pléiade (Paris: Gallimard, 1988–1989 (first edition, 1974–1979), II, 83; I, 1169; II, 1239; II, 347; I, 815. All references to Maupassant's stories are to this edition.
25. Mérimée, *Correspondance générale*, XIV, 245.
26. Quoted by Michel Crouzet in his edition of Barbey d'Aurevilly, *Les Diaboliques* (Paris: Imprimerie Nationale, 1989), 42.

Brooks has noted, a preoccupation with framed stories, with contact between teller and listener, which is uncharacteristic of nineteenth-century novels.[27] Finally, having its origin in the world of journalism, as something made to order, short fiction enjoyed less critical esteem than the novel,[28] and was often denounced as an example of the commercialisation of literature, what Sainte-Beuve was to term in 1839 'la littérature industrielle'. Désiré Nisard attacked the proliferation of collections and periodicals devoted to it, worried that this 'littérature facile' was finding a wide readership; for Philarète Chasles, 'l'impulsion ne venait plus de l'esprit, mais de la caisse, ni des gens qui dirigeaient la plume, mais de ceux qui les payaient,'[29] and it was in consequence regarded as just 'délassement d'esprit' rather than 'objet d'étude', as the *Figaro* put it in 1830.[30] Its practitioners were often novelists who had recourse to short fiction at a particular stage of their career, as in the case of Balzac, Stendhal and Flaubert. They frequently sought to avoid too close an association: Balzac wrote in a letter to Amédée Pichot, then editor of *La Revue de Paris*: 'Quant à ne faire que des contes, quoique ce soit à mon avis, autre hérésie peut-être, l'expression la plus rare de la littérature, je ne veux pas être exclusivement *contier*. Autre est ma destinée.'[31] Some writers, like Champfleury, attached more importance to their unsuccessful novels, neglecting a real talent for short fiction, which Balzac had urged him to treat as no more than an amusement.[32] Even Maupassant became increasingly impatient with the form and sought critical esteem with his novels; Mérimée largely abandoned literature for a career as an inspector of historical monuments, only intermittently writing tales

27. Peter Brooks, 'Le Conteur: réflexions à partir de Walter Benjamin,' *Maupassant miroir de la nouvelle*, ed. by Jacques Lecarme and Bruno Vercier (Paris: Presses Universitaires de Vincennes, 1988), 225-42.
28. This remains true: see, for example, Hanson, *Rereading the Short Story*, 1.
29. Respectively in *La Revue de Paris* (December 1833), and in *Etudes sur les hommes et les mœurs au XIXe siècle* (Paris: Amyot, 1849), 333; both quoted by Bryant, *Short Fiction*, 40-41 and 27.
30. Bryant, *Short Fiction*, 67.
31. Letter of 3 December 1832, Honoré de Balzac, *Correspondance*, ed. by Roger Pierrot, 5 vols (Paris, Garnier, 1960-1969), II (1962), 185.
32. See Michael Wetherilt's Introduction to Champfleury, *Le Violon de faïence* (Geneva: Droz, 1985).

which he feigned to regard as 'petites drôleries'.[33] Short fiction is also produced in large quantities: a survey of 1832 was forced to limit itself to 500 texts of this 'enormous production';[34] and as we have seen, the end of the century saw a second explosion.[35] Inevitably much of this production has little lasting interest. Even the 'giants of the magazine field', the *Revue de Paris* and the *Revue des Deux Mondes*, rely on the 'recipe forms of short fiction for the bulk of their material' and show that talent and high quality were in short supply,[36] and a recent exhaustive trawl through the periodical publication between 1829 and 1841[37] has confirmed that that there are few forgotten treasures hiding there. But the fact that production was driven by the market did not impose one uniform formula; the public wanted variety and novelty.

Storytelling and the possibility of analysis

To say that one cannot provide any distinct criteria for the short story beyond the problematic fact of brevity need not, as Mary Louise Pratt observes, preclude establishing recurrent features, even if not all of these are present in all texts. In analysing narrative technique today, the reader of the short story is arguably in a particularly advantageous position. The critical study of narrative in the twentieth century, though concerned with a general theory that can range from history to bed-time stories and jokes, has (with the notable exception of the work of Gérard Genette) generally taken short fiction as its starting-point. This has been the case from the initial impetus given to narratology through the study of folk-tales by the Russian Formalist Vladimir Propp, to Roland Barthes's sentence-by-sentence analysis of Balzac's *Sarrasine*, A. J. Greimas's similarly exhaustive treatment of Maupassant's 'Deux amis', and Tzvetan Todorov's *Grammaire du Décameron*. Todorov argued that with its limited number of characters and few plot links, a brief work

33. For example, *Correspondance générale*, XV, 16, 67 (on 'Djoûmane').
34. Frank Paul Bowman, 'La Nouvelle en 1832', *Cahiers de l'Association Internationale des Etudes Françaises*, 27 (1975), 189-208.
35. See Goyet, *La Nouvelle*, 92-94.
36. George, *Short Fiction*, 62.
37. Bryant, *Short Fiction*.

presented fewer difficulties for analysis than the novel: 'au stade de connaissances où nous sommes, il est préférable de choisir des exemples plus simples.'[38] Exhaustive analysis is obviously more manageable with a short work, viewed as a rudimentary form of the novel, what Bruno Monfort has termed 'un récit-laboratoire'[39] showing its characteristics in miniature. But it could be that the features that such critics focused on: recurrent thematic patterns, significant oppositions, a narrative dominated by plot to which a schematic characterisation is subordinate, are more characteristic of short fiction than of other kinds of narrative. The novel tends to avoid too clear a structure and stereotyped characters who are little more than their role.[40] The result is that narratology has provided tools for the study of short fiction rather than of narrative in general.

The short work also offers itself for analysis without dissimulating its tricks and devices. One consequence of brevity is, as Todorov has noted, an awareness of artificiality: reading a short work, you do not have time to forget that it is only 'literature' and not 'real life'.[41] More specifically, brevity means that we are conscious of a tale being told, recently begun and shortly to end, whereas the nineteenth-century novel seeks to create an image of comprehensiveness and continuity, to immerse us in a world that in Balzac or Zola extends beyond the confines of individual novels: 'Un roman c'est plus confortable, le lecteur se laisse porter jusqu'au bout. Pour la nouvelle il faut toujours recommencer.'[42]

38. Tzvetan Todorov, *Grammaire du Décaméron* (The Hague and Paris: Mouton, 1969), 11.
39. Monfort, 'La Nouvelle et son mode de publication', 155.
40. See Goyet, *La Nouvelle*, 84–87.
41. Tzvetan Todorov, *Poétique de la prose* (Paris: Seuil, 1971), 151; a similar point is made by Angus Martin of the early eighteenth century: 'Le conte est conçu comme un genre qui ne permet au lecteur d'oublier ni la présence du narrateur, ni la nature artificielle de l'histoire qu'on lui raconte' (Introduction to *Anthologie du conte en France 1750–1799* (Paris: Union Générale d'Editions, 1981), 34).
42. Carmen Camero Perez, 'Le Temps de la nouvelle', *La Licorne*, 21 (1991), 125–33 (129). A similar opposition is made by Antonia Fonyi, 'Nouvelle, objectivité, structure: un chapitre de l'histoire de la théorie de la nouvelle et une tentative de description structurale', *Revue de Littérature Comparée*, 50 (1970), 355–75 (370).

Rather than a deficiency, this feature can be seen as one of the pleasures of literary short fiction, just as it is of the oral tale: the sense of the presence and voice of a narrator, whether a fictional character telling the tale or an external narrator, and of structure in the narrative. Hence the usefulness, in the analysis of short fiction, of the categories elaborated by Gérard Genette in 'Discours du récit'.[43] These were developed from an analysis of Proust, reminding us that narrative fiction is a continuum that moves from short story to novel, and that no one technique is the exclusive preserve of either.[44] The questions posed by Genette about who is talking and to whom, about the order and frequency of the narration of events, about shifting viewpoints (or focalisation), and about levels of narration, are crucial to both. But in short fiction such questions present themselves in a more obtrusive way than in a novel; they provide an immediate handle with which we can get to grips with narrative techniques.

These categories, however, sometimes fail to account for the interaction of teller and listener, and overlook the extent to which (as speech-act theorists of narrative such as Barbara Herrnstein Smith, Mary Louise Pratt, or Ross Chambers in his study of 'narrative seduction', have insisted),[45] story-telling is not just an account of events, but an act. A story is always 'someone telling someone that something has happened', and for a purpose: in literature as in life, 'the fact that something is true is never a sufficient reason for saying it',[46] and the purpose can be to 'justify, seduce, revenge, gain time...'.[47] Even a story told to entertain seeks something in exchange: attention, appreciation.

43. *Figures III* (Paris: Seuil, 1972).
44. The point is made in Dietrich Bonheim's exhaustive demonstration in *The Narrative Modes*: 'Short story and novel, then, overlap' (169).
45. Ross Chambers, *Story and Situation: narrative seduction and the power of fiction*, (Manchester University Press, 1984); Mary Louise Pratt, *Towards a Speech Act Theory of Literary Discourse* (Bloomington: Indiana University Press, 1977).
46. Barbara Herrnstein Smith, *On the Margins of Discourse: the relation of literature to language* (University of Chicago Press, 1978), 17, 195-6. See also Richard Shryock's study of embedded narratives in this light, *Tales of Story-telling: Embedded Narrative in Modern French Fiction* (New York: Lang, 1993).
47. See Shryock, *Tales*, 3-4.

As important as the question 'how' is 'why': why a narrator tells a tale, why the audience listens, why the narration affects them.
The reader is particularly conscious of these issues when a tale is told by a character. Mérimée, Maupassant, and Barbey d'Aurevilly often represent an act of narrating in a specific context in imitation of the oral tale. An example from Maupassant can show the usefulness of Genette's categories, but also what can be added by viewing story-telling as an act. In 'Le Garde' (II, 347), M. Boniface takes his turn to tell a story to a group of old friends who have been relating hunting adventures after dinner. Before starting he warns them that his tale, which he has never told before, does not have the standard interest — excitement, amusement, emotion — expected of the hunting tale, and defies classification. He moves through a whole series of definitions, finding them all inadequate — it is 'une histoire de chasse, ou plutôt un drame de chasse assez singulier. Il ne ressemble pas du tout à ce qu'on connaît dans le genre [...] Il n'a pas cette espèce d'intérêt qui passionne, ou qui charme, ou qui émeut agréablement' — before finally presenting it bluntly as 'la chose'. Boniface has been rapidly characterised at the start of the tale as robust, witty, 'd'une philosophie ironique et résignée'. He rapidly situates the events: several years ago, when he was thirty-five. He introduces the main characters: his gamekeeper, Cavalier, a retired *gendarme*; the gamekeeper's nephew of fourteen, Marius; and an elderly woman who comes to cook when Boniface is at his small estate. Then Boniface relates the 'aventure'. On his arrival at the estate in 1854, the gamekeeper tells him that he has caught his nephew poaching and has beaten him, and repeats the punishment in the presence of his master until Marius begs for forgiveness. That night a fire is started in the house: Boniface escapes, wakens Cavalier by firing his gun; Cavalier escapes, but the old woman dies in the flames. Boniface realises Marius was responsible: as the boy runs from the stable where he has been hiding, Cavalier seizes Boniface's gun and shoots him dead. The gamekeeper is later tried and acquitted, on Boniface's evidence, but leaves the region.

What might seem a simple tale of punishment and revenge that takes a gruesome turn provides plenty of material for formal analysis. In the standard 2,500 to 3,000 words of a tale published in a newspaper in the 1880s (it first appeared in *Le Gaulois* in 1884), we have three levels of narration. (Here and subsequently I shall term an initial unnamed narrator who is distinct from the author, 'the Narrator'.) There is the presentation, by the Narrator, of the after-dinner group, of which he is one ('nous'), and of Boniface; the main embedded or framed narrative, Boniface's tale; and inside that, two further embedded narratives: Cavalier's account of Marius poaching, given verbatim, and Boniface's brief report of his account to the court ('je racontai les faits par le détail, sans rien changer').

We are conscious of three distinct elements distinguished by Genette. First, the events narrated (in Genette's terms, the *histoire*, what Maupassant refers to as 'les faits'): these are the poaching, the punishment, the fire and shooting, the trial, and much later the after-dinner gathering. Second, the narrative formed from them in Maupassant's text, 'Le Garde' (the *récit*). Third, the role in this of *narration*, the act of narrating (by Boniface to the group and to the court, and by Cavalier to him). The order of events as they occurred is manipulated in the *récit*, as we move from the after-dinner narration, back to Boniface's arrival at the estate, and further back to Cavalier's narration of Marius's poaching and his punishment, then forwards to the second punishment and its consequences, up to the trial which includes the mention of Boniface's evidence summing up all the preceding events. We then return to the point where we began, as Boniface addresses his after-dinner audience. The characterisation relies on stereotype and opposition, as frequently in short fiction: the upright but violent *gendarme*-gamekeeper is contrasted with his 'sournois' (II, 351) and malformed nephew, 'maigre, long, un peu crochu', who squints and whose 'mains géantes' (II, 348) become 'monstrueuses' (II, 351). The thematic patterning is underlined by verbal echoes and images. It is 'une histoire de chasse' with no real hunting, but the gamekeeper is responsible for his nephew and cannot 'le chasser' (in the sense of 'send him away' (II, 351)), yet ends up shooting him. Marius is compared initially to vermin, a polecat or a fox; dying, he still attempts to flee 'à la façon des lièvres blessés à mort qui voient venir le chasseur' (II, 354).

The formal complexity of the tale is evident: Maupassant has rearranged the order of his fictional events, has constructed oppositions and thematic echoes that hold the story together. But much of the effect of the tale has not yet been touched on. This becomes clearer if we ask why the characters are telling their tales and what impact they have. Maupassant contrasts both Boniface's formal tone and Cavalier's more colloquial style, and their motives. Boniface's tale to the after-dinner group is set in the context of story-telling to amuse. But it is a tale that evokes the role of unpredictable impulse in human life, and the pointlessness of judgement, justice and punishment: a tale less likely to entertain than to disturb and provoke reflection. The abrupt ending, with no comment on the audience's reaction, corresponds to an implied silence, a numbed response to the nihilistic implications of the story. Cavalier's narration to his master does not just seek to inform him about Marius's misdeed and his punishment, but is predominantly an expression of complex emotions: pride at his vigilance, shame at his nephew's act, anger and the need for absolution: 'Est-ce que j'ai bien fait, monsieur?' In telling of the punishment and then repeating it before Boniface, the emotions he reveals anticipate the final punishment he inflicts on Marius. The exchanges between Cavalier and Boniface, between Boniface and his nephew do not just elucidate past events, but provoke future ones: Marius's act of revenge is prompted as much by his humiliation and being forced to apologise to Boniface as by the physical pain of the beating.

Boniface interrupts his account of events between Cavalier's first punishment and the second beating with a comment directed at his after-dinner audience: 'Je savais qu'il était inutile d'essayer de dissuader le vieux d'un projet. Je le laissai donc agir à sa guise' (II, 351). The aside reveals the variety of roles Boniface is playing in his own story. He is, as narratee (the person to whom a narrative is addressed), the master to whom the gamekeeper confesses, and from whom Cavalier seeks approval for the punitive role he will repeat later. As character in his own tale, Boniface's comment reveals his own more detached attitude towards Marius's poaching: he has neither the shame that the gamekeeper feels for this betrayal of trust, nor the responsibility of the uncle for the orphan. Boniface's attitude is straightforward distaste: 'Dans la race humaine, il me faisait l'effet de ce que sont les bêtes puantes, chez les animaux' (II, 348). As a comment addressed by Boniface as narrator to his audience, the aside guides them to the less more general meaning that we expect from a literary narrative: the account is not just of a striking and singular event, it implies a view of life — an attitude of resignation in a world where people are victims of their characters and impulses, and where any intervention to guide or restrain them is futile. And when Boniface comes to retell the events to the court, 'sans rien changer' (II, 354), even if what he actually says is identical, the purpose of his narration changes again: to secure the acquittal of an honest servant, rather than to convey a message about life.

Questions about why stories are being told and how they are functioning lead us to the pessimistic point of the tale. In studying the processes of literary story-telling it is important to recall that storytelling occurs in real life as well. Analysts who have studied natural oral tales can also provide insights into the construction of narrative and the interaction of teller and listener, notably the tradition that has sprung from William Labov's seminal study of Black English vernacular narratives (BEV) of personal experience.[48] Labov analysed a series of oral accounts where speakers rehearsed or relived events of their past in response to the question: had they ever been in danger of being killed? He found a single underlying pattern, six characteristic features found in part or completely in all the narratives. The elements that he distinguished can be seen as responses to basic questions: the *abstract*, or initial summary (what is the story about?); the *orientation* that identifies time, place, characters, situation, with past present clauses, which in French would be in the imperfect (who? what? when? where?); the *complicating action*, the series of events (then what happened?); *evaluation*, the key feature which guides the listener to the point and without which the narrative becomes meaningless and difficult to follow (so what?); the *resolution* (so what finally happened?); and the *coda* as an optional way of restoring listeners to the present (and now?). This provides both a model for distinguishing the elements of the narration, and in some cases formal features, such as different tenses, for doing so.[49] Moreover, the model and its linguistic features map neatly on to Boniface's narrative in 'Le Garde'. The abstract, as often with Maupassant, takes the form not so much of a naming of the event,

48. William Labov, *Language in the Inner City: Studies in Black English Vernacular* (Oxford: Blackwell, 1972), Chapter 9: 'The Transformation of Experience in Narrative Syntax', 354-96. For an earlier version of the analysis, see William Labov and Joshua Waletzky, 'Narrative Analysis: Oral Versions of Personal Experience', *Essays on the Visual and Verbal Arts*, ed. by June Helm (Seattle and London: University of Washington Press, 1967), 12-44.
49. The point is stressed by Ronald Carter and Paul Simpson, 'The Sociolinguistic Analysis of Narrative', *Belfast Working Papers in Linguistics*, 6 (1982), 123-52 (126, 147).

but of its type, or rather its ambiguous generic status as not quite 'une histoire de chasse', and its emotional tone: 'Il n'est pas sympathique'. The orientation, using the imperfect: 'J'avais alors vingt-cinq ans environ', is baldly highlighted by Boniface: 'Vous connaissez donc les personnages et le local. Voici maintenant l'histoire' (II, 348). The evaluation is provided by elements that break the sequence of narrated events: Boniface's interposed comment to the listeners just noted, his generalising comments on Cavalier's motivation: 'Un de ces mouvements irréfléchis, instantanés, qu'on ne saurait prévoir ni retenir', and the image which compares Marius to a dying hare (II, 354). The resolution is the shooting of the nephew; the coda is provided by Cavalier's acquittal and disappearance, where Boniface shifts in tense from past historic to perfect to return us to the present of his narrating: 'Je ne l'ai jamais revu'.

Labov's study shows the verbal skill of his narrators, able 'to command the total attention of an audience in a remarkable way';[50] in effect it shows how the oral tale from the streets is just as much constructed as a literary tale. The problems of story-telling — 'finding a place to stand in order to report the goings on in another world'[51] — problems of tense, of point of view, of consistency, are the same in conversation and in literature, and are solved using the same devices. Richard Bauman has likewise created an awareness of the oral narrative tale as artful, one where the storyteller can show creative individuality in 'performance'.[52] In consequence the study of literary short fiction and natural oral tales is a two-way process. On the one hand analyses of literary story-telling can provide a stimulus to see similar patterns in oral narration: Mary Louise Pratt notes that Labov's analysis and categories seem obvious in part because they correspond to the kind of organisation we are traditionally taught to observe in literary narrative.[53]

50. Labov, *Language in the Inner City*, 396.
51. Livia Polanyi, 'Literary complexity in everyday storytelling', in *Spoken and Written Language: exploring orality and literacy*, ed. by Deborah Tanner (Norwood, New Jersey: Ablex, 1986), 155-70 (169). See also Pratt, *Towards a Speech Act Theory*, 61-62.
52. Richard Bauman, *Story, Performance and Event*, Cambridge Studies in Oral and Literary Culture, 10 (Cambridge University Press, 1986), 7-8.
53. Pratt, *Towards a Speech-Act Theory*, 50-51. Compare Bauman's analysis of focalisation in first-person narratives about practical jokes: *Story, Performance*

At the same time socio-linguistic analyses like Labov's enable literary criticism to approach short stories with a new emphasis on interaction, performance and stylistic features, provide us with a new series of questions to ask. If we sometimes get different answers from those provided by the analysis of oral narratives, this can indicate the different priorities of literary story and real-life tale.

What characterises much of the most interesting French short fiction of the nineteenth century is a refusal or a subversion of the natural pattern defined by Labov and his successors. If, as Richard Bauman has argued, 'it might be profitable to think of literary narration as akin to oral story-telling,'[54] oral models can help us define both how literary tales work and how they transgress. Even in such a conventional and easily consumed tale as 'Le Garde', the evaluative elements that guide us to the significance of the story (so what?) are less overt than we would expect in an oral tale, leaving the reader with more work to do to discover the point. Boniface's abstract provokes by refusing a classification for his story: it is 'la chose', something awkward, and Cavalier significantly echoes the word when he hesitantly introduces his ashamed account of his nephew's poaching: 'Voici la chose, monsieur.'

A recurrent feature is the extent to which the constants of the narrative contract of natural tales is violated: rather than fostering the identity of a cultural group, they can unsettle, provoke, disturb; rather than creating identity, interpreting events and experiences, they can be used to portray narrators who dissimulate or try to mislead; rather than embodying a point that the audience can grasp, the reader can sometimes be left baffled, or with ambiguous or even contradictory points. The literary tale is an 'independent disembodied unit',[55] unlike the natural tale that arises from the flow of conversation that situates it and clarifies its meaning. A standard pattern of real-life oral storytelling is to produce a chain of related stories, or to be followed by 'exit talk', 'a chunk of talk' consisting of at least two exchanges which revolves around the story and integrates it into the conversation after the extended 'turn' of the narrator.[56] Boniface's narrative in 'Le Garde',

and Event, Chapter 3.
54. Bauman, *Story, Performance and Event*, 113.
55. Livia Polanyi, 'The Nature of Meaning in Stories in Conversation', *Studies in Twentieth-Century Literature*, 6 (1981–1982), 51–65 (59).
56. Polanyi, 'Literary Complexity', 164, and 'The Nature of Meaning', 57, 51.

like several similar cases in Maupassant and Barbey, reduces the group to silence. Not only is the literary narrative more inclined to this effect of decisive closure, its meaning is generally more open. The priorities of literature,[57] its aesthetic and destabilising function, differ from those of everyday exchanges and their role in creating solidarity. The majority of nineteenth-century French stories may merely seek to provide 'une lecture qui occupe l'esprit sans le fatiguer, qui éveille l'attention pour le lendemain et devienne sujet de causerie qui fasse diversion aux dialogues un peu monotones des cercles de province',[58] and suffer from the defects of lack of concentration, unchallenging escapism and an excessively moralising tone.[59] In the best, however, one can find works that both offer immediate narrative pleasure and meaning, and also repay rereading to discover that their point might not be as simple as it seemed at first, or to explore more fully their unsettling and critical thrust, that can range from the disconcerting irony of Mérimée, or the bewilderment induced in the narrators of Théophile Gautier ('Je ne savais que penser de ce que je voyais,' confesses the narrator of 'La Cafetière'),[60] to Villiers's more outrageous onslaught: 'Il faudra affoler le lecteur'.[61]

I shall start in the first two chapters with the most obvious constituents of story-telling, narrator and audience, asking who is telling, why, and to whom, to see how factors such as the motives of tellers and listeners, their desire not simply to relate events, but to influence each other, or even paradoxically not to give or receive the narrative, can be a key feature of the interest of stories. Tellers and listeners will continue to be a preoccupation in subsequent chapters, which will explore how typical features of short narrative in the nineteenth century are handled to control the narrative and intrigue the reader: the use of objects to trigger narrating and concentrate events, the presence of verbal and thematic patterning, the exploitation of

57. On this difference, see Smith, *Margins*, 193.
58. A *feuilleton* in *La Presse* (1832), quoted by Bryant, *Short Fiction*, 108.
59. See Bryant, *Short Fiction*, 100.
60. Théophile Gautier, *Œuvres*, ed. by Paolo Tortonese (Paris: Laffont, 1995), 4.
61. To Mallarmé, 27 September 1867 (Villiers de l'Isle-Adam, *Correspondance générale*, ed. by Joseph Bollery, 2 vols (Paris: Mercure de France, 1962), I, 113).

focalisation or point of view, and finally, the imposition of temporal deadlines or physical constraints.

1. Tellers and Listeners: 'making the frame part of the story'

Mérimée, 'Carmen'; Maupassant, 'Les Bécasses'; Villiers, 'Sombre récit, conteur plus sombre'

In 'Le Garde' Maupassant's fictional setting serves as a 'frame' in which one character tells other characters a tale, this framed or embedded tale being the main narrative. Framing is a recurrent feature of French nineteenth-century short fiction: Mérimée uses it early in his career in 'La Partie de trictrac' (1830), in 'Carmen', and towards the end of his life in 'Lokis'; Maupassant exploits it in about half his stories, as does Barbey d'Aurevilly in all of *Les Diaboliques*. It clearly descends from the model established by Boccaccio's fourteenth-century *Decameron* and followed by many subsequent writers with brief tales to tell. In this model, a circle of storytellers, in Boccaccio's case, a group of young people who have fled the plague in Florence in 1348 to a palace in the countryside nearby, takes turns to tell stories to entertain, 'pour adoucir l'ennui,'[1] and sometimes to instruct or to support an argument: for 'pleasure' and for 'useful advice'. The reader's interest lies in the tales and to some extent in the reactions and comments they provoke; the story-telling context is established initially and sometimes rounded off at the end, but does not provide a developing plot, and frequently it is treated perfunctorily, 'a convenient pretext for assembling individual tales'.[2] The circle of rotating story-tellers in these miscellanies is a convenient literary artifice, but it also reflects social realities, whether in aristocratic literary society or in popular *veillées* where individuals gathered to hear tales told.[3] Some other long works do offer a framing narrative with an ongoing interest of its own, in a

1. Marguerite de Navarre, *L'Heptaméron* (Paris: Garnier, n.d.), ix.
2. Ian Reid, *Short Story*, 50.
3. Madeleine Jeay, *Donner la parole: l'histoire-cadre dans les recueils de nouvelles du XVe-XVIe siècle* (Montréal: Ceres, 1992), 8, 180.

model that goes back at least to Apuleius's *The Golden Ass*, the framing tale being interrupted by autonomous intercalated tales.

Some narrative structures in the nineteenth century still conform to the model of the *Decameron* and Marguerite de Navarre's similar *Heptaméron*, both of which were frequently reprinted in the period,[4] by setting up frames for telling and discussing tales, such as Vigny's *Stello* and *Servitude et grandeur militaires*, and Balzac found the structure a useful way of inserting earlier brief narratives in a larger framework, as in *Autre étude de femme*. Two key features, however, distinguish most French tales, from 'La Partie de trictrac' onwards. First, the framing situation generally introduces a single embedded tale. Authors tend to avoid a series of stories, as if the force of the tale, as we saw in 'Le Garde', was heightened by closure: a humorous anecdote that could not be capped, or a disturbing tale that reduced the audience to silence. Secondly (and this is true of the collections by Vigny and Balzac), the tale told in this framing context is an aspect of that individual's experience, something lived or witnessed at first hand. In Genette's terms, the narrators of the framed tale are homodiegetic, and play a role in the diegesis or storyworld and storyline they are evoking,[5] whereas those in Boccaccio or the *Heptaméron* are heterodiegetic; though they may assert in a conventional formula that what they are relating is recent and authentic, the narrators evoke a storyworld other than the world in which they recount. Narrators in Boccaccio and Marguerite de Navarre do not tell their own story, and only very rarely ones they have witnessed: the tales are generally hearsay.[6] In this respect a nineteenth-century framed tale like 'Le Garde' is more like the episode in a novel when characters meet for the first time (say the old woman in Chapters 11-12 of *Candide*), or after a gap in time (say Cunégonde in Chapter 8, Pangloss in Chapter 28), tell their companions of their past or of what has happened in the intervening time. The nineteenth-century framed

---

4. René Godenne, 'Un premier inventaire', in Gratton and Imbert, *La Nouvelle hier*, 334.
5. Again there are exceptions: in tales like Maupassant's 'Madame Parisse' (II, 703) or 'Le Rosier de Madame Husson' (II, 950) the narrators tell of events and characters known about by hearsay, not at first hand, and the narrative is in effect heterodiegetic.
6. See Nicole Cazauran, 'Les Devisants de l'*Heptaméron* et leurs nouvelles,' *Revue d'Histoire Littéraire de la France*, 96 (1996), 879-93 (881).

tale is the representation of a single narrative act, in a particular context, by a character generally directly implicated in the events he or she is narrating.

This key difference, as Théophil Spoerri[7] has put it, enables the frame to become part of the story. The general frame for a miscellany of narratives provides a pretext for their narration or discussion,[8] but, except when the narrator's character is linked to the type of tale told, as in *The Canterbury Tales*, frame and tale are not linked. But the single framed narrative can set up complex relationships between the two. Frames can have advantages in abbreviating the inner narrative, or focusing it on a key issue, for instance in a trial. Aesthetically, they can be useful in providing parallels between frame and story: a tale of violence and passion told on a stormy night, a tale of murder told on a hunting trip. Judgementally, they can guide the reader's response to the embedded tale or prompt disagreement.[9] But whatever the function of the frame (and I shall return to some of these later), narrators of embedded tales need to be provided with a reason for relating them. As Barbara Herrnstein Smith has stressed, things are always happening, and given the amount of information in the world, the fact that a story is true 'is never a sufficient reason for saying it'.[10] The ostensible reasons can still broadly be grouped under the two main categories that apply in collections like the *Decameron*: pleasure and useful advice. After-dinner stories like 'Le Garde' and stories told to pass the time on boring journeys entertain. Those that inform can range from explanations: why a captain regards a knife as so special that he will not let anyone play with it in 'La Partie de trictrac'; to warnings: in Maupassant's 'Au

7. Theophil Spoerri, 'Mérimée and the Short Story', *Yale French Studies*, 4 (1949), 3–11 (3).
8. Jeay, *Donner la parole*, 72.
9. The question has been studied especially in Maupassant: See notably Angela Moger, 'Narrative structure in Maupassant: frames of desire', *PMLA*, 100 (1985), 315–27; Andrea Calí, 'Histoire encadrante et histoire encadrée, ou de la réception du conte maupassantien', in *La Narration et le sens* (Lecce: Milella, 1986), 101–29; Mary Donaldson-Evans, 'Beginnings to understand: the narrative "come-on" in Maupassant's stories', *Neophilologus*, 68 (1974), 37–47; Tuula Lehman, *Transitions savantes et dissimulées: une étude structurelle des contes et nouvelles de Guy de Maupassant* (Helsinki: Societas Scientiarum Fennica, 1990).
10. Smith, *Margins*, 16–17.

printemps' (I, 284), a man on a boat tells a fellow-traveller, attracted to a young girl, how he got married, to apprise him of the dangers of spring love; as well as exploring issues like the nature of fear, as in Maupassant's 'La Peur' (II, 198).

But not all tales are told solely to inform or to amuse. The accused persons in the dock in stories such as Maupassant's 'Rosalie Prudent' (II, 699) and 'Le Trou' (II, 381) are trying to secure acquittal: what is said by them is governed not just by what happened in the past but by their present situation in the courtroom. The baronne in Maupassant's 'Le Signe' (II, 725) is both telling of an awkward situation her imprudence had led to the previous day when imitating a prostitute and being forced to act accordingly, and seeking advice about how to deal with the consequences when the client returns. The narrator of an after-dinner story seeks not just to entertain, but also to elicit appreciation, even applause. As in real life, we do not just talk from a disinterested desire to inform others; what we tell forms a verbal act which seeks to have 'appropriate consequences for the performer — that is [...] serve [our] interests, and enable us to obtain and achieve what we desire'.[11] Literary narrative in particular can turn these motives into sources of interest. Questioning of the reasons for telling and listening can often lead us to see the frame as something contributing to the coherence of the tale. Three stories in particular, by Maupassant, Mérimée and Villiers, can demonstrate how short fiction can call into question the motives of narrators and their listeners and contribute to our awareness of their point.

'Les Bécasses': why tell? why retail?

The complex narrative structure of Maupassant's 'Les Bécasses' (II, 563), with one tale, but three narrators and as many narratees, prompts us to enquire into these motives. The text of the tale (the *récit*) consists entirely of a letter written by the unnamed first Narrator to a woman ('Ma chère amie'). His attitudes may be close to Maupassant's, but in the overall economy of the tale he is a fictional figure. She had asked why he has not returned to Paris; his letter alleges his enthusiasm for

---

11. *Ibid.*, 86.

CHAPTER 1. TELLERS AND LISTENERS

hunting: 'Est-ce qu'un chasseur rentre à Paris au moment du passage des bécasses?' In it he describes his life in the Normandy countryside, contrasting it with life in the capital, then his first day's hunting with the two d'Orgemol brothers and their farmer, maître Picot. In the course of the shoot Picot and the Narrator encounter the deaf-mute shepherd, Gargan. This prompts Picot to reveal that Gargan has killed his wife the previous winter, saying: 'Je vas vous conter ça' (II, 567), having aroused the curiosity of the Narrator by presenting someone simultaneously as a murderer and a free man. He tells of Gargan's marriage to a poor orphan, known as la Goutte because of her taste for 'eau-de-vie'; of her notorious infidelities, unnoticed by the deaf Gargan, as she yields to every offer of alcohol; of how her husband caught her with a lad 'occupés à leur besogne criminelle', and strangled her. Picot then gives an account of the trial, where by prompting nods and shakes of the head from the shepherd, and finally a miming of the murder, he obtains Gargan's acquittal. Gargan's *histoire*, the marriage and murder, is in effect told three times, in reverse chronological order: by the first Narrator in the letter; by Picot, orally, to the Narrator (though we read the Narrator's account of this, not Picot's actual words: Maupassant avoids the potential distraction of extended narration by an uneducated character);[12] and finally, in slow questions and mime, by Picot and Gargan to the court. But what are the motives of these three narrators for telling the tale? The last two differ: the account to the court seeks to ensure Gargan's acquittal; Picot retells to interest the Narrator. But what are the implied reasons retelling the story in the letter? Is the Narrator simply explaining his absence, and, as he also suggests, passing on the emotion he has felt?

Each successive act of narration is by a less urbane, less educated narrator, concluding with the inarticulate Gargan's brutal mime of copulation and murder:

> Il s'était dressé, entre les deux gendarmes, et, brusquement, il imita le mouvement obscène du couple criminel enlacé devant lui.

---

12. On the distraction created by the representation of accents, regional speech, etc., see Vivienne G. Mylne, *Le Dialogue dans le roman français de Sorel à Sarraute* (Paris: Universitas, 1994), 145–8, and Sylvie Durrer, *Le Dialogue romanesque* (Geneva: Droz, 1994), 43.

> Un rire tumultueux s'éleva de la salle, puis s'arrêta net; car le berger, les yeux hagards, remuant sa mâchoire et sa grande barbe comme s'il eût mordu quelque chose, les bras tendus, la tête en avant, répétait l'action terrible du meurtrier qui étrangle un être.
> Et il hurlait affreusement (II, 570).

We are conscious that Picot's account is being relayed to the female narratee in Paris by the Narrator, using the farmer's terms; the Narrator interpolates an apology for using the word *cocu*: '(pardon pour ce vilain mot!)' (II, 569), and adds at the end: 'Je vous ai raconté [cette aventure] en termes bien grossiers, pour ne rien changer au récit du fermier' (II, 570). What does the implied presence of the woman add to the tale?

It seems initially to point to an opposition between the primitive and the civilised. As frequently in short fiction, we rapidly see that the constituents of the story fit into an underlying antithetical structure.[13] At first the opposition seems to be simple: between Paris, civilisation, and elegance on the one hand, and instinctive sex, jealous rage and murder on the other, between the *bois* of Normandy evoked at the start, and the fashionable Bois de Boulogne referred to in the final sentence. But the narrative of events is interrupted by descriptive remarks. Gargan, according to Picot, is not a brute but 'un excellent berger, dévoué, probe' (II, 568); and he comments to the court, after the account of the killing: 'Il a de l'honneur, cet homme-là'. These interruptions to the narrating of events serve, in Labov's terms, as an evaluative guide to the point of the story. Picot's comment, ostensibly addressed to the court to make them acquit, also guides the Narrator and the reader. We are led to see that the opposition between primitive and civilised is not clear-cut, and that Gargan embodies positive values: fidelity, honour. The contrast underlying the tale is rather between what are presented as male and female worlds. When we see this, we realise why the Narrator has evoked at such length hunting (four pages) before the encounter with Gargan and Picot's tale of the shepherd's marriage and murder (three pages). The contrast between the intial 'vie simple, la vie rude d'automne du chasseur' (II, p. 563) and the final comment of the Narrator: 'tandis que vous allez aussi voir passer au bois les premières

---

13. On the role of antithesis in short fiction, see Chapter 4, and Goyet, *La Nouvelle*, 28-47.

CHAPTER 1. TELLERS AND LISTENERS

toilettes qui passent' (II, p. 571) points to the artifice of elegant Parisian life and the superiority of the 'male' values embodied in the shoot, which is moreover punctuated by the shooting of the woodcock, the *bécasses* of the title, a word also used colloquially of a featherbrained woman. The male Narrator implies throughout the superiority of simplicity, honour, and solidarity; the more so as we are aware that he is telling the woman a tale told him by another man of a woman's infidelity and punishment.

In discussing natural oral tales, the term 'recipient design' has been given to the tendency to make a story target the knowledge or ignorance of its listeners,[14] who in a sense mould the tale. Picot tells the Narrator of the peasants' amusement at the exchange of alcohol for sex, of male voyeurism ('des messieurs' come from a neighbouring town to watch la Goutte's infidelities), of jokes in the café; but his account to the court remains in contrast serious and respectful. But reporting Picot's account to the woman in Paris, the Narrator does not politely censor it for his audience; he leaves the humour about sexuality and the directness about death in their original form. If we ask: 'Who is telling the tale, to whom, and why?', we can see how the implied frame gives an edge to the narration in the form of provocative and undeniably misogynistic overtones, as the Narrator confronts his narratee in Paris,[15] and how the opposition of 'male' and 'female' values unifies the story and underpins the other oppositions that can be seen in it: honour/infidelity, nature/artifice, crudity/elegance, fidelity/flirtatiouness, directness/decorum.

'Carmen': why tell? why listen?

In 'Les Bécasses', an awareness of the twin frames affects our response to the tale. Without the female narratee, we would have only two loosely linked Norman anecdotes, a shoot and a murder. In the case of a

---

14. Harvey Sachs, *Lectures on Conversation*, ed. by Gail Jefferson, 2 vols (Oxford: Blackwell, 1992), II, 231; Livia Polanyi, 'The Nature of Meaning', 54.
15. This Narrator is one constructed by Maupassant, implied by the narrative. At the same time these attitudes are clearly close to those of Maupassant himself.

much longer tale, Mérimée's 'Carmen',[16] there is again an apparent disproportion: the frame is almost as long as the embedded narrative, the well-known tale of Don José's love for the gypsy Carmen, and there is a similar lack of apparent overall unity. Can the motives of tellers and listeners contribute to our desire for unity?

The frame is provided, as in 'Les Bécasses', by an unnamed homodiegetic Narrator, an archaeologist recalling in 1845 his travels in Spain in 1830 to find the site of the battle of Munda. He meets the brigand José three times: first, in the countryside, when he helps the bandit escape from the law; then in Cordoba, when José breaks in unexpectedly on Carmen and the Narrator, whom she has invited to her room to tell his fortune; and finally in prison awaiting execution, when José recounts his life with Carmen. This embedded tale is pseudo-oral: the Narrator claims to report José's actual words, but after the first three sentences the brigand falls into the past historic of written narrative to recount the key moments of his life, from leaving his home village to her murder. After the end of José's tale, the frame is resumed with a substantial final chapter by the Narrator on gypsy customs and language.

The frame clearly provides a context that makes José's narration plausible. The Narrator of 'Les Bécasses' gives his account of the shoot because the woman in Paris has asked him to explain his absence; Picot relates Gargan's killing of his wife to satisfy the Narrator's curiosity; so too José has reasons for giving an account of his life to his narratee, both retrospective, as he is indebted to the archaeologist, and also prospective, in that he wants him to tell the bandit's mother that her son is dead. Other events in the lengthy frame-narrative help explain this final encounter in prison: the coincidental encounter with Carmen in Cordoba leads to the theft of the Narrator's watch; its recovery leads to the meeting in gaol. The frame also provides a way of leading the civilised French reader into an alien and exotic world. But the frame is overlong if its sole function is to provide a context for narration, as if Mérimée were reluctant to adopt or anticipate the psychologically implausible[17] but now accepted convention whereby murderers in prison

16. All references in the text are to *Théâtre de Clara Gazul. Romans et Nouvelles*, ed. by Jean Mallion and Pierre Salomon, Bibliothèque de la Pléiade (Paris: Gallimard, 1978).
17. On this implausibility, if the aim is not self-justification or public confession,

awaiting execution, as in Poe's 'The Black Cat', Schwob's 'L'Homme voilé', or Camus's *L'Etranger*, are allowed to 'unburthen [their] soul'[18] in an autonomous and uncontextualised monologue. Moreover, the contextualisation cannot justify the closing chapter on gypsy customs after José's confession. This chapter has indeed been dismissed as irrelevant: a pedantic dissertation that weakens the story, a 'wilfully perverse' addition, or 'little more than a learned appendix', and even treated as one in a recent English translation.[19]

A different approach to the frame of 'Carmen' has been to justify it as a tactic adopted by the author towards his audience (Mérimée wants to display his philological knowledge, or to affect detachment from an exciting narrative), or to guide the reader's response by creating a character whose 'intrusive erudition' will make us identify rather with José.[20] But to approach the frame this way still treats it as something extraneous to José's narrative. Indeed the word 'frame', though a useful metaphor, is misleading in that its associations of enclosure, of a separate container for something contained, implies that it is not fully 'part of the story'.[21] This underplays what is going on between José and the archaeologist throughout the bandit's narration, when we do not forget the Narrator, now acting as narratee, any more than we forget the woman to whom the Narrator of 'Les Bécasses' is writing. Don José is not just relating his life, but relating to the archaeologist: not with veiled aggression, like the Narrator of 'Les Bécasses', but generously

see Dorrit Cohn, *Transparent Minds: Narrative Modes for Representing Consciousness in Fiction* (Princeton University Press, 1978), 181.
18. Poe, *Selected Writings*, 320.
19. Respectively by Pierre Trahard, *Prosper Mérimée et l'art de la nouvelle* (Paris: Presses Universitaires de France, 1952), 39; A.W. Raitt, *Prosper Mérimée* (London: Eyre and Spottiswoode, 1970), 197; and Mérimée, *Carmen, et autres nouvelles choisis*, edited by M.J. Tilby (London: Harrap, 1981), 36; and Nicholas Jotcham (trans.), Mérimée, *Carmen and Other Tales*, The World's Classics (Oxford University Press, 1989).
20. Respectively, Maurice Parturier, in his edition of the *Romans et nouvelles*, 2 vols (Paris: Garnier, 1967), II, 342; Auguste Dupouy, *'Carmen' de Mérimée*, Les Grands Evénements littéraires (Paris: Malfère, 1930), 118-19; and Frank Paul Bowman, *Prosper Mérimée: Heroism, Pessimism, and Irony* (Berkeley: University of California Press, 1962), 88, 171.
21. Jean Rousset has expressed such reservations: *Le Lecteur intime* (Paris: Corti, 1986), 58.

'giving' the story. This might lead us to ask what he seeks in exchange, apart from the repayment of a debt and the message to his mother. If we do so, a second set of relationships needs to be borne in mind: that between narrators and their younger selves. With homodiegetic storytellers like Don José and the archaeologist, there is always a gap between the narrator recalling events and the self acting in his own narrative. These two aspects of the same person have often been distinguished: as the narrating self and the experiencing self,[22] or as *narrator* and *hero* (Genette).[23] An example from another tale by Mérimée, where the question of focalisation, of whether events are perceived by the narrating or the experiencing self, can show how the gap can be crucial to storytelling. In 'Il Vicolo di Madama Lucrezia', the Narrator relates an adventure in Italy in his youth, in which he imagines himself caught up in a love affair, and the target of an assassination attempt; in fact, as he discovers at the end of his stay, he has been mistaken for don Ottavio, the son of an old friend of his father, the marquise Aldobrandi, with whom he is staying. Events are narrated just as they were experienced by the younger self. The older self may intervene on occasion to judge ironically the naïvety and vanity of his younger self: 'Je croyais pieusement à l'inflammabilité des dames allemandes, espagnoles et italiennes à la seule vue d'un Français. Bref, à cette époque, j'étais encore bien de mon pays' (1016). But he gives no hint of discoveries that are yet to come; these we can only guess at with the help of clues planted by Mérimée that the hero misses. This preserves the ambiguity of the tale, as we are uncertain if the events are supernatural or rationally explicable, and also the suspense: we can see what is going on, but not why.[24] The hero, as experiencing self, imagines himself at the centre of the increasingly mysterious events: a

---

22. Leo Spitzer's *erzählendes Ich* and *erzähltes Ich*. See F.K. Stanzel, *A Theory of Narrative*, trans. by Charlotte Goedsche (Cambridge University Press, 1986), 81–82; Cohn, *Transparent Minds*, 170.
23. Genette, *Figures III*, 259.
24. Bauman has highlighted similar manipulation of focalisation in oral narratives about practical jokes given by their perpetrators, who thus control the information available to the listener about what is going on in the narrated event: for example, by adopting external focalisation for a younger self so that we see what is going on, but not what he has planned, see *Story, Performance and Event*, 37.

CHAPTER 1. TELLERS AND LISTENERS   31

woman throws him a flower from a window in a deserted house, a shot is fired at him from the same window; in fact they are directed at don Ottavio, by his mistress and by her hostile brother respectively. The ambiguity is perhaps sustained only by a trick, even, in Alan Raitt's terms, 'a bare-faced hoax':[25] the narrating self omits any mention of the resemblance of his younger self to don Ottavio (it is implied that they are half-brothers). But since we witness events solely as perceived by his younger self, it is natural that he did not notice the family resemblance, especially given the vanity and imperceptiveness that the older narrator does foreground, which is evident in his admiration of his own lucidity and his confident misreading of don Ottavio as preoccupied with politics rather than a love-affair.

So when we ask about a homodiegetic narrator: 'who is perceiving things, the narrating self or the younger self as protagonist?', we are not faced with a clear-cut alternative. The use of the two focalisations is above all a question of emphasis, that can be varied as the tale proceeds to create different effects. Of the two focalisations available,[26] Mérimée adopts in 'Il Vicolo' the perspective of the narrator to generate ironic amusement at the expense of the character of his younger self, but slides to that of the hero to perceive events in order to create ambiguity and suspense. The gap between the two lies in part in the amount of information each possesses: the narrator knows of the resemblance and probable relatiship between the hero and don Ottavio, but the hero does not. But the gap is also a product of experience: the hero's juvenile vanity versus the narrator's mature detachment. If we ask the same question of 'Carmen', it becomes clear that Mérimée exploits through his two narrators both possible focalisations (hero or narrator) and the two differences on which they can be based (knowledge of facts or character development).

José overwhelmingly adopts the point of view of his older, narrating self. As he tells his tale to the archaeologist in prison, having been led by Carmen from duty to a life of crime, under sentence of death for

25. Raitt, *Prosper Mérimée*, 196.
26. See Genette, *Figures III*, 214. Genette uses the term 'focalisation' to avoid the exclusively visual associations of 'point of view'; what is at issue is who perceives a given scene, whether by seeing, hearing, feeling... But arguably focalisation too has predominantly visual associations, and there is no difficulty extending 'point of view' to cover perception in a wider sense.

several murders including hers, he views the successive scenes of his life in the light of these later developments. He constantly intervenes in his account of events with comments loaded with hindsight. These correspond to Labov's 'external evaluation': a narrator's comments made from outside the sequence of events being narrated, often spread throughout the story,[27] that point to the meaning that the events have for him and the response that he desires in his listener. The interventions of José's narrating self contribute to the sense of fatality that, resigned to death, he seeks to instil in his listener. His evaluative remarks to the archaeologist frequently take the form of comments on the critical nature of various scenes. They are marked by a shift from the past historic to a combination of present (and sometimes future) and perfect (all emphases are mine): 'L'on me fit étudier, mais je ne profitais guère. J'aimais trop jouer à la paume, *c'est ce qui m'a perdu*' (956). Thus when he first sees Carmen: 'C'était un vendredi, *et je ne l'oublierai jamais*' (958), or when he is on guard duty at the colonel's after his release from prison: 'C'est de ce jour-là, *je pense*[,] que je me mis à l'aimer pour tout de bon' (964). Significantly, perfect and present take over from past historic again in the coda when José bridges the gap between the end of his narrative and the moment of narration, and makes a final comment on Carmen's life: 'Pauvre enfant! Ce sont les *Calé* qui sont coupables pour l'avoir élevé ainsi' (988). Evaluation is equally evident in asides that warn of misfortunes to follow: Carmen throws him a flower, and 'je ne sais ce qui me prit, mais je la ramassai [...]. Première sottise!' (958). These external evaluative remarks are reinforced by reporting in direct speech Carmen's own proleptic insistence on fatality (in Labov's terms, an embedded evaluation), such as her recurrent 'C'est écrit' (985, 987).

How does José's consistent adoption of this focalisation help guide us to his motives, and what do they suggest of his relationship to the archaeologist? In real life, story-telling is not the disinterested imparting of information; like other verbal acts, it disposes others to react so that we can attain what we desire: approval, applause, co-operation... A fictional character's enlightenment of listeners can equally be tainted by ulterior motives. Behind the ostensible reasons for José telling the Narrator his tale we can detect, in the interventions that create a sense

---

27. Labov, *Language in the Inner City*, 368–9.

CHAPTER 1. TELLERS AND LISTENERS 33

of inevitability, a strategy of self-exculpation. He is presenting things with hindsight, and it is only after the event that one can seek to apportion, or in his case, to shift, blame. He blames Carmen when he kills her: 'Pourtant, tu le sais, c'est toi qui m'as perdu; c'est pour toi que je suis devenu un voleur et un meurtrier' (987); he also presents her (as she does too) as 'le diable' (975) and 'un démon' (988),[28] while at other moments blaming Carmen's character on her gypsy upbringing (988). Inconsistent explanations, perhaps; what they have in common is that they shift any blame from José as hero. The José as narrator who seeks to do this repeatedly apostrophises the archaeologist in a manner characteristic of external evaluation. He appeals for sympathetic understanding of his position, for instance to convey his shock when she throws the flower at him: 'Monsieur, cela me fit l'effet d'une balle qui m'arrivait' (958), or to stress his humiliation at being reduced to guard duty: 'Vous ne pouvez vous figurer ce qu'un homme de cœur éprouve en pareille occasion' (963). This apostrophe occurs when he underlines her power and his helplessness: 'Monsieur, quand cette fille-là riait, il n'y avait pas moyen de parler raison' (978). It is therefore unsurprising to find it when he is on the point of killing her: 'Tout, monsieur, tout! je lui offris tout, pourvu qu'elle voulût m'aimer encore!' (988).

In relating his past to the Narrator, the older José retrospectively invests it with inevitability, exculpates himself, and appeals for understanding. But also, since giving an account of one's life can be a way of making sense of it, he shapes the image of his own character. This can be seen in the way that he manages the tempo[29] of his narrative, the relative length and emphasis given to the narration of particular events. He glosses over his life before meeting Carmen, but we can detect in his rapid account hints of a young José who is resistant to discipline and study: 'On voulait que je fusse d'église, et l'on me fit étudier, mais je ne profitais guère. J'aimais trop à jouer à la paume' (956); someone whose lack of self-control in a quarrel leads to a fight:

> Quand nous jouons à la paume, nous autres Navarrais, nous oublions tout. Un jour que j'avais gagné, un gars de l'Alava me chercha querelle, nous

---

28. See also 'cette diable de fille' (972); 'un sourire diabolique qu'elle avait dans de certains moments' (980); and for Carmen herself, 968.
29. What Genette terms *durée* (duration).

primes nos *maquilas*, et j'eus encore l'avantage; mais cela m'obligea de quitter le pays. (956)

The narrating José again shifts responsibility, first to 'national character', then to his opponent for instigating the fight. What the fight actually leads to is not clear (death?[30] fear of revenge?), but the evasiveness about its consequences is suspicious. His perfunctory account of how he left his home town means that he can make his life of dishonour and crime begin with the moment when he meets Carmen. Once we note this, we can see that the recourse to violence and the flight from its consequences are recurrent features of his account of their relationship. He discovers his love for her, on duty at the Colonel's party, when prompted by a jealous impulse to run through the *freluquets* flirting with her in the patio (964). When he relates the quarrel with the lieutenant in the rue du Candilejo, he stresses his own inability to move, conveniently forgets his retort, and suggests that the officer not only acted first (so his response is self-defence), but in effect impales himself on the sword of José, hampered by the elderly Dorothée's intervention:

> Je ne pouvais faire un pas; j'étais comme perclus. L'officier, en colère, voyant que je ne me retirais pas, et que je n'avais pas même ôté mon bonnet de police, me prit au collet et me secoua rudement. Je ne sais ce que je lui dis. Il tira son épée, et je dégainai. La vieille me saisit le bras, et le lieutenant me donna un coup au front, dont je porte encore la marque. Je reculai, et d'un coup de coude je jetai Dorothée à la renverse; puis, comme le lieutenant me poursuivait, je lui mis la pointe au corps, et il s'enferra. (970)

Swift transitions elide the stages between being a fugitive from justice and a deserter to involvement at Carmen's suggestion in the smugglers' band: 'Pour le faire court, monsieur' (972), and in the space of ten lines he is out of uniform and the smugglers have become 'nos gens'. Similarly, in his account of his shift from smuggler to thief, rapidity implies that he did not have time to think, and his external evaluation presents his jealous violence as the defence of a young girl: 'Monsieur,

30. As some critics have assumed, for instance Dominique Maingueneau, *Carmen: les racines d'un mythe* (Paris: Sorbier, 1984), 24.

on devient coquin sans y penser. Une jolie fille vous fait perdre la tête, on se bat pour elle, un malheur arrive, il faut vivre à la montagne, et de contrebandier on devient voleur avant d'avoir réfléchi' (976). If we fail to differentiate the protagonist from the narrating José who is presenting an image of his life to the archaeologist, it is easy to perceive him as a man, weak perhaps, but essentially virtuous, destroyed by love; he 'tries to remain true to his duty as soldier and firmly resists Carmen, but he weakens and his passion plunges him into a world of crime'.[31] A sceptical reading of José's controlling role as narrator of this deceptively linear life, in which he plays down the role of impulse, sees his career fatalistically in terms of its outcome, and elides elements like the earlier violence, reveals a more complex figure. Such a reading also needs to take account of the prominence he gives to certain elements. At the start of his narrative, introducing himself as 'don José Lizarrabengoa', he mentions his entitlement to the *don*, his genealogy; he is equally proud of his Basque origins and his language. Having achieved the rank of corporal in the army, he dwells on his desire to occupy himself usefully, making a chain, while the other soldiers play cards and sleep, and expects promotion. Imprisonment and demotion after Carmen escapes just mean that he will have to work harder for it; his 'honneur de soldat' (963) makes him reject the chance to escape from prison, just as he ascribes his rejection of Carmen's proposal to get Garcia killed while ambushing the Englishman to his national honour: 'Pour certaines choses, je serai toujours franc Navarrais, comme dit le proverbe' (980). The narrating Don José strives to create the image of someone true to a certain ideal throughout the vicissitudes of his past. In response the archaeologist endorses this by always referring to him as 'don José', whereas for the guide he is José Navarro (945) or le Navarro, losing his nobility and acquiring a nickname like his fellow-smuggler le Remendado.

The archaeologist, José's narratee in Chapter 3 of 'Carmen', is also both a character in the frame, travelling in Spain in 1830, and homodiegetic narrator of the escapades of his younger self after a gap of fifteen years (950). Whereas José's narrative is dominated by the

31. Bowman, *Heroism, Pessimism and Irony*, 47. See also, for example, Trahard, *Mérimée et la nouvelle*, 35. Exceptions to such readings are Maingueneau, *Racines*, 24, and Claude-Gilbert Dubois, 'Métamorphoses de *Carmen*: un cas de réalisme mythologique', *Eidôlon*, 25 (October, 1984), 9-62 (20-21).

perspective of his narrating self, the archaeologist seems initially to adopt the other available focalisation by restricting his narrative to what he perceived as events occured, in ignorance of what would happen next. When he first meets José, we are aware of his suspicions, as he notes details like the stranger's ignorance of the region and his knowledge of horses; but the narrative goes no further than the conclusions that the archaeologist as hero draws at the time: he sees that his guide Antonio distrusts the stranger, but cannot yet tell why. This distinction between the focalisations adopted by José and the Narrator, however, hinges on the difference in information possessed by their older and younger selves. But, as we saw with the narrator of 'Il Vicolo di Madama Lucrezia', a difference can also spring from a development in self-awareness between the two selves. José is telling of events that led up to Carmen's death only a few months, perhaps even a few weeks, earlier,[32] whereas fifteen years have elapsed between the Narrator's Spanish experiences and the moment of narration.

The older Narrator wryly presents himself as a pedantic academic, about to resolve the question 'qui tient toute l'Europe savante en suspens', namely the site of the battle of Munda in 45 B.C., but for the moment entertaining his readers with 'une petite histoire' (938), a travel episode from his youth. The perceptions of his younger self in Spain in 1830 suggest a very different person. Then he was naïve: he innocently relates how Carmen asks him the time, no doubt to see if he has a watch worth stealing before inviting him to the *neveria*, and enquires if it is really gold; no surprise when it goes missing. He shows the same traveller's vanity as the Narrator of 'Il Vicolo di Madama Lucrezia', with his confident pronouncements on Spanish pronunciation (940) and character (941). He is fascinated by exotic sexuality: we deduce this is why he is down by the Guadalquivir at nightfall at the moment when the women bathe, 'écarquill[ant] les yeux' with the other men and fondly imagining Diana and her nymphs (948). He lets himself be picked up by Carmen, as she uses smoking to initiate a conversation, and his curiosity about magic enhances her allure. Even at the time, he seems

32. José's tale ends with the murder of Carmen and his surrender (988). Some months (953) elapse between the Narrator meeting Carmen and José in Cordoba and the final interview. José situates the meeting in Cordoba (984) shortly before the affair with Lucas and her death; the chronology is coherent, but we are clearly not meant to reconstruct it too exactly.

CHAPTER 1. TELLERS AND LISTENERS

ashamed of what he has exposed himself to in accompanying Carmen, and we deduce that the 'diverses considérations' that prevent him going to the *corregidor* after the theft of his watch (953) include the difficulty of explaining why he was with her. He is, moreover, fascinated with bandits. He stays with José because he wants to get to know what a brigand is like: 'On n'en voit pas tous les jours, et il y a un certain charme à se trouver auprès d'un être dangereux' (941).

Thus we sense a gap between the young archaeologist's only half-avowed curiosities in the marginal and the forbidden and the aloofness of his older self who treats them with a certain irony: mocking himself for gaping down at the river, confessing shame at his interest in magic. The narrative filters events through the eyes of the younger self to contribute to effects of drama and surprise, but also allows us to view them with the self-awareness of the older Narrator, conscious now both of the comedy and of the recklessness of his youthful escapades. This dual perspective is clearly seen in the dramatic moment when José bursts in on the Narrator and Carmen. The younger Narrator does not yet know the intruder's identity, is worried about what is to happen, seeks to defend himself, and cannot (ignorant as he then was of Romany) understand the argument. The calm older Narrator has the time to formulate these anxieties with circuitous caution in a literary style:

> Le mot de *payllo*,[33] souvent répété, était le seul mot que je comprisse. Je savais que les bohémiens désignent ainsi tout homme étranger à leur race. Supposant qu'il s'agissait de moi, je m'attendais à une explication délicate; déjà j'avais la main sur le pied d'un des tabourets, et je syllogeais à part moi pour deviner le moment précis où il conviendrait de le jeter à la tête de l'intrus. Celui-ce repoussa rudement la bohémienne, et s'avança vers moi; puis, reculant d'un pas:
>
> — Ah! Monsieur, dit-il, c'est vous!
>
> Je le regardai à mon tour, et reconnus mon ami don José. En ce moment, je regrettais un peu de ne pas l'avoir laissé pendre. (952)

---

33. The Pléiade text here has the awkward 'le mot du *payllo*'; other reliable editions, including *Nouvelles*, ed. by Michel Crouzet (Paris: Imprimerie Nationale, 1987), II, 171; *Romans et nouvelles*, ed. Parturier, II, 362, have 'le mot de *payllo*'.

The frame in the first two chapters preserves this dual perspective. When we shift to José's narrative in Chapter 3, the frequent footnotes that explain Romany phrases or Spanish customs are a constant reminder that we are not just hearing José relate his life to the Narrator in prison, but reading the written record of it by an older Narrator who now knows Romany. Once we see how this double perspective is guiding our response, the nature of the shift in the final chapter becomes clearer: the voice heard here, as the frame resumes, is unambiguously that of the older Narrator. The chapter is not simply a study of gypsies, but a sign of the death of youthful curiosities and the survival of a purely scholarly self. As he works methodically through a series of points (distribution, jobs, morality, origins, language), we see that gypsies are no longer fascinating individuals, but specimens for study. As regards sexuality, he now knows that 'la beauté est fort rare parmi les gitanas d'Espagne' (989), and shows the cynicism of an older man; his fascination with magic has given way to the view that their 'spells' are a way of fooling the naïve *payllo* out of money. Overall the chapter offers a deromanticised view of gypsy life: smuggling and other illicit activities feature alongside the more conventional ones of horsetrader and tinker. The triumph of the academic can be seen in the Narrator's ostentatiously self-deprecating references to 'mes minces connaissances' (994), after comparing conjugation in German and Spanish Romany dialects.

Distinguishing between the two selves, narrating and experiencing, of Don José and the archaeologist highlights the different narrative interests of the frame and the embedded tale. In the frame we find an ironic tension between the academic and the naïve curiosities of the young traveller, between calm retrospection and anxious experience; José's account of his life feeds the traveller's fascination with the exotic and dangerous. In José's narrative, we find at first a tale of infatuation and self-destruction, the 'degenerative or pathetic tragedy' that has been seen as a typical mode of the novella,[34] and on closer examination a narrative dominated by hindsight, in which we can explore how José as narrator moulds his career to exculpate himself and seek for sympathetic understanding from his narratee.

---

34. Mary Doyle Springer, quoted by Reid, *Short Story*, 45.

CHAPTER 1. TELLERS AND LISTENERS

The final chapter functions as a coda, bridging the gap between the end of the narrative and the present; after it, we cannot ask: 'what happened next?' It moreover makes the frame part of the story by linking it thematically with José's narrative. Running through both is an opposition between forms of constraint and aspirations to freedom. The central conflict is between jealous José, the soldier, who desires fidelity, and Carmen the gypsy and smuggler, who desires freedom. But beyond that, both figures show an internal tension: in José, this lies between his pride and ambition, and his instability and violence. After the brawl that causes him to leave his village he seeks social integration as a soldier. When Carmen seduces him from the path of duty, we know that the various forms order takes (honour, family, military duty, marriage) are the more important to him because of his lapses. Carmen herself is no more a simple embodiment of freedom than José is of duty. She may tell José: 'Ce que je veux, c'est être libre et faire ce qui me plaît' (982), or that 'Carmen sera toujours libre' (987). But she frequently invokes the gypsy code and 'notre loi' (967) in argument, and her attitude to gypsy law, together with her fatalism (another form of constraint), contributes to her death. She evokes the possibility that she could become José's *romi* under 'la loi d'Egypte' (967). While Garcia is alive, José has no rights to command her (978); after José has killed him, 'Comme mon rom, tu as le droit de tuer ta romi' (987); her desire for freedom can now realise itself only in death. In this light we can see that the young Narrator, too, is caught in the tension between constraint and freedom: seduced from the rigours of scholarship first by his curiosity about a bandit, then by a gypsy girl and the attractions of magic.

The narrative voices, the tellers and listeners, that Mérimée has constructed, bring out the tensions in all three main figures between various forms of constraint and impulses of passion, violence, and individualistic self-assertion. What is important is not so much the superiority of one or the other as the tensions set up between the two. There is a potential moral issue, one that the Narrator toys with when he allows José to escape: should he have saved a thief, perhaps a murderer, from the law, simply because he has eaten with him? Has he not exposed his law-abiding guide to the vengeance of a bandit? But the incident does not serve to pose a choice between law and illegality, and the dilemma is eluded by the soldiers arriving to interrupt the Narrator's reflections. The sort of point we expect from literature is not so much unambiguous endorsement of one or the other but rather food for thought, and in short fiction in particular, the crystallisation of a central issue. The incident alerts the reader to this central thematic tension. Garcia's attitude to Carmen is straightforward: as le Dancaïre observes after José has killed him, he would have sold her for a piastre (981); he owns and uses her, but is neither obsessed nor fascinated. It is more interesting to hear of her from a representative of order, a soldier, and even more when that soldier has a very ambivalent relationship with the law, as a man of impulse aspiring to social reintegration. The interest is augmented in that this soldier/bandit's account of his relationship with Carmen is listened to by someone who is both a restrained academic and also a voyeur seeking excitement abroad. In Carmen and José's cases, the irreconcilable demands of constraint and freedom lead to their deaths; in the case of the Narrator, the triumph of the law is embodied in the final chapter in the death of his younger self.

'Sombre récit, conteur plus sombre': why listen? why retell?

What we find in 'Carmen' is a sense of the ambivalence of the tellers; but what of the listeners? Mérimée's tale can usefully be set against one where the ambivalent role of the listener is highlighted. The title of Villiers de l'Isle-Adam's 'Sombre récit, conteur plus sombre',[35] first published in 1877 and included in his collection *Contes cruels* (1883), announces a tale about story-telling, although implying initially that the teller is the main centre of interest. In it, Genette's distinction between the events narrated (*histoire*), the narrative account given of them (*récit*) and the act of narrating (*narration*), is useful in clarifying the story's structure, and the role of another puzzling concluding section.

An anonymous voice, as in 'Les Bécasses' and 'Carmen', similar to but distinct from the author, opens the story with a rapid orientation (later details indicate contemporary Paris as the setting): 'J'étais invité, ce soir-là, [...] à faire partie d'un souper d'auteurs dramatiques.' The homodiegetic narrator is characterised at first only by his ironic attitude

---

35. Villiers de l'Isle-Adam, *Œuvres complètes*, ed. by Alan Raitt and Pierre-Georges Castex with Jean-Marie Bellefroid, 2 vols, Bibliothèque de la Pléiade (Paris: Gallimard, 1986), I, 686. All references in the text are to this edition.

CHAPTER 1. TELLERS AND LISTENERS 41

which sets him apart from the group of diners; and at the end he leaves as the other members approach the celebrated dramatist D***, to congratulate him on the story he has just told. The tale D*** relates in the course of the dinner, with self-indulgent drama and pathos, is of his involvement in a duel: his friend Raoul had called on him to serve as his second, he had done so, and the duel had ended in the Raoul's death.

The levels of narration in the story present a succession of homodiegetic narrators, each relating events in which he played a part: the Narrator relates the dinner to the reader (level 1, the text we read); that tale evokes D*** narrating to his audience (including the Narrator) his tale (level 2), in this tale (level 3), Raoul calls on D***, relates his challenge to his adversary (level 4), asks D*** to serve as second, and is killed. Chronologically the series of narratives contains two discrete sequences of events, separated by a brief gap. The first is of the events leading up to the challenge, Raoul's visit to D***, the duel, and Raoul's death. Here our interest is held by suspense: we want to know how the duel will end. D*** (like the archaeologist in 'Carmen') adopts the focalisation of his earlier self as second in recounting it, without revealing its outcome in advance. The second sequence of events is that witnessed by the Narrator, namely D***'s narration at the dinner and subsequent events. Here the point of the first story, the tragic 'sombre récit' of a duel, is changed by its new context, just as Picot's tale in 'Les Bécasses' changes in emphasis when the Narrator relates it to the woman in Paris. Told by D***, it entertained and moved his audience; relayed by the narrator, it becomes an illustration of how D*** (the 'conteur plus sombre') has been corrupted by his profession as a dramatic author.

Villiers sustains to the end what Pierre Citron terms an 'atmosphère double',[36] a curiosity about the outcome of both the duel (level 3) and the narrating of the duel (level 2). It is a consequence of the structure that, even more than in 'Les Bécasses' and 'Carmen', we cannot simply ask who is a narrator and who a narratee: someone who is a narrator on one level (for instance, D*** in level 2) can become a listener in another (D*** to Raoul, in level 3). Before he begins his narrative, D*** points to this interchangeability of functions by asking his

---

36. *Contes cruels*, ed. by Pierre Citron (Paris: Garnier-Flammarion, 1980), 245.

audience: 'Ah! que diriez-vous, messieurs, s'il vous était arrivé mon aventure de l'autre jour?' (686), putting them, as listeners, into his position as potentially both experiencing and narrating the duel.

But the most striking feature about the sequence of embedded narratives is that none is watertight: inside each level there are constant interruptions. When Raoul is relating his challenge (level 4) to D***, the dramatist reacts to what he sees as the theatrically unmotivated or clichéd nature of this account, and interrupts him:

> 'Je compris qu'il [Raoul] me jouait la première scène de sa "machine".
> '"Oh! oh! dis-je, comment amènes-tu cela? [...] le motif? L'agencement de la scène? [...]
> '— Il s'agissait d'une injure faite à ma mère, mon ami, — répondit Raoul, qui semblait ne pas m'écouter. — Ma Mère, — est-ce un motif suffisant?"'
> (Ici D*** s'interrompit, regardant les convives qui n'avaient pu s'empêcher de sourire à ces dernières paroles.) (688)

But what is also happening here (in the parenthesis, on level 2) is that both D*** (stopping) and his audience (smiling) are interrupting D***'s account of events. In fact, more than a fifth of the text given over to D***'s narrating, which one might expect to relate straightforwardly the events of the duel, consists of such interruptions. Many of these interruptions are D***'s comments and asides to his audience in level 2, which (like José's appeals to the archaeologist) form an external evaluation, guide the listeners to the point he wants to make, and characteristically switch from the past historic of narration to the present.[37] Pausing to note that they follow appreciatively, he remarks: 'Il me parut très convenable pour la circonstance. Vous voyez cela d'ici, n'est-ce pas?'; or he inserts an aside: '(Entre nous, je trouve qu'ils sont un peu en retard, dans la vie réelle!)' (689). But we also find their reactions: they smile at D***'s report of Raoul's account of the motive for the duel; they associate themselves out of vanity with a psychological observation by D***: 'C'est vrai! on est comme ça!...

---

37. As well as this external evaluation, there are also instances of embedded evaluation (Labov, *Language in the Inner City*, 372) taking the form of thoughts of characters at the time: 'Je me dis que...' (687).

s'écrièrent les convives, qui tenaient à bénéficier de la remarque' (689). These audience reactions also include the Narrator's responses during the dinner, congratulating D*** at the end, and making an aside to himself and the reader: '— Succès d'*estime*! pensais-je' (693). These intrusions are all the more noticeable in that the Narrator had introduced D***'s narration by affirming (the emphasis is his): '(*Je lui laisse, strictement, la parole*)' (687), as if we were to have an uninterrupted block of D***'s narrative (level 3) with his words reported without comment. Maupassant's Narrator in 'Les Bécasses' had similarly claimed not to change Picot's words to guarantee the authenticity of the narrative. Here, however, it is clearly not true, and the claim calls attention to what interrupts D***'s narration — notably the audience, but also the Narrator himself.

Are there intrusions like this at every level? The Narrator's implied audience in his account of the dinner (the reader) is of course in no position to interrupt him. At the same time the Narrator appeals to us both directly and indirectly from the outset. When he notes: 'Le souper fut d'abord naturellement triste' (686), implying that celebratory dinners for others are generally gloomy occasions, the irony establishes a knowing complicity. More obviously, the just-quoted '(*Je lui laisse, strictement, la parole*)' is clearly an aside to the reader as it is in the present tense and in parentheses. The use of *ici*, on five occasions (688, 689, 690, 692, 692), introducing comments on D***'s appearance or gestures, is a further sign of the Narrator's direct appeal to the reader. In any narrative we are more or less conscious of the presence of a narrator; the Narrator's irony, the way he underlines how D*** is performing for his audience,[38] means that rather than having the illusion of being confronted directly with events, we are conscious of a high-profile narrator 'telling', and not just 'showing', or in Ross Chambers' terms, making the narrative less duplicitous and more self-designating. What is obviously true of D*** is also true of the Narrator.

38. This use of *ici* is also frequent in Barbey's stories, where we are likewise very conscious of the performance of narrators and of audience reactions: see, for example, 'Le Dessous de cartes d'une partie de whist' (*Œuvres romanesques complètes*, ed. by Jacques Petit, 2 vols, Bibliothèque de la Pléiade (Paris: Gallimard, 1964-1965), II, 133: 'Ici, il fit une légère pause'; II, 164: 'Ici encore le conteur s'arrêta'; 'Le Plus Bel Amour de don Juan', II, 68, 70. All references in the text are to vol. II of this edition.

We are conscious on every level of storytellers, but equally of their narratees. The tale is dedicated to an actor, Coquelin *cadet*, which points to performance and the link between performer and audience as central to the story,[39] as well the theme of *déformation professionnelle* in the dramatist-narrator D***.[40] It is true that the tale concerns a dramatist who treats life merely as material for art, and in this respect is similar to other tales by Villiers like 'L'Héroïsme du docteur Hallidonhill' (*Histoires insolites*), where the doctor sacrifices normal human concerns (he has cured a patient) to professional duty (he kills him to find out why the cure worked). The dramatist D*** responds to Raoul's account of his situation as if he were outlining a plan for a drama, and his friend's natural behaviour is read as a sign of superior theatricality: 'Raoul semblait pensif, distrait. Il avait le regard et la voix tranquilles, ordinaires. Il avait beaucoup de Surville en ce moment-là... de Surville dans ses bons rôles, même' (687). He rapidly realises his error: 'Je m'aperçus qu'il me parlait d'une chose de la vie! de la vie réelle!' (688), and continually underlines the contrast between the theatre and Raoul's real-life duel, turning on a member of the audience who criticises the events he is narrating as stage clichés (689). But he remains incapable of viewing the events he has lived through except in terms of theatrical schemata. He has recourse to theatrical parallels for that very reality, and his use of 'se jouer' ('be played out') is revealing. The situation may have its conventional side, he says, alluding to a famous melodrama of the mid-nineteenth century,[41] but 'son côté *Closerie des Genêts*, sans offense, disparaissait à mes yeux quand je songeais que ce qui allait se jouer, c'était la vie de mon pauvre Raoul!' (689). His behaviour similarly is modelled on the theatrical: 'J'entrai dans la chambre de Raoul. Il avait passé la nuit à écrire. Nous avons

39. Villiers, himself, was renowned for the bravura oral performance of his stories, whereas Mérimée's performance, when he read his tales to a circle of friends, was by all accounts flat and verged on the monotonous (see A.W. Raitt, *The Life of Villiers de l'Isle-Adam* (Oxford: Clarendon Press, 1981), 68-9; Mérimée, *Nouvelles*, ed. Crouzet, I, 14).
40. Stressed in most accounts of the tale: see Castex's edition of the *Contes cruels*, 463; Villiers, *Œuvres complètes*, I, 1317. The phrase was first used by Max Daireaux, *Villiers de l'Isle-Adam* (Paris: Desclée de Brouwer, 1936), 367-8.
41. Frédéric Soulié's *La Closerie des Genêts*, first performed 1846, revived 1875. Villiers's story was first published in 1877.

CHAPTER 1. TELLERS AND LISTENERS

tous mûri de ces scènes-là. Je n'avais qu'à me rappeler pour être naturel' (690). His idea of what is natural springs from theatrical cliché, and he acts in both senses in conformity with it. This is increasingly the case towards the end of his narrative: he feels 'le trac' (690), sees his position in terms of the stage set (I, p. 691), reacts to Raoul's death with applause (I, p. 692).

D***'s criticism of the guest who could see things only 'à travers une lorgnette de théâtre' (689) makes the point that his audience wants to see the affair in this light just as much as D*** does. Dramatic presentation and performance, like story-telling, imply an audience, whose role is not simply to decide a success, but (by 'recipient design') to mould the content and the shape of a public work of art. If we think of the role of the audience the end of the story adds a crucial twist. The events narrated by the Narrator continue after the dinner, and the Narrator leaves, meets a friend, and tells him of D***'s narration. But what exactly does he tells his friend? By referring to it as 'l'histoire de M. D*** *telle que je l'avais entendue*' (692: his emphasis), he brings himself in as a member of the audience, listening to D*** and then relating his own version. We imagine that what the Narrator gives his friend is level 2, the account of the dinner and D***'s narration there (rather than simply D***'s words, level 3), because that is the form in which we have read it so far as a *récit*. The oddity of this is that it could end with the Narrator telling his friend of his meeting with him, narrating the dinner... and an infinite regress sets in.[42]

The final line looks forward, as at the end of *A la recherche du temps perdu*, to the future (re-)narrating of what we have already heard/read, with the same ambiguity as in Proust's novel, which is a *roman du roman* rather as Villiers's tale is a *conte du conte*:[43] will the Narrator's future retelling be level 2, or a reworking of it?

'Eh bien! lui demandai-je en finissant: qu'en pensez-vous?
— Oui, C'est presque une nouvelle! me répondit-il après un silence. —
Ecrivez-la donc!'

42. For this natural tendency of what Ross Chambers terms 'narrational embedding' (Chambers, *Story and Situation*, 33-35); see also Lucien Dällenbach, *Le Récit spéculaire: Essai sur la mise en abyme* (Paris: Seuil, 1977), esp. 139-48.
43. Dällenbach, *Récit spéculaire*, 119-20.

Je le regardai fixement.
'Oui, lui dis-je, *maintenant* je puis l'écrire: elle est complète.' (693)

But why can he narrate it only now? What has the friend added to make it complete? If a story is always 'someone telling someone else that something happened',[44] — something that *relates*, in both senses — the audience's role is essential. The friend has made the Narrator turn events into a tale for him, has provided the crucial audience response and confirmed its potential: 'C'est presque une nouvelle'. If the Narrator looks at him 'fixement' after this, it could be interpreted, as it is sometimes,[45] as a sign of shocked recognition that *he* has fallen into the narratorial trap of dramatising and playing on his audience's reactions that he was satirising in D***, and has finally seen the significance of D***'s appeal to his audience: 'Ah! que diriez-vous, messieurs' (686) — every listener is a potential (re)teller. But Villiers is also suggesting that it is being a listener that makes the other into a teller, just as, in the world of 'industrial literature' of the nineteenth century, public and editors play a decisive role in moulding the short story.

What do we see of audience response in the tale? In level 3, D*** sees the 'potential' in Raoul's situation and encourages him to continue: 'Va! va!' (688). Similarly the guests in level 2 exclaim to show how they share D***'s emotion: 'On est comme ça!' (689); they are 'très émus' (691, 693) by his narrative, just as he was by the events he witnessed. And just as the friend's remark gives approval to the Narrator's 'nouvelle', the guests endorse D***'s use of the clichéd mother-motif:[46] 'Le "ma pauvre mère" passa donc comme une lettre à la poste' (691-2). Without audience response there would have been no performance by D***, no narration to the friend, and no *récit* for us to

---

44. Barbara Herrnstein Smith, 'Narrative versions, narrative theories', *Critical Inquiry*, 7 (1980-1981), 212-36 (232).
45. See Jean-Paul Gourevitch, *Villiers de l'Isle-Adam et l'univers de la transgression* (Paris: Seghers, 1971), 36-37; the Pléiade edition, I, 1317; Bertrand Vibert, *Villiers l'inquiéteur* (Toulouse: Presses Universitaires du Mirail, 1995), 230-1.
46. Probably based on a play by Théodore Barrière, *Les Parisiens de la décadence* (first performed 1854), where a character fights a duel over an insult to his mother (Villiers, *Œuvres complètes*, I, 1395).

read. Narrating is always motivated by something more than a simple desire to tell the truth. José is motivated by self-justification, as D*** is by his desire for applause: seduction, the desire to capture the other, and narcissism, the quest for attention, have often been seen as the two factors that lie behind story-telling.⁴⁷ But it is the narratee who authorises the act of narration, and for a specific purpose: here, not for satisfying curiosity as in 'Carmen', but for entertainment. At the end, the guests applaud, captivated 'tant par le côté impressionnant de son histoire que par la vivacité de son débit' (693). They initially demand the narrative: D***: 'Voyons! si tu nous racontais — mais là, franchement! — comment cela s'est passé?' (686); they ask for more: 'Continue! dirent les convives' (690); and they call for the end: 'Achève! crièrent, de toutes parts, les convives, très émus à leur tour' (691): they see the event as a self-contained narrative unit and impose a structure on it.⁴⁸

D***'s theatre-going audience wants the story in theatrical terms. The Narrator is a writer; the *récit* we have read is prompted by the Narrator's friend, but we know that the audience it is designed for is ourselves. His constant violations of his claim of non-intervention show that he has arranged the story for his audience. The discredit that attaches to narrating — treating reality, including the death of a friend, as material for art and responding to it only in so far as it conforms to what art tells us is real — attaches to the Narrator as much as to D***, although the more obviously caricatural portrayal of D*** disguises this. If Raoul has become story-fodder, 'a subject of declamation' for D***, in the terms of the epigraph from Juvenal (*Satires*, X, 167),⁴⁹ so has D*** for the Narrator. At the same time his remark: '*telle que je l'avais entendue*' reminds us that he was a member of D***'s audience; the discredit that attaches to audience promptings and expectations attaches to all narratees. In level 3, this means D*** (responding to Raoul); at the dinner, this includes the other guests and the Narrator ('Je crus devoir joindre mes humbles félicitations à celles de ses amis'

---

47. See, for example, Peter Brooks, *Reading for the Plot: Design and Intention in Narrative* (Cambridge, Mass.: Harvard University Press, 1992), 236.
48. See Polanyi, 'The Nature of Meaning', 54, on this 'recipient design', and Shryock, *Tales*, 10.
49. See Villiers, *Œuvres complètes*, I, 1394.

(693)); are we likewise implicated by our response to the story we have read?

If we respond to the story as a fiction, we avoid the trap into which D*** falls as narratee of Raoul, and D***'s guests do in their turn: that is, to fail to distinguish art from life. In a sense D***'s error is not so much the exploitation of friends in art for entertainment, as thinking that he can turn life into art and at the same time insist that it is real. His tears were real: 'Tout mon jeu était contenu. ... J'avais les larmes aux yeux, non pas les larmes de rigueur, mais de vraies' (691). But the theatrical parallel ('mon jeu') points to his dishonesty. The key sign of this confusion is the emotion D*** repeatedly lays claim to, an emotion which is the reaction of an audience to a spectacle: 'Raoul m'enlevait' (690); 'mon cœur faisait le trémolo!' (691). The same is true of the guests at the end, both moved and at the same time congratulating D*** on his talent (693). We can escape from the criticism being levelled at narratees if we sense that the Narrator is offering us a little fable: if we do not fall into the trap of emotion, but think. Indeed Villiers, when he was editor of the *Revue des Lettres et des Arts* in 1867, made 'faire penser' its motto, and it is a recurrent aim in other stories: by ironic reversal in 'Les Demoiselles de Bienfilâtre' (545), by provocation in 'Le Plus Beau Dîner du monde' (650), and in this tale by questioning the motives behind story-telling and listening. To the extent that we have been gripped by the duel — and even feel that D*** has exploited this situation 'heartlessly' — we are involving ourselves emotionally with a purely fictional character and situation. 'Sombre récit, conteur plus sombre' thus becomes an insidious attack on emotional reading, disconcerting to readers who suddenly finds themselves in the position, *vis-à-vis* dramatising narrators, of their egoistic audiences who want both 'a good story' and emotional involvement.[50]

All three stories have at their core events that are the staple of short fiction in nineteenth-century France: infidelity, sexual jealousy and murder in 'Les Bécasses' and 'Carmen', a duel and sudden death in 'Sombre récit, conteur plus sombre'. The tendency to push simplified feelings and events to extremes is very much a product of the brevity of

50. Other *Contes cruels* of Villiers denounce the manipulation of public opinion (by journalism in 'Deux Augures', by a fanciful anticipation of canned laughter in 'La Machine à gloire') in a way that attacks not only those who seek to control opinion, but also the gullibility of the public.

CHAPTER 1. TELLERS AND LISTENERS							49

the form.[51] So too is the concentration on the effects of intensified emotions rather than on their causes. Why does Don José fall for Carmen? The fact that they seem totally opposed enables Mérimée to make us accept this without asking further. The intensification and the emphasis on consequences lead to a world where passion, instinctive violence, and chance subvert any attempt to understand and control the individual's destiny. But in all three stories what holds our interest is not the simple bones of the stories themselves, but their telling.

The framed tale provides each with a convenient way to encapsulate a tragic incident or, in the case of 'Carmen', a whole life. It enables the author to set in the confined space of a letter, or the chapel where José is held, or a Parisian restaurant, a contrasting world of violence, passion, and honour. Framing can also open up a 'multiplicity of perspectives' on a single event.[52] Narrators have to be provided with reasons for narrating, and their audiences with motives for listening. The pseudo-oral nature of the narrative can intensify our awareness of the relationship between teller and listener. The written representation of a real oral narrrative inevitably means the loss of features like emphasis, gesture, intonation, accent, a loss that the transcribers of oral narratives often underline.[53] But adding to the narration of José and D*** features such as appeals to their narratees, hesitations, gestures, though these remain part of a written text, represents a gain. They turn our attention to the relationship between tellers and listeners, and provide ways of linking frame and tale, of creating overall coherence. All three stories are also typical in developing a thematic opposition that runs through the different levels of each. In the case of Maupassant and Villiers these are very basic antitheses: in 'Les Bécasses' between 'masculine' and 'feminine' worlds, between nature and artifice; in 'Sombre récit, conteur plus sombre' between life and literature. These lead us beyond the singular incident to the sort of point that we expect in literature: something more general in value, but also less explicitly

51. The point is stressed by Goyet, *La Nouvelle*, 28-47.
52. Paulin, *The Brief Compass*, 36.
53. See Bauman, *Story, Performance and Event*, ix; Jeanne Demers and Lise Gauvin, 'Le Conte écrit, forme savante', *Etudes françaises* 12 (1976), 3-24 (6); Dennis Tedlock, *The Spoken Word and the Work of Interpretation* (Philadelphia: University of Pennsylvania Press, 1983), 115.

stated, than in a real-life tale.[54] The parallels between the archaeologist and José are at first sight not obvious; the *littérateur*-narrator of Villiers seems poles apart from the crudely successful D***, on whom we look condescendingly until the double-take of the ending.

Villiers's tale self-consciously sets out to foreground and undermine the acts of narrating and listening. The way he reminds us, not least by the artifices of his style, of the artificiality of what we are reading could be seen as a way of turning to advantage the fact that Todorov noted, that in the brief span of short fiction we cannot forget that what we are reading is literature, not life. If the nineteenth-century novelist, exemplified by Balzac, seems to believe in his world, the writer of short fiction is often more sceptical. Mérimée frequently highlights in his tales his awareness that story-telling is able not only to captivate, but also to deceive, and consequently can be either frivolous or dangerous:[55] it is a way of passing the time, but only, as he suggests in 'La Partie de trictrac', when there is nothing better to do. At the end of 'Carmen' the Narrator quotes a gypsy proverb: 'En close bouche n'entre pas mouche'; the storyteller might do better keeping his mouth shut. The unsettling quality of Villiers's tale, exploiting the final twist that the short story lends itself to,[56] is that this time it is the reader whose role and motives are called into question. For all that, the narrators in all three stories still want to tell their tales, and their narratees (audience?), to listen, which seems the obvious framing situation for a writer to invent. But can there be advantages in narrators who do not want to tell, narratees who do not want to listen? This is the possibility to be explored in the next chapter.

54. On the explicit formulation of the moral point or maxim in the real-life tale, see Alan R. Ryave: storytellers 'do not leave this matter to be understood from the specifics of the story' ('On the achievement of a series of stories', *Studies in the Organization of Conversational Interaction*, ed. by Jim Schenkein (New York: Academic Press, 1978), 113-32).
55. See Frank Paul Bowman, *Heroism, Pessimism and Irony*, 161, and, for 'La Partie de trictrac', Chapter 3.
56. See Goyet, *La Nouvelle*, 48-52, for a discussion of how this can be understood in terms of the tendency of short fiction to antithetical opposition and intensification.

2. Hesitant Tellers, Reluctant Listeners

Maupassant, 'Un cas de divorce'; Barbey, 'Le Rideau cramoisi'

The Narrators and their narratees in the previous chapter showed in different ways a desire to tell, a readiness to listen. But this pattern was set up not just to offer direct access to events: the motives of narrators affected both the telling of the story and our interest. Narrators target their audience; narratees are not neutral recording devices, but play a role in shaping the tale that is told to them. Narrators, influenced by their own desires and the wishes of their audience, not only select what to tell, but also gloss over or 'omit' elements that they could have included — something obviously useful in short fiction. This prompts the question: if a narrator is unable, or does not want, to tell, or if a narratee does not want to listen, how might this contribute to the interest of the story?

The question could be approached by looking at Maupassant's attitude to frankness. Maupassant's stories, like his journalism, consistently emphasise the need to go beyond consoling illusion, 'la grande menteuse', and to see 'la vie, la vraie vie'.[1] He aims to reveal a truth, as he sees it, about life, mankind, society; he is responsible perhaps more than any other writer of short stories for the view that 'the nature of the medium is revelation and exposure'.[2] A recurrent preoccupation is, as Edward Sullivan has argued, the attempt 'to lift the mask of appearance'.[3] So it seems natural that Maupassant should be opposed not only to the hypocrisy or the comforting blindness which refuse to acknowledge the truth, but also to any censorship which seeks

1. 'Causerie triste', Guy de Maupassant, *Chroniques*, edited by Hubert Juin, 3 vols (Paris: Union Générale d'Editions, 1980), III, 410.
2. Sachs, 'Emergence of a poetics', 149.
3. Edward D. Sullivan, *Maupassant: the Short Stories* (London: Arnold, 1962), 57. See also David Bryant, *The Rhetoric of Pessimism and Strategies of Containment in the Short Stories of Guy de Maupassant* (Lewiston: Mellen, 1993), 6-7; Mariane Bury, 'Maupassant pessimiste?', *Romantisme*, no. 61 (1988), 75-83 (81-82).

to hide it. Early in his career, Maupassant had, like Flaubert before him, difficulties with public controls on the written word. In 1880 his poem 'Une fille' had been threatened with prosecution for 'outrage à la morale publique et religieuse et aux bonnes mœurs'; in 1883 Hachette had briefly banned his first novel, *Une Vie*, from sale on railway bookstalls. He would not compromise his vision, but he was ready, as a writer living from his work, to adapt to different publications. Since newspapers offered less freedom to be explicit than books,[4] he angled different stories to different outlets; aware that the *nouvelle* 'L'Héritage' might be a bit 'vive' for *Le Figaro*, Maupassant thought of publishing it in *Gil Blas*[5] (in the event, for reasons of timing, it appeared in *La Vie Militaire*). But he remained implacably opposed to censorship by newspaper editors,[6] and his *chroniques* frequently stress the artist's duty to show the brutal truth, both as regards what is shown and how it is shown. He attacks the public's desire for a sentimental idealisation of reality in a literature that is '*invraisemblable, sympathique* et *consolante*'.[7] This desire is ultimately hypocritical in that the reader knows, even if not admitting it, that what it represents is a lie. 'La société moderne attache une idée de honte au fait brutal de l'accouplement [...] Et voilà que l'hypocrisie mondaine nous veut forcer à l'enguirlander de sentiment pour en parler dans un livre.'[8] He attacks not just this falsification of what he terms 'la chose', but also the suppression of 'le mot', explicit language:[9]

4. Maupassant remarked to his mother, on the subject of the early poem 'Vénus rustique': 'En livre bien, mais pas dans un journal' (letter of 3 April 1878; quoted in Gustave Flaubert, Guy de Maupassant, *Correspondance*, ed. by Yvan Leclerc (Paris: Flammarion 1993), 386 (Suffel no. 90).
5. Guy de Maupassant, *Correspondance inédite*, edited by A. Artinian and E. Maynial (Paris: Wapler, 1951), 177.
6. 'Tous les directeurs des journaux où j'ai écrit savent également que je n'ai jamais toléré qu'on supprimât un seul mot. J'ai cessé ma collaboration régulière au *Gaulois* après une modification, ou plutôt une coupure faite *en mon absence*, à un article sur *Manon Lescaut*, cet article ayant paru *un peu vif* (*Correspondance inédite*, 228; see also page 231).
7. 'Autour d'un livre', Maupassant, *Chroniques*, I, 283.
8. 'Les Audacieux', Maupassant, *Chroniques*, II, 281.
9. Maupassant, *Chroniques*, III, 356.

CHAPTER 2. HESITANT TELLERS, RELUCTANT LISTENERS 53

Nous n'avons plus le droit de parler franchement de l'accouplement des êtres, acte aussi utile à la race et aussi innocent en soi que celui de la nutrition, [...] sans exciter dans le public pudibond mais débauché un ouragan d'indignation.[10]

This refusal both to acknowledge and to name explicitly known realities is satirised in a humorous *chronique* of 1882, 'Conflits pour rire',[11] prompted by a law introduced to counter a flood of cheap obscene publications by restricting press freedom.[12] Maupassant tells how a village priest, shocked by the primitive sculpture of a naked Adam and Eve on his church porch, first attempts to conceal the 'groupe trop naturel' by fixing trousers on Adam with sealing wax, and is then caught 'en train d'amoindrir Adam' by night. The priest is attempting to suppress sight of *la chose*; in his narrative, Maupassant refers to the offending genitalia only by a series of oblique expressions, suppressing the explicit *mot*: Adam 'se dressait dans le costume originel'; after his diminution, 'le morceau que venait de perdre le générateur du genre humain' is kept as evidence. Maupassant is satirising false modesty, but his euphemistic language ironically imitates the censoring attitude that he is mocking.

Maupassant may express his preference for the sexual explicitness of earlier French writers and their 'cru' and 'chaud' language,[13] and call for 'des vers hardis et passionnés' on sexual love without 'gros mots, ni polissonneries, ni sous-entendus'.[14] But 'Conflits pour rire' shows paradoxically the advantages of *not* naming the contentious parts. Sexuality is an area where there is no neutral and direct language; social constraints impose limits, and when Maupassant did write explicit poems and a farce set in a brothel,[15] they were not so much direct and

10. 'Fille de fille', Maupassant, *Chroniques*, II, 329; see also 'Chez le ministre', *Chroniques*, II, 146.
11. Maupassant, *Chroniques*, II, 45-49.
12. *Histoire générale de la presse*, III, 24. The law made 'outrages aux bonnes mœurs' in newspapers punishable by a *tribunal correctionnel*; books still went before a jury.
13. Maupassant, *Chroniques*, I, 288.
14. 'Celles qui osent!', Maupassant, *Chroniques*, II, 335.
15. See *A la feuille de rose, maison turque*, edited by Alexandre Grenier (Paris: Encre, 1984).

simple as outrageously obscene, delighting in the fact that they could not be publicly performed or printed. Restrictions exist; but inhibitions about *la chose* and *le mot* can be turned by a writer to his advantage.

If the aim of a tale is to 'lift the mask of appearance' and reveal a brutal truth, the shock can be intensified by characterising appropriately the person to whom the truth is shown. Narratees who do not want to know can also mirror inside the story the effect on the reader outside it. 'En voyage' (I, 431) is an anecdote embodying a recurrent theme of short fiction: cruel and pointless death, chance, and the helplessness of mankind in the face of nature, a tale 'bien sombre et bien navrante, [...] et bien banale en même temps'. A boy is forced to watch his brother drown in a well in the countryside into which he has fallen, unable to help him or to leave him to get help. The tale is told by a traveller in a letter addressed to a woman; she, in contrast, is distant and safe in a protected urban room. In 'La Veillée' (I, 445) two children read their dead mother's letters as they watch over her body. The letters reveal an unsuspected passionate affair. Neither the affair nor its discovery is that remarkable, but the children, a magistrate 'aux principes inflexibles' and a nun, represent the respectability of law and religion. Their response is condemnation and rejection: in silence, the letters are bundled back in a drawer and the curtains drawn round the bed.[16] Jean Rousset has noted how a fictional narratee can react defensively to an embedded tale: events, however fascinating, must be kept at a healthy distance.[17] Maupassant's narratees frequently go further in their desire not to know; their wilful social, sexual or moral blindness is representative of the desire of humanity not to know. The upper-class shooting party and their wives who are a retired doctor's audience in

---

16. For a very similar response, see 'La Confession' (II, 371).
17. Rousset, *Lecteur intime*, 63. Recent studies on narrator and narratee in Maupassant include Calí, 'Histoire encadrante'; Carmen Licari, 'Le Lecteur des contes de Maupassant', *Francofonia* 3 (1982), 91–103; Jaap Lintveldt, 'Pour une analyse narratologique des *Contes et nouvelles* de Guy de Maupassant', in *Fiction, narratologie, texte, genre*, ed. by Jean Bessière (New York: Lang, 1989), 65–75, and 'La Polyphonie de l'encadrement dans les contes de Maupassant', in *Maupassant et l'écriture*, ed. by Louis Forestier (Paris: Nathan, 1993), 173–85; Tuula Lehman, *Transitions savantes*; Moger, 'Narrative structure'. With the exception of Lintveldt and Moger, the emphasis tends to be on classification of technique rather than defining of effect.

'La Rempailleuse' (I, 546) are reluctant to hear his tale of life-long passion because of the social status of the heroine, a woman who repairs chair seats and who loves the local chemist from afar; the frame situation is echoed in the embedded story where the chemist and his wife are indignant at the devotion she shows.[18] At the end of 'Une ruse' (I, 560), the female narratee is shocked by '"cette épouvantable histoire"' (II, 565) told by her doctor, relating how he solved the problem of getting the body of a woman's lover out of the house before the husband returned; it represents a way of life she does not want to acknowledge.[19] Shocked reactions can also be used playfully: narratees can pretend not to want to hear simply to preserve appearances. In the frame of 'Joseph' (II, 506), two young aristocratic women, drunk after a dinner together, exchange confidences; the *baronne* reveals gradually how she manipulated and seduced her manservant, and her tale is punctuated by the protests of her tipsy narratee: ' — Oh! ma chère!...' and '— Oh! Andrée.' The tone here is humorous, but the desire not to hear of all these narratees represents a cosy, dishonest world into which realities intrude: the fragility of human life and the unfairness of chance; passion and sexuality; obsessive love. Even a slight tale like 'Joseph' serves to highlight how easily caprice and instinct can break down unquestioned conventions like marital fidelity, class distinctions and male initiative in love. In this respect the reaction of shock or refusal is essentially an element of evaluation placed in the frame, guiding the reader beyond the embedded anecdote to the point.

The role of the unwilling narratee in these tales of revelation is clear. The narrator who does not want to tell seems a paradoxical reversal of what we expect in a narrative situation. But here too narrators, both homodiegetic and heterodiegetic, may show reluctance to confront certain realities and express them (*la chose* and *le mot*). In 'Boule de Suif', the small group travelling in the carriage from Prussian-occupied Rouen towards Dieppe represents a cross-section of respectable society, 'des honnêtes gens qui ont de la Religion et des Principes', together with two nuns and the republican Cornudet. Their hypocrisy is revealed as their initial hostility towards their fellow-traveller, the prostitute

18. This parallel is also noted by Calí, 'Histoire encadrante', 104.
19. As Peter Brooks notes (*Reading for the Plot*, 217-8). On the function of the frame and narrator/narratee relationships here, see also Angela Moger, 'That Obscure Object of Narration', *Yale French Studies* 63 (1982), 129-38.

Boule de Suif, gives way successively to friendliness when she shares her food with them, then to hostility when she patriotically refuses to sleep with the Prussian officer who has halted them in Tostes. The heterodiegetic narrator points out during the conversation at dinner, when the characters join forces to persuade Boule de Suif to yield, that the women are hypocritical and enjoying the situation vicariously: 'Elles s'épanouissaient dans cette aventure polissonne' (I, 111). But their euphemisms veil the reality of what they are suggesting: 'C'était fort convenable du reste. Ces dames surtout trouvaient des délicatesses de tournures, des subtilités d'expression charmantes, pour dire les choses les plus scabreuses' (I, 111). The narrator echoes this evasion by playing with focalisation and ellipsis. If we ask what Maupassant's potentially omniscient narrator chooses to show and what not to show, we can see that he stays largely with the group of travellers. The exchanges and encounters between Boule de Suif and the Prussian officer take place 'off stage', and we know of them only from what she reveals to the group after the event. Moreover, the narrator switches point of view to create a sense of not being allowed to see or hear key sexual activities or conversations. The encounter between Cornudet and Boule de Suif in the corridor, when he too seeks her favours and is rebuffed, is observed not directly by the narrator, but indirectly by the watching wine-merchant Loiseau. We have to guess, with Loiseau, Cornudet's proposition. The subsequent narrative follows Loiseau and his actions as he returns, excited by what he has seen, to his room and his wife in bed. But with his ritual: '"M'aimes-tu, chérie?"', the narrative is teasingly cut short, hinting at but refusing to show what follows. During the celebratory dinner, when Boule de Suif has retired with the Prussian, Loiseau makes jokes 'd'un goût déplorable' (I, 116) about their activities. The narrator's humour is less coarse, but just as Loiseau appeals to the group's awareness of what is going on upstairs, so does the narrator to the reader's awareness that what keeps the passengers awake that night is not the champagne:

> Et toute la nuit, dans l'obscurité du corridor coururent comme des frémissements, des bruits légers, à peine sensibles, pareils à des souffles, des effleurements de pieds nus, d'imperceptibles craquements. Et l'on ne dormit que très tard, assurément, car des filets de lumière glissèrent longtemps sous les portes. Le champagne a de ces effets-là; il trouble, dit-on, le sommeil. (I, 117)

CHAPTER 2. HESITANT TELLERS, RELUCTANT LISTENERS

The heterodiegetic narrator's hints in 'Boule de Suif' throw into relief the hypocrisy that we are observing in the story. Similar evasions in 'L'Héritage' (I, 3) highlight what cannot be acknowledged fully by either the characters or the teasing narrator: the link between sex and money. Other tales use reticent narrators to create a detached amusement from the incongruities that result from the necessary social constraints on language, in particular from the opportunity to construct a complex story from meagre anecdotal material. A frank *histoire* is intensified by an awareness of what cannot be said, conveyed in the narrative by euphemism, elision and restricted focalisation as well as in the characters' own inhibitions.[20] In 'La Serre' (I, 855), the dormant love-life of a retired married couple, the Lerebours, is revived when they witness their maid Céleste's nocturnal rendez-vous in the greenhouse. What was merely an episode in 'Boule de Suif' here becomes a whole story. The opening characterises from an external point of view (with hints of the husband's thoughts) the Lerebours and their relationship, above all Mme Lerebour's unexplained but growing hostility to her husband and his bafflement at her behaviour. The action commences with a conventional transition: 'Or, une nuit [...]' (I, 857). The heterodiegetic narrator could theoretically follow the actions of any or all of the characters: here the action begins with the couple in their bedroom. Hearing noises in the house on two successive nights, Mme Lerebour dispatches her husband to investigate what she suspects is a burglar. At this point we stay with her in the bedroom. The narrative allows us to see her thoughts as she remains alone for forty-five minutes, gripped with fear. When her husband returns, the narrative merely reports the incoherent account he gives to his wife: he is laughing, but also cannot find the words for what he saw. '"C'était... c'était... Céleste qui avait un... un... rendez-vous dans la serre... Si tu savais ce que... ce que... ce que j'ai vu"'. The following events, as he embraces his wife, are cut short by an ellipsis: 'Mais lui, la tenant à pleins bras, l'entraînait doucement vers le lit...' (I, 859). This is followed by a blank line and a cut to the next morning, when the narrative resumes from the point of view of Céleste, surprised that they

---

20. See Christopher Lloyd's remarks on the role of humorous euphemism and circumlocution in 'La Farce' ('Maupassant trichologue: histoires de poils', in *Maupassant conteur et romancier*, edited by C. Lloyd and R. Lethbridge (Durham: University of Durham, 1994), 161-2).

are so late rising. In a coda in the present tense we see the couple revisiting the greenhouse. The initial state (marital disharmony) is now replaced, after the singular events of one night, by a new state (harmony):

> Par les nuits claires quelquefois, les deux époux vont, à pas furtifs, le long des massifs et des plates-bandes jusqu'à la petite serre au bout du jardin. Et ils restent là blottis l'un près de l'autre contre le vitrage comme s'ils regardaient dedans une chose étrange et pleine d'intérêt. (I, 860)

The narrator does not say what they are watching; the reader can imagine the elided scenes teasingly cut off on the basis of what Umberto Eco calls our repertory of 'intertextual scenarios' derived from life and reading (or now, films);[21] here from ready-made erotic memories or scenes. The interest of the story lies not so much in events as in presentation, built up from Lerebour's stumbling inability to explain what is happening in the greenhouse, and from truncated scenes. Each time these are witnessed by the character who is *not* fully aware of what is going on: first M. Lerebour, then his wife, then Céleste, finally an external narrator who feigns not to know.

With fictional characters relating their experiences to a narratee in a frame, it is more obvious that they might be reluctant to be frank. But here too their inhibitions and the hesitant narration can be linked to the themes and the point of the *récit*. In 'La Bûche' (I, 352), the elderly Narrator is explaining to a friend, 'une vieille aux cheveux blancs', why he has remained a bachelor. When he was young, his best friend married. He relates how, dining with the couple one day, his friend had to leave 'pour une affaire', leaving him alone after the meal with his friend's wife, and a prey to her advances; fortunately a log falling from the fire saves him from yielding and being caught when the husband unexpectedly returns early. The Narrator dwells on the 'gêne singulière' of the time when he was alone with the young wife, his vain attempts to

---

21. See Umberto Eco, *Lector in fabula: le rôle du lecteur*, trans. by Myriem Bouzaher (Paris: Livre de poche, 1990), 101-105. For an analysis of 'La Serre' in terms of a suppressed predictable story that the reader has to supply, see Armine Kotin Mortimer, 'Second Stories', in *Short Story Theory at a Crossroads*, ed. by Susan Lohafer and Jo Ellyn Clarey (Baton Rouge: Louisiana State University Press, 1989), 276-98 (285-6).

CHAPTER 2. HESITANT TELLERS, RELUCTANT LISTENERS 59

fill the 'silences embarrassants' and to fend off her advances (I, 354). When she unambiguously embraces him, the older Narrator finds the narration of events increasingly difficult: he cannot bring himself to use to his woman friend the direct but socially unacceptable words that would explain what was about to happen: lover, mistress, infidelity, cuckold. So too his embarrassed younger self had been unable to respond decisively to his friend's wife: should he yield and betray his friend? or play the role of Joseph and resist — something both difficult at this point, and dangerous with someone 'perverse et rusée'?

> Enfin, une minute de plus... vous comprenez, n'est-ce pas? Une minute de plus et... j'étais... non, elle était... pardon, c'est lui qui l'était!... ou plutôt qui l'aurait été, quand voilà qu'un bruit terrible nous fit bondir. (I, 356)

At this point his narration can resume without further hesitation. The Narrator's younger self is saved by the log and the husband's premature return; his older self can continue the narration with unembarrassing events. The embedded story is about an awkward moment from which the Narrator had been saved; the frame echoes this with the Narrator's hesitations.

More elaborately, in 'Enragée?' (I, 939) the female Narrator is responding in a letter to a friend: 'Tu me demandes de te raconter mon voyage de noces'. But the subject inhibits her: 'Comment veux-tu que j'ose?' (I, 939). Her tale is one of comic misapprehensions: she cannot understand her husband's advances in bed, thinks that he is going mad and is going to kill her; she mistakes her subsequent sexual pleasure for the onset of rabies. Her mistakes spring from her ignorance of sexual realities (a problem that Maupassant explores seriously in *Une Vie*): her family have not informed her, her husband assumes she is mischievously feigning innocence. The reasons they have not told her are precisely the inhibitions that constrain her as she relates events to her friend: 'Oh! ma chère, comment dire ça? Enfin voici' (I, 941). She can evoke her experiences only obliquely as she brings out the rabies/orgasm parallel: 'Les irritantes obsessions de mon mari déterminèrent un nouvel accès, qui fut plus long que le premier. J'avais envie de déchirer, de mordre, de hurler [...]' (I, 945). The story is permeated by a network of references to telling/not telling that draw out her anxieties. Her mother dared not 'effleurer ce sujet délicat' of sex (I, 939); nor do her parents write to her about her pet dog, which had bitten her before she left, increasing her fears of rabies. She is of course reluctant to express her fears on this score to her husband: 'Vingt fois je faillis lui dire mon abominable secret, mais je me tus' (I, 943). Even her husband's tardy explanations are 'sommaires' (I, 942) and do not prepare her to understand her physical reactions. The resultant confusions and misunderstandings are intensified by her vivid imagination. As in 'La Bûche', a Narrator's embarrassment at narrating events (here in a letter) echoes the inhibitions that played a central role in the events recalled.

The usefulness of inhibited narrators to tease, to create suspense and thematic complexity out of a slender anecdote, is even more evident when Maupassant underscores the problem of telling by a proliferation of *re*tellings. 'Le Remplaçant' (I, 700) is, in terms of its *histoire*, a mildly salacious anecdote: a respectable, *dévote* widow, Mme Bonderoi, hires the regular sexual services of a soldier, Siballe; when he cannot make the appointment one week, he sends a friend as a substitute; this prompts an initial quarrel and a duel over the sharing of the proceeds, then a resolution when both are taken on to provide the service twice a week. This could be summarised schematically: an arrangement is set up; → it is threatened; → substitute arrangement; → new threat; → new arrangement. At the centre seems to be the point that shocks the narratee in the frame narrative: the false respectability of Mme Bonderoi.

In the story there is clearly an element of playful gender role reversal. The unnamed narrator, who presents the story to a friend, suggests that we would not be surprised by the male version of these events: preying on young women, sexual exploitation in the workplace (Mme Bonderoi uses her husband's *clercs* while he is alive), prostitutes supporting their families on the proceeds, as the soldiers do their parents. But it is not just a tale of hypocrisy unmasked, of Mme Bonderoi's 'vices secrets' (I, 700). The secret has to be told to the appropriate persons if the supply of lovers is to be maintained. This creates a paradoxical pattern where characters are recurrently sworn to secrecy, told the secret, and then themselves divulge it. However, conventions restrict what they can say: neither Mme Bonderoi (talking to Siballe) nor Siballe (embarrassed by the subject, but also by talking about it to his captain) can mention sex directly, which leads to a series of euphemisms and oblique references.

CHAPTER 2. HESITANT TELLERS, RELUCTANT LISTENERS 61

Maupassant's frame presents conventionally a conversation in which one character's surprise prompts a narrator to reveal 'tous les détails' about a surprising discovery — here, about Mme Bonderoi. But rather than giving a direct account of 'l'aventure invraisemblable arrivée jeudi dernier', the second narrator reveals that he has heard it from a friend, Captain Jean d'Anglemare, who had heard it from one of the soldiers involved. So before we reach the embedded tale, Siballe's first-hand oral narration of events, we know that the story has passed through a succession of narrators. Siballe relates his first encounter with Mme Bonderoi from the point of view of his innocent self at the time, unaware of what she is proposing (the reader who has been told that 'elle aimait les beaux garçons' can guess). She swears him to secrecy: '"Alors ell' se fit comprendre ouvertement par des manifestations. Quand j'vis de quoi il s'agissait, je posai mon casque sur une chaise; et je lui montrai que dans les dragons on ne recule jamais, mon cap'taine"'. He too, rather than being explicit, alludes and naturally raids military language for his metaphors.[22] His friend Paumelle, the *remplaçant*, is similarly sworn to secrecy. After the soldiers' quarrel and duel, Siballe now tells the captain, who tells his friend (the second narrator); and the friend repeats all this to his narratee: 'Mais il [d'Anglemare] m'a fait aussi jurer le secret qu'il avait garanti aux deux soldats. "Surtout, n'allez pas me trahir, gardez ça pour vous, vous me le promettez?"' The friend of course promises and tells his narratee of this promise... which he is now breaking: '"Oh! ne craignez rien"' (I, 703). On one level the story may seem to have at its centre the joke about the *remplaçant*, singularly appropriate for soldiers, since until 1872 a *remplaçant* had been a substitute paid to perform military service in place of someone called up by lot. It is also a revelation of 'vices secrets' in bourgeois women. But the *récit* is constructed around attempts to swear to secrecy (by Mme Bonderoi with both soldiers, by Siballe with the captain, by the captain with his friend) and their failure. Without these attempts and their subversion by gossip there would be not only no story-telling, but no *histoire*, since the replacement and the

---

22. With possible salacious overtones: 'Quand la corvée a été faite, mon cap'taine, je me suis mis en position de me retirer' (I, 702).

quarrel it provokes all depend on Siballe breaking his vow of secrecy and telling his friend, desperate not to lose Mme Bonderoi.[23]

Such stories derive narrative complexity and verbal play from a minimal anecdotal content. But these tales are comic, as are the passages in 'Boule de Suif' where Maupassant plays with evasions and euphemisms, and in the main they were destined for the licentious *Gil Blas*. One of Maupassant's tales with the courtroom context that he frequently exploits as a frame suggests that hesitation and inhibition can also create more disturbing effects.

'Un cas de divorce' (II, 777) centres on the state of mind of a husband whose wife is seeking divorce. The title and the most rapid of orientations from a heterodiegetic narrator ('L'avocat de Mme Chassel prit la parole') establish a courtroom setting; the lawyer then takes over the whole narration, save for one brief interruption. He outlines the husband's character ('d'âme noble et exaltée'), his love for a young woman, their marriage; followed by apparently inexplicable neglect, revulsion, and violence. Then he evokes in parallel, without naming him,[24] the eccentric Ludwig II of Bavaria, his idealistic dreams and an incident one evening when he threw in the lake a singer who had kissed him, apparently repulsed by her physical advances. Both cases are presented as 'bizarres, incompréhensibles', and by implication due to individual eccentricity. At this point we expect an explanation from 'inside', a revelation of the husband's point of view. Maupassant's courtroom stories (such as 'Une vente' (I, 1207), 'Rosalie Prudent' (II, 699), 'Le Trou' (II, 831), 'Un parricide' (I, 553)) frequently hinge on the accused being allowed to present their account of what happened. In general this leads to an understanding of their motives or of the chain of events which led to the act, and to their acquittal. Here this inside view is provided by the husband's diary, from which the lawyer reads extracts; but these reveal a more complex situation than we anticipated, and a character whose motivation remains ambiguous.

23. Bernard P.R. Haezewindt comes to a similar view of the story from a different approach: see *Guy de Maupassant: de l'anecdote au conte littéraire*, Faux Titre, 70 (Amsterdam: Rodopi, 1993), 180-1.
24. The story contains, as Forestier notes, several allusions for a contemporary reader: as well as the death of Ludwig II (13 June 1886), Huysmans's *A Rebours* (1884) and Des Esseintes's response to flowers, and Maupassant's feud with Jean Lorrain.

CHAPTER 2. HESITANT TELLERS, RELUCTANT LISTENERS 63

The ambiguity is in part due to changes Maupassant made to the story after its first publication. In the original version a highly discursive passage of the diary explains the husband's rejection of his wife.[25] He reveals himself as a misanthropic idealist who thinks that he has found ideal love, but realises after marriage that 'love' is an illusion: both man and animals couple merely out of 'un instinct bestial qui les force à continuer la race' (II, 780). In this respect he echoes, as Maupassant often did, the view of the philosopher Schopenhauer that 'L'amour a toujours pour fondement un instinct dirigé vers la reproduction de l'espèce'.[26] He has also been revolted by discovering that Nature (or God), by combining the organs of reproduction and elimination, has sabotaged the attempts of sensitive people to poeticise the reproductive instinct. Other organs (eyes, mouth, nose, ears) also have multiple functions, but all are elevated; for love, however, mankind only has 'les organes ridicules et honteux par où s'écoulent les ordures du corps' (II, 1575). In contrast, flowers have a beautiful reproductive system without this degrading dual purpose. In the series of fragmentary entries that form the second half of the diary, the husband presents his exalted love for flowers, which we understand in terms of the previous arguments and the flight from human love. He evokes the sexualised flowers in his greenhouse, 'rouges, charnues, entr'ouvertes, plus troublantes que des bouches de femme, et profondes, avec des lèvres retournées, dentelées, grasses, et d'où sortent des parfums qui grisent comme des caresses' (II, 1575), to whow that they are the plants' reproductive organs but nothing else. Nevertheless, the final paragraph of the diary hints that his absorption is becoming self-destructive: 'Elles ont tous les charmes, toutes les grâces,

---

25. *Gil Blas*, 31 August 1886. These arguments echo those Maupassant expresses elsewhere through fictional characters: Forestier notes echoes of 'Les Caresses' (I, 952). But the husband is not just a spokesman for Maupassant: his condemnation of 'pratiques immondes' is the opposite of the views expressed in 'Les Caresses' and 'Celles qui osent!' (*Chroniques*, II, 334-5).
26. Schopenhauer, *Pensées et fragments*, trans. by Jean Bruneau (Geneva, Slatkine, 1979), 98. See René-Pierre Colin, *Schopenhauer en France: un mythe naturaliste* (Lyon: Presses Universitaires, 1979), 135, for the debt of Naturalist writers to this translation, and 197-9 for Maupassant's possible debt to Schopenhauer in his revulsion at the physicality of reproduction and his sense of the God, or Nature, as behind it.

toutes les formes qu'on peut rêver [...] . Et je me tue, à les caresser' (II, 1577). This is cut short by the lawyer, who denounces the 'folie' of both Ludwig and the husband: their excessive sensibility and inability to come to terms with reality have led them to seek refuge in a private world. But having quoted the diary *verbatim*, Maupassant leaves it open to us to judge it for ourselves. We can see that the husband is a disillusioned idealist, but a logical one; the diagnosis of *folie* and *démence* is used by the lawyer and by society to dismiss a truth that they do not wish to acknowledge. The lawyer reading the diary aloud and the listening court play the role of narratees who do not want to hear; the husband is spokesman for an unsettling truth.

If the first version of the story thus evokes one category of shocked and hypocritical narratees, the situation is more complex in the final version, published in the volume *L'Inutile Beauté*. (Maupassant probably made the changes, not to reduce the sexual explicitness, as publication in volume allowed more freedom than newspapers, but because the theme of a sensitive character revolted by his awareness of the dual function of the organs of love had been developed in almost identical terms in the title story of the volume (II, 1216-7)). A large part of the husband's diary is rewritten, Maupassant deleting, adding, and moving key passages. The Schopenhauerian argument that 'love' is Nature's way of tricking mankind into reproduction is reinforced ('Elle est ma femme [...] l'être dont la nature s'était servie'). But the argument of the first version about the dual function of human sexual and eliminatory organs is deleted. In consequence the theme of physical revulsion, still present, is no longer clearly motivated: 'Le dégoût de l'étreinte amoureuse, si vile, qu'elle est devenue, pour tous les êtres affinés, un acte honteux' (II, 780). When the husband talks of 'la chair, fumier séduisant et vivant, putréfaction qui marche, [...] où les nourritures fermentent', we interpret this now as a more generalised awareness of the human body subject to decay and mortality.[27] When the husband turns to flowers, metaphors feminise and sexualise them even more than in the first version:

---

27. This is, in fact, how Mary Donaldson-Evans reads it (*A Woman's Revenge: the Chronology of Dispossession in Maupassant's Fiction* (Lexington: French Forum, 1986), 55).

CHAPTER 2. HESITANT TELLERS, RELUCTANT LISTENERS 65

> Comme elles sont grasses, profondes, roses, d'un rose qui mouille les lèvres de désir! Comme je les aime! Le bord de leur calice est frisé, plus pâle que leur gorge et la corolle s'y cache, bouche mystérieuse, attirante, sucrée sous la langue, montrant et dérobant les organes délicats, admirables et sacrés de ces divines petites créatures qui sentent bon et ne parlent pas (II, 782).

In the original the flowers appeared as a natural development of the argument; flowers evoked the female body (flesh, lips, perfumes, orifices, folds) but in a purer form. In the final version we do not see why the husband flees to the flowers, but their sexuality is paradoxically intensified, with descriptions that suggest explicit parallels with erogenous zones (mouth, breasts, genitals: often confusing the first and the last, in a traditional way), and constant references to smelling, kissing, licking. So the evocation of the flowers comes across as a choice springing from a bizarre individual temperament, which is reinforced by the ambiguous phrasing with its overtones of oral/genital contact.

The second part of the diary now shows the husband seeking in flowers the very characteristics (sensuality, sexuality, decay, mortality) that he has fled in his wife. His 'favourites' among the flowers are paradoxically those orchids 'qui viennent, ces filles étranges, de pays marécageux, brûlants et malsains. Elles sont attirantes comme des sirènes, mortelles comme des poisons' (II, 782): curious praise given that he denounced woman as a trap of nature, 'rose, jolie, tentante, trompeuse' (II, 780). The husband's development seems increasingly confused, indeed perverse.

The result is a story more complex and disturbing than the first version. The diary is no longer simply the embedded confession that enables us to understand the husband and see the condemnation by the lawyer and by society as blind and hypocritical. The husband has become an eccentric; but he is also right in his disillusionment over love as a reproductive trap. The ambiguity leaves the reader hovering between possible explanations: is he a repressed homosexual, like Ludwig II? Do the husband's oral contacts with the flowers betray some other sexual obsession? And the final paragraph provides a suitably unsettling close with its suggestion of a sadistic male possessing a captive female (flower) in a 'prison de verre',[28] and then watching it die:

> On l'enlève [...] et on l'enferme dans un mignon cabinet de verre où murmure un fil d'eau contre un lit de gazon tropical venu des îles du grand Pacifique. Et je reste près d'elle, ardent, fiévreux et tourmenté, sachant sa mort si proche, et la regardant se faner, tandis que je la possède, que j'aspire, que je bois, que je cueille sa courte vie d'une inexprimable caresse (II, 783).

From the formal point of view, the most obvious feature of the story is Maupassant's use of two devices he frequently uses elsewhere: the courtroom and the diary. Here, unusually, they are combined. The courtroom has clear narrative advantages in a short story: witnesses, lawyers or accused, used as narrators, can focus on the issue to be raised. Here the lawyer can skip what is irrelevant (which might be considerable in a diary)[29] and read only 'quelques fragments d'un journal écrit chaque jour par ce pauvre homme, par ce pauvre fou' (I, 777), jumping rapidly between key points. The courtroom frame is also itself limited in terms of time and space. But Maupassant's frame gives us two narrators, the lawyer and the husband, both of whom are reluctant to tackle and express directly the issues at stake, having difficulties with both *la chose* and *les mots*. The judges and the courtroom clearly inhibit the lawyer, who censors the diary in the name of 'la décence' (II, 783). The husband in contrast might seem a more honest narrator, writing only for himself. But there are things he will not say: after his marriage the diary refers in a conventional periphrasis to 'l'étreinte amoureuse', which he qualifies as 'si vile, qu'elle est

---

28. Only he and the gardener visit the greenhouse, which recalls the places of isolation which seem to offer refuge, but where we sense madness, that are a constant in the tales of madness: the isolated houses of 'Qui Sait?' and 'Apparition', the asylums of that story and 'La Chevelure', the solitude of the hero in 'Lui?' See Guy de Maupassant, *Apparition et autres contes d'angoisse*, ed. by Antonia Fonyi (Paris: Flammarion, 1987), 17-19.
29. The implausibility of using this form in fiction (as when the narrator of 'Le Horla' notes things whose significance he doesn't realise at the time — the arrival of the boat — but nothing that is not significant) is generally overcome by our acceptance of the convention and by the compelling nature of the tale.

CHAPTER 2. HESITANT TELLERS, RELUCTANT LISTENERS 67

devenue, pour tous les êtres affinés, un acte si honteux qu'il faut cacher, dont on ne parle qu'à voix basse, en rougissant' (II, 780). There is shame (the word *honteux* reappears in the lawyer's final condemnation) in the act, and in the naming of it. If this does still hint at the 'base' nature of the organs involved in the act of love, it is something that he cannot put into words. As he retreats into his private world, argument gives way to a self-absorbed fantasy whose implications he seems unable or unwilling to clarify. The final version leaves us baffled at the husband's combination of remorseless logic (love is a mask for reproduction) and a bizarrre obsession with flowers: are they an escape from human sexuality, or a transposed obsession with the female body?

In his *Chroniques* Maupassant denounces the twin aspects of hypocrisy in his time: the sentimental refusal to acknowledge *la chose*, and the *pudibonderie* which leads to euphemism or silence. But in 'Un cas de divorce' we are aware of the narrative interest in characters reluctant to face and say things, in a way that disturbs rather than amuuses. Both types of tale still work because inhibitions are felt about certain areas; as Harvey Sacks noted, with some bodily functions, notably sex, direct language is impossible and 'crude': 'The properly literal way to talk about sex is allusively'.[30] These inhibitions are the centre of the husband's predicament in 'Un cas de divorce': he cannot accept the realities of human sexuality. In the comic tales they are echoed in the framing context. The lawyer of 'Un cas de divorce' admits that the case is a medical one in a judicial setting, and this sense of inappropriateness and awkwardness runs through the tale: the lawyer's sense of indecency, the reading aloud of the husband's *journal intime*, the public presentation of private fantasies and reference to unseen organs. Saying/censoring, public/private become key thematic oppositions that give coherence to a short story, and are brought out in the frame.

The complex textual history of 'Un cas de divorce' makes it an interesting but perhaps marginal case. Barbey d'Aurevilly's *Les Diaboliques*[31] provides a second instance of narrative interest created by

30. Sacks, *Lectures on Conversation*, II, 434.
31. References in the text to this work are to vol. II (1966) of Barbey d'Aurevilly, *Œuvres romanesques complètes*.

obstacles in the telling and receiving of tales. The six stories exploit possible relationships between a character, usually a homodiegetic first Narrator, and the narrator of an embedded tale. In most cases they follow the expected pattern. The first character is eager to hear the tale, requesting it in 'Le Bonheur dans le crime': 'Docteur, mon cher et adorable docteur, — repris-je, avec toutes sortes de câlineries dans la voix, — vous allez me dire tout ce que vous savez' (88); demanding it in 'Le Plus Bel Amour de Don Juan': 'Dites-nous cela, comte!' (67). The narrator may initially play with his audience, like Mesnilgrand in 'A un dîner d'athées', but he is ready to respond: 'Il y a une histoire là-dessous... Quand elle sera dite, vous comprendrez peut-être' (203–204). But in the opening tale, 'Le Rideau cramoisi', both narrator and audience erect barriers to straightforward narration. The unnamed first Narrator tells how he met vicomte de Brassard on a coach, travelling to Normandy. A breakdown halts them in the middle of the night in a provincial town. Brassard notices a lighted window: his reaction points to some personal experience that is waiting to be told. But he is reluctant to tell his tale and takes the conversation away from the window; moreover, it is clear that he has not told the tale before. To extract the tale, the first Narrator initially feigns indifference, even though (as he admits to the reader) he is 'le chasseur aux histoires' (21). But Brassard's hesitation seems to be more than a conventional way of intriguing the reader. Barbey is a writer for whom (perhaps more than any other in the nineteenth century) conversation is interaction,[32] and not just a way of imparting information. From the beginning, he sets up the relationship between the two characters in a way that makes us think about how they relate to the embedded tale, and how this can influence its interpretation.

The story, reduced to its bare bones, is as simple and as implausible as some of Maupassant's comic tales. Brassard tells of an experience he had when garrisoned in the town at the age of seventeen, inexperienced in love and war. He had lodgings with an elderly couple, 'tout ce que vous pouvez imaginer de plus bourgeois' (49). After several months, a young girl appears, attractive but reserved, whom he discovers with surprise to be their daughter, just out of boarding school. She initiates

---

32. Underlined notably by Michel Crouzet in his edition of *Les Diaboliques* (Paris: Imprimerie Nationale, 1989), 13–21.

CHAPTER 2. HESITANT TELLERS, RELUCTANT LISTENERS 69

an intense and reckless sexual relationship with Brassard, which is concealed from her parents. Brassard narrates it in terms of three key scenes: the first time she seizes, unnoticed, his hand beneath the table at dinner; her first visit, unannounced, to his room one night; then, after months of silent passion, her sudden death in his arms on his canapé one night, followed by his panic flight.

If (as in 'Carmen') one looks at the relationship between a narrator and his younger, experiencing self, the two here are strikingly different. The first Narrator presents Brassard in the frame as an officer possessed of *sang-froid* whose military courage is matched by his amorous conquests (even having, allegedly, seven mistresses at once). He is a dandy resistant to 'toute espèce de discipline et de routine' (14): this is exemplified during the 1830 Revolution when he recklessly led his company down the centre of the boulevard while they kept to the sides. In contrast, his younger self is innocent, inexperienced and timid.

Brassard has not told the tale before, although it represents a key moment of his life, 'mordant sur ma vie comme un acide sur de l'acier' (24): it is clearly something he has not wanted to go back over. Brassard says that in the three crucial moments of the affair, Alberte had brought him intensity of feeling, 'émotion'; but what emotion? We might assume in a tale of 'first love' that it is reciprocal passion. But, as he reminds his narratee in an evaluative comment just before the climactic moment (he had made the point earlier (24), but his narratee had forgotten the hint), his central discovery in the affair is 'la peur complète, [...] cette panique qui fait prendre la fuite à des régiments tout entiers' (50). After telling of Alberte's death and his panic-stricken disarray, trapped with her body in his room, Brassard ends his tale rapidly and unconvincingly: he had fled from the house to his colonel, and then from the town, and the subsequent military campaign conveniently killed those who could have told him 'what happened next' in his lodgings. The over-hasty conclusion reinforces the initial hesitation: his flight reflects the way that has shied away from knowing and facing his past. Even as he narrates, Brassard is not fully aware of the significance of the adventure. Prompted by the frame, we can now see why his life developed as it did. Instead of the older Brassard's account throwing light on his youth, it is his youth, as revealed in the story, that throws light on what he has become: someone blocked in a career of heroism and sexual exploits, who has failed to attain maturity and self-knowledge.[33] His present display of recklessness, impenetrability and virility paradoxically repeats Alberte's. As the frame is resumed and the two passengers move on in the repaired coach, we realise that Brassard's shock and panic, buried in the past, are something that have not been, or cannot be, resolved. Frame and embedded narration are linked; his fear of loss of control has given way to a life of control.

Brassard has recalled the adventure of his youth without really learning from it. What of the narratee who, in spite of his feigned indifference, does want to hear the tale? He much more obviously is somone who fails to see things. As frequently in Barbey, Brassard's embedded story is characterised by interruptions in the form of comments and anecdotes by its recipient. In real life, making a comment or telling a story can be a way of underlining the point of a previous story, or of showing that one has got the point.[34] But here the narratee's over-eager interventions show him repeatedly misinterpreting. He treats Brassard's tale as a 'leste aventure de garnison' (37); he breaks in with two anecdotes about women who succeed in duping their husbands or family during love affairs, which he thinks echo the tone of Brassard's. Brassard receives the first coldly; not only is his tale one that will end in the woman's death, but also its point is not sexual initiation, but discovering fear. The narratee's anticipations are equally misguided: he thinks the lighted window will lead to a tale of amorous conquest: Brassard corrects him, saying that *he* was 'pris' (24); when Brassard recounts the daughter's first visit, the narratee's ironic comment: 'Mais elle va bien, votre Alberte' (44) is to prove wide of the mark. As the account of the affair continues, he expects Brassard's narrative to lead to 'une fin', the discovery of what motivated the mysterious Alberte. Brassard compares her to a sphinx; for the narratee, 'les Sphinx sont des animaux fabuleux. Il n'y en a point dans la vie'; and he presumes, both disrespectfully and crudely,

---

33. The point is made by Timothy Unwin, 'Barbey d'Aurevilly conteur: discours et narration dans *Les Diaboliques*', *Neophilologus* 72 (1988), 353-365 (361-2), and in more detail by Dietmar Rieger, '*Le Rideau Cramoisi* von Barbey d'Aurevilly: Versuch einer tiefenpsychologischen Interpretation', *Germanisch-Romanische Monatsschrift* 22 (1972), 176-92.
34. Livia Polanyi, 'Nature of meaning', 55-57.

CHAPTER 2. HESITANT TELLERS, RELUCTANT LISTENERS   71

that 'vous finîtes bien par trouver, que diable! ce qu'elle avait dans son giron, cette commère-là!' (47). Brassard has again to correct him: there is 'une fin', but not in the sense that his narratee means it.

If there is an unanalysed gap in Brassard's development, one that he does not face, the narratee's interruptions make clear that there is another gap at the heart of the tale: Alberte's secret. 'Est-elle effrontée? Est-elle folle?' Brassard asks himself after her first advances (34–35); and is no wiser when she dies, admitting: 'Je n'ai jamais bien compris ce que j'avais pour elle et ce qu'elle avait pour moi, et cela dura plus de six mois!' (48). Her motive is left ambiguous. The reader can guess at a range of possibilities: sexual curiosity? lust? perverse recklessness? defiance of her family and background? madness? But Brassard gives no explicit pointer. The only clues we have appear in the images he uses. Images can be a key evaluative guide, especially if they form a consistent pattern. Here they play on the idea of heat beneath surfaces that are cold or hard: 'Elle me produisait l'effet d'un épais et dur couvercle de marbre qui brûlait, chauffé par en-dessous... Je croyais qu'il arriverait un moment où le marbre se fendrait enfin sous la chaleur brûlante, mais le marbre ne perdit jamais sa rigide densité' (47). This combination of exterior impassibility and inner passsion, like the image of the sphinx, serves to reinforce Alberte's paradoxical nature. Brassard, recalling his past life in a homodiegetic narrative, sees her only from the outside. This external focalisation, common to many of Barbey's female protagonists,[35] is coupled with her own silence about her inner feelings:

> Sa bouche triste demeurait muette de tout [...]. Elle ne disait mot... [...] Elle fut toujours aussi *difficile à confesser* que la première nuit qu'elle était venue. Je n'en tirai pas davantage... Tout au plus [...] un monosyllabe qui ne faisait pas grande lumière sur la nature de cette fille. (47)

Brassard suggests various possible but conflicting causes for her sudden death: the cold could have caused a 'maladie de poitrine' (50), her recurrent *pâmoisons* (51) could be a symptom of some medical condition. But it remains inexplicable. In one sense, the reader is left,

---

35. On this, see Anne Giard, 'Le Récit lacunaire dans les *Diaboliques*', *Poétique* 11 (1980), 39–50 (45).

as we are frequently in short fiction, with gaps to complete: we can guess what Cornudet asks Boule de Suif in the corridor, what Mme Bonderoi proposes to the soldier Siballe, what occupies Céleste during her rendez-vous in 'La Serre' as the Lerebours watch. Barbey's other tales consist of incomplete narratives which leave similar gaps in the events related, after which 'chacun [...] complétait, avec le genre d'imagination qu'il avait, ce roman authentique dont on n'avait à juger que quelques détails dépareillés' ('Le Dessous de cartes d'une partie de whist', 170). But the revelation is never complete; even if we can reconstruct most of the events (the *histoire*), the central characters remain, like Alberte, enigmatic and paradoxical.[36] External focalisation and 'narrative reticence'[37] are central to the reader's curiosity about motivation. And our inability to understand fully Alberte's motives contributes to the disquiet that the story leaves. To explain would enable us to pin down the characters, to control the unpredictable, and would reassure rather than disturb.

These problematic narrators and narratees, inhibited, reticent, or unaware, are perhaps not what we normally expect in a story. They are not the over-motivated tellers of 'Carmen' or 'Sombre récit, conteur plus sombre', nor their eager listeners. But they too can sustain interest in a narrative of events that provide little more than a meagre and often bizarre or implausible anecdote. Just as with a willing narrator, it is worth bearing in mind that a story is 'someone telling someone else that something has happened': the motives, characters, and attitudes of both parties can be crucial to the sort of interest, comic or disturbing, given to the story told. In a successful framed story, frame and embedded story cannot be considered separately.

Maupassant's comic tales with hesitant narrators let us fill a teasingly suppressed gap from our 'intertextual scenarios' based on knowledge of the world and of literature. The narrator is very much in charge, and part of his game is to make sure that we can guess what narrative ellipses or shifts in focalisation have hidden. The gaps in 'Un cas de

36. For the main exception, the duchess in 'La Vengeance d'une femme', see Chapter 3.
37. The term is Herta Rodina's, 'Textual Harassment: Barbey d'Aurevilly's *Les Diaboliques*', *Nineteenth-Century French Studies* 24 (1995-1996), 144-53 (148).

CHAPTER 2. HESITANT TELLERS, RELUCTANT LISTENERS

divorce' and 'Le Rideau cramoisi' are more disturbing. They show how narrators who are inhibited or uncomprehending, and narratees who reject, are baffled by, or misunderstand what they are being told, can serve to evoke realities that are unknowable: Alberte's passion, the mind of the husband in 'Un cas de divorce'. The gaps left in short fiction can be easily filled by the reader, as in 'La Serre', or left to provoke the reader as something that cannot be rationally controlled or explained, as in 'Le Rideau cramoisi'.

'Le Rideau cramoisi' also shows that for short fiction, the intense and unexplained sexual obsession is more manageable than a more complex and slowly developing emotion that could be called 'love'. Brassard is revealingly reluctant to pin a label on it: 'Notre amour, notre relation, notre intrigue, — appelez cela comme vous voudrez' (47). In short fiction intensification of effect can be more important than spelling out causes. Events are pushed to extremes: comically in 'le Remplaçant', where prostitution leads to a duel, or in 'Enragée', where a wedding night leads to fear of rabies. So are emotions: Alberte, who perhaps does not love Brassard, who perhaps does not love her, leads him to 'des sensations que je ne crois pas avoir éprouvées jamais depuis avec des femmes plus aimées que cette Alberte' (42). Not explaining is not a limitation, as it might be in a novel, where it would frustrate, but a feature of short fiction with positive advantages.

3. Singular Things: prompting and focusing

Mérimée, 'Le Vase étrusque', 'La Partie de trictrac';
Barbey, 'La Vengeance d'une femme'

In Barbey's 'Le Rideau cramoisi', Brassard reacts to the lighted window with its crimson curtain seen from the coach by exclaiming: 'C'est singulier! ... On dirait que c'est toujours le même rideau' (21). From this point, however reluctant he may be to go back over the experience of his youth, neither he, nor his companion, nor the reader can doubt that there is a tale to be told. Throughout the nineteenth century, particular objects, incidents and phrases in frame narratives serve to trigger an exchange between characters that leads to a tale about a specific experience. The 'singular' object or phrase can sometimes release an experience that has profoundly marked the character, as with Brassard. Sometimes it just provides the occasion for an amusing anecdote. In Maupassant's 'Le Moyen de Roger' (II, 473), a friend asks Roger about a phrase frequently used by his wife, which always makes him blush: what is 'le moyen de Roger'? Roger's tale reveals not only the event his wife is referring to: his overcoming temporary impotence on his wedding night, but also the fact that she remains unaware of the means that he used to solve the problem: a quick trip to a local brothel. In both these tales the curiosity of a narratee sets in motion the narrative process.[1] But it can be the narrator of the embedded tale whose memory, like Brassard's, is jogged: Picot seeing Gargan on the shoot in 'Les Bécasses' is prompted to tell the Narrator how he killed his wife; a log falling from the hearth in 'La Bûche' prompts an elderly man to recall an incident in his youth, and explain why he never married.

Other means can obviously be used to trigger a narrative. A dramatic change in a person or a place can prompt an enquiry about how this happened: the narratee of 'Garçon, un bock!' (I, 1123) is shocked by the appearance of an old school friend met by chance in a brasserie; in

---

1. Other examples are 'Mon oncle Jules' (I, 931) or 'Ce cochon de Morin' (I, 641).

'La Mère Sauvage' the narratee sees a house, once 'propre, vêtue de vignes, avec des poules devant la porte' (I, 1218), that is now ruined and 'morte'. In both cases the embedded tales reveal what lay behind the change: a sudden disillusionment about life, an act of revenge during the Franco-Prussian war. But the small object, odd phrase, or trivial incident can be more than 'un simple prétexte, sur lequel il n'y a pas lieu de s'arrêter'.[2] They have the advantage of singularity (to recall Brassard's term) that will enable them to stick in the mind. They frequently provide a title for the tale; the fact that they are small makes them appropriate triggers for tales that are themselves often limited, either in terms of the nature of the event or incident, or, in the case of oral tales, in the time taken by their narration.

In most of these examples from Maupassant what could be termed the 'prompt' is a convenient device to trigger the embedded narrative. The prompt is more interesting when it also arouses expectations, and focuses our attention not just on events, but on the inner meaning of the tale. This role is similar to that of the 'falcon' that German criticism of the *Novelle* has sometimes singled out as a characteristic feature of the genre, a feature that takes its name from Boccaccio. In tale V, 9 of the *Decameron*, a young and noble Florentine, Federigo Alberighi, falls in love with a married woman, Giovanna, who is chaste and takes no notice of his attentions. Rapidly ruined, he retires to live frugally on a small farm in the country, keeping only his falcon, which is 'of the finest breed in the whole world'. Giovanna's husband dies; she withdraws to a nearby country estate with her young son. The son becomes fascinated with Federigo's falcon; falling seriously ill, he asks his mother for it, believing it will help him recover. Giovanna visits Federigo; indigent, but wishing to receive her appropriately, he kills his falcon and serves it to her as a meal; only then does Giovanna reveal the purpose of her visit. Federigo is distraught at the impossibility of satisfying her request; the son dies, either through disappointment or because he was already mortally ill. But some time later, Giovanna, urged to remarry, remembers Federigo's generosity and choses him, saying: 'I would rather have a gentleman without riches, than riches

---

2. As René Godenne judges the knife-throwing in Mérimée's 'Une Partie de trictrac' (Godenne, *La Nouvelle*, 58).

CHAPTER 3. SINGULAR THINGS

without a gentleman'.[3] When Paul Heyse first picked out this story as exemplifying a key feature of the *Novelle*, and used the question: 'Where is the falcon?' as a test for the success of others, he saw the 'falcon' just as the feature that differentiated one particular tale from a thousand others,[4] something that gave 'a strong and clear silhouette'. Later critics extended this: the 'falcon' was an object that not only made the story memorable, but also served as the centre of the tale and possessed a symbolic value — or indeed, multiple values.[5] In Boccaccio's tale, not only is the falcon central to the plot and its cruel twist, but all the characters relate in different ways to the bird: it consoles Federigo, the son desires it, and its sacrifice reveals Federigo's nobility to the widowed Giovanna, making it a symbol of unconditional love.

It is obviously not the case that a 'falcon', either as a memorable feature or as a focus of meaning, is an essential feature of short fiction.[6] At the same time the examination of such focusing objects often provides a useful way of getting to grips with narrative technique. Mérimée can already be seen using an object in this way in his earliest stories. In 'Le Vase étrusque', first published in *La Revue de Paris* in 1830,[7] the elegant but discreet Auguste Saint-Clair is in love with Mme de Coursy, a young widow admired by the élite of society. Not only is his love reciprocated, but he is convinced of his special status: '"Elle

3. Giovanni Boccaccio, *The Decameron*, trans. by G.H. McWilliam (Harmondsworth: Penguin, 1972), 469.
4. 'Das Specifische, das diese Geschichte von tausend anderen unterscheidet': see Paul Heyse's introduction to *Deutscher Novellenschatz* (1871), quoted in Josef Kunz (ed.), *Novelle* (Darmstadt: Wissenschaftliche Buchgesellschaft, 1973), 68, 75.
5. Hermann Pongs, 'Über die Novelle', *Zeitschrift für Deutsche Bildung* 5 (1929), 175-85, reprinted in *Novelle*, ed. Kunz, 139-53 (esp. 141-6); see also E.K. Bennett, *A History of the German 'Novelle'* (Cambridge University Press: 1938 (1st edition 1934)), 13-16; and Daniel Grojnowski, *Lire la nouvelle* (Paris: Dunod, 1993), 23-24.
6. For criticism of the theory, see, for example, John M. Ellis, *Narration in the German Novelle: Theory and Interpretation* (Cambridge University Press, 1974), 4.
7. On the charged role (literal and symbolic) of objects in Mérimée's fiction, see Bowman, *Prosper Mérimée*, 111-3; compare also the role of the watch and the gun in 'Mateo Falcone' (1829).

n'a jamais aimé avant moi"' (514). When Saint-Clair is at a bachelor dinner with his friends, Thémines speaks confidently of a past affair between Mme de Coursy and the well-dressed but inept and boring Massigny. Saint-Clair suddenly recalls Massigny's gift of an Etruscan vase to his mistress; this to him proves their affair. Tortured by retrospective jealousy and wounded vanity, he hides his suspicions from Mme de Coursy. While out riding, he meets Thémines by chance, and in his irritation with him as the source of his distress, provokes him to a duel. The day before it is fought he discovers, too late, his error, when Mme de Coursy tells him of a prank which she and a cousin had played on the infatuated Massigny in order to humiliate him. Overwhelmed by remorse and love, Saint-Clair confesses his suspicions. Mme de Coursy forgives him, laughs when she hears the vase was the 'proof' and breaks it. After this reconciliation he dies in the duel.

How does Mérimée use the Etruscan vase of the title? As regards plot, Saint-Clair's suspicions crystallise around it: it is first mentioned as 'proof' of them. Later, it reawakens his fading jealousy when he taps 'le vase odieux' with a key (the very key that gives him access to Mme de Coursy's house at night), as she snatches it from him to protect the ornament: '"Vous allez casser mon beau vase étrusque!"' (526). Coincidentally she mentions Massigny just afterwards, reinforcing the irritation that is to lead to the duel. Finally, Mme de Coursy breaks it into a thousand pieces after their reconciliation. But it is more than a trigger and a focus for his jealousy. Each time the precious and delicate vase is mentioned, it is in close proximity to a reference to breaking. It is first mentioned just after Saint-Clair had noted how easy it was to 'mettre en pièces' a woman's reputation (his friend Jules had exclaimed in surprise at hearing that Mme de Coursy had yielded to Massigny: '"*Frailty, thy name is woman!*"' (519)). Later, Mme de Coursy was worried that Saint-Clair would break it. The reader is alerted to the forms taken by fragility in the story: Mme de Coursy, having broken Saint-Clair's watch, then gives it back to him, mended, with her portrait inside; Thémines discards his fashionable English pistol after the duel and breaks its hammer. We see the fragility of a woman's reputation, and of human life and happiness, vulnerable to misunderstanding, mood, chance and coincidence. The vase of the title provides a memorable detail that reinforces the themes and points to the more general meaning.

CHAPTER 3. SINGULAR THINGS

In 'Le Rideau cramoisi' the curtained window seen by Brassard triggers his memories, prompts his companion's question, and also contributes to the story's unity and key themes. In the embedded tale window and *rideau cramoisi* play a role both on the literal and the symbolic level. On the level of plot, it is the window of Brassard's room from which he watches for Alberte (41), and from which he fleetingly thinks of throwing her dead body. Thematically, 'Le Rideau cramoisi' is a tale of lovers who violate convention. Barbey underlines the elements of formality and routine: the boredom of the provincial town, the old-fashioned manners of the couple at dinner, the 'politesse la plus froide' between him and Alberte in public (32)) against which the intense and illicit affair stands out. Brassard violates hospitality, Alberte, and parental trust; the window of his room, in which this is accomplished, comes to stand as a synecdoche for desecrated house and family, order and morality. 'Le Rideau cramoisi' is a tale of hidden passions and unexplained motives, and the window is explicitly linked to hidden dramas and spying. The first Narrator cannot see a window lit at night 'sans imaginer derrière ces rideaux des intimités et des drames' (20), and Brassard draws the curtain to prevent curious neighbours from seeing 'le fond de [sa] chambre' (42). It also becomes charged with the emotional content of his experiences: when he looks at it as he flees the town, its connotations are of sexuality, fear, and guilt. Its colour, red, alerts us to references running through the story to things that are conventionally red, evoking violence and passion, namely fire and blood. Brassard's blood is 'allumé' when Alberte first takes his hand (33, 42), he kisses her 'belles lèvres rouges et érectiles' in a 'baiser de feu' (45); and the references to fire are contrasted with Alberte's exterior 'froideur' (41) and the final pallor of her 'corps glacé' (52). Mérimée's vase and Barbey's curtain are not so much straightforward symbols, planted by the author to embody an idea, as objects linked to the themes of the story and invested with emotion by the characters. At the end of 'Le Rideau cramoisi' Brassard falls silent and we return to the frame. Brassard points out the passing shadow of a woman at the lit window, which then resumes 'son carré vide, rouge et lumineux' (57): this typical reminder of the initial prompt provides an effect of resolution and completeness, reinforced here as the coach departs and life in the present resumes.

Such objects can serve as narrative prompts or as central focusing devices. Maupassant often uses them at the end of the tale to sum it up.

The octopus tortured by the internal narrator in 'Un Soir' (I, 1069) finally embodies his hatred of his unfaithful wife and of women. In 'Hautot père et fils' (II, 1056) a pipe (with its obvious sexual connotations) is passed on by the secret mistress of the father, killed in a hinting accident, to his son, who now discovers not only a half-brother but no doubt a future mistress too. As prompt, central focus, or symbol, such objects can become rather mechanical tricks in short fiction. But two stories from different ends of the nineteenth century show not only their usefulness, but also how they guide the reader in a less obvious way to the point of rather enigmatic stories.

Mérimée's 'La Partie de trictrac' presents a framed narrative that tells of a naval lieutenant, Roger, generous but impulsive and obsessed with honour, who wins a mistress, cheats once when playing backgammon, and whose life falls apart when the loser in the game commits suicide. This tale of remorse is made more complex, as Danielle Mihram has noted,[8] by Roger's character (he a typical protagonist of short fiction in that he is simplified to a few extreme traits): his susceptibility and insecurity, his desire always to be in the forefront of events, play a key role in his disintegration.

A dagger provides the narrative prompt for the narrative. The tale is told by Roger's friend, now a Captain, to an unnamed initial Narrator during a period of flat calm towards the end of a long sea journey. The officers and the Narrator are on deck, bored, after dinner. The Narrator wants to borrow the Captain's knife to join in a game being played by the other officers; the Captain refuses because it belonged to his friend Roger; and as we expect, it does not just function as a trigger to the telling of the tale, but is also present in its key scenes. But compared to the role of the Etruscan vase, or Barbey's curtained window, the dagger's role is incoherent and incomplete: it fails to play its expected part in the final climax, and indeed this climax is evaded. The Captain sketches in Roger's character, tells how the actress Gabrielle became his mistress, and of the fatal game of backgammon. There follow three scenes between Roger and Gabrielle in which Roger confesses his act and gradually reveals his motives and present anguish. After the first of

8. Danielle Mihram, 'La Partie de trictrac, nouvelle aux résonances tragiques', Nineteenth-Century French Studies, 8 (1979-1980), 53-61. See also Lorina Todorova, 'Observations sur la composition et le style de la nouvelle "La Partie de trictrac" de Prosper Mérimée', Philologia, 4 (1978), 56-61.

CHAPTER 3. SINGULAR THINGS

these scenes he is already thinking obsessively of suicide; and after the second, he draws the dagger in a fit of anger, throws it at her feet and leaves the apartment 'pour ne pas céder à la tentation qui l'obsédait' (544). It reappears (with no explanation of how it got there!) in Roger's room that same evening: the Captain takes it, together with his pistols, after a further suicide threat by Roger. But he does not accomplish his 'funeste dessein' (546) before he has to leave on a naval mission. During that mission he makes a final confession to the Captain: his despair is such that (says the Captain) 's'il m'avait demandé ses pistolets pour se tuer, je crois que je les lui aurais donnés' (548). This confession is followed by a lengthy engagement with a more heavily armed English frigate, which inflicts severe damage; the main mast falls and Roger is seriously wounded. The reader expects the guilt-ridden and suicidal Roger to die,[9] as the Captain first mentioned him as 'un brave officier mort malheureusement dans la dernière guerre' (535); moreover, he has just made the Captain promise to throw him overboard if he is wounded. At this point we may expect the knife to play a part in this death: indeed, just before he is wounded, the Captain sees him busy 'à faire couper les haubans qui retenaient encore le mât abattu' (549). But the Captain's dramatic narrative is interrupted at this point by the sighting of a whale; 'transporté de joie et laissant là son récit' (550), he organises a pursuit; and Mérimée elides the outcome of the battle, Roger's death, and any reappearance of the knife.

Why does Mérimée interrupt the Captain's narrative here? The reader expecting a conventionally turned tale, with an end and a point, anticipates Roger's death as the logical consequence of his moral disintegration. We are frustrated at the lack of climax or resolution; we feel we can still ask: 'what happened next?'.[10] There are other instances in Mérimée of what has been called[11] 'narrative aposiopesis', by

---

9. All the more so as it would conform to some literary models: Bowman instances George Sand's *Mauprat* and Mme de Duras's *Edouard* (*Prosper Mérimée*, 73), though only the latter predates Mérimée's tale.
10. The interruption is, on reflection (but it is a short story, and Mérimée does not give us time to think), doubly a trick: it is arbitrarily introduced by Mérimée, and the first Narrator could presumably have asked the Captain later how his tale ended, though they are admittedly only a few days from land (536).
11. Thierry Ozwald, 'La Nouvelle mériméenne: entre atticisme et mutisme', *La Licorne*, 21 (1991), 91-102 (97).

analogy with the rhetorical figure in which a sentence, notably a threat, is left uncompleted: 'If you do that again... '. His tales can end with a silence or sudden abbreviation at the moment when explanations seem needed. But in Mérimée, this silence is generally a trick. The clues are there, and in the tales where a realistic explanation of events is finally possible, the reader can retrospectively use them to provide the missing ending or explanation. Indeed, to follow the implications of Ozwald's term, a rhetorical aposiopesis does not just interrupt a sentence; the recipient is perfectly able to fill in the drift of what has not been said: in the case of a threat, to guess that punishment is in store. At the end of 'Arsène Guillot', we are not told what becomes of the devout Mme de Piennes and her friend Max de Salligny after the death of Max's former mistress Arsène, but we deduce an affair between them from the handwritten inscription on her tombstone: '"Pauvre Arsène! Elle prie pour nous."' Why else would Arsène have to pray for them, when it is normally the living who pray for the dead? In 'Les Ames du Purgatoire' the central event of the story is an apparently supernatural vision which turns the hero from a life of evil to one of repentance. This vision is framed by symmetrical suspension points (719–20). Together with other clues, like the hero's fatigue, the fact that he is outside the church both before and after the vision, which ends *inside* the church), these provide clear enough pointers for the alert reader to realise that the 'vision' was just a dream. It is only in *contes fantastiques* like 'La Vénus d'Ille' and 'Lokis', which leave the reader hesitating between supernatural and rational interpretations of events, that the gap left by the narrator is genuinely enigmatic and leaves unresolved what actually happened. With the provocative narrative aposiopesis of 'La Partie de trictrac', Roger's death is in no doubt; and in the teasing suspension of closure, with the Captain embroiled in the description of the battle, the reader begins to see that the real point, as the title indicates, lay in the game.

The presentation of the game itself, like the story as a whole, is characterised by a certain amount of narrative 'cheating'. We hear of Roger's life not directly, from an omniscient narrator, but from the Captain. His narrative, however, contains substantial elements of hearsay, enabling him to relate events he did not witness: Gabrielle's break with her former protector in Paris, the riot in the theatre when she refused an encore. Indeed, since the Captain was absent from so many key events, why did Mérimée chose him as narrator? Mérimée's later narrators and witnesses are frequently notable for their

CHAPTER 3. SINGULAR THINGS

inappropriateness or incongruity. In 'La Vénus d'Ille' we have an erudite bachelor, in 'Lokis' a pastor for whom etymology is more urgent than marriage, who are both involved in weddings that end in violent death; in 'Carmen' and 'Colomba' we find a Parisian archaeologist and staid British tourists who are plunged into tales of banditry and murder. The gap between the witness and the events portrayed creates effects of irony, but also puts in sharper focus what the narrators observe, characters and events that are seen as both fascinating and dangerous. This contrastive function is already evident in the character of the Captain — at least the older, narrating Captain. He is 'le plus doux des hommes' (536), embodying experience and calm, responsible authority. He tells a tale of a character who, because of his illegitimacy, is insecure, dependent on the esteem of others, and also impulsive and reckless. Roger's immature infatuation with Gabrielle veers between talk of marriage (539) and contempt for a 'fille de joie' (545). His megalomaniac streak is accompanied by a tendency to defy authority and conventions, when he provocatively offers money with flowers to Gabrielle, when he proposes and threatens suicide, when he provokes a mass duel with a visiting regiment.

The Captain, then, is a useful narrator because of the contrasts his character sets up, just as the becalmed boredom of the narrative frame contrasts with the youthful energy of the events related.[12] But as he narrates the key scenes of the story, it is difficult to tell whether he was actually present, and who is actually observing the events narrated. In the crucial gambling scene, for instance, we are not told where it takes place or who (apart from the Dutchman, Roger, and another officer) is there. We enter the game in mid-play: 'Il s'appliquait horriblement; aussi la partie fut-elle longue et disputée. Il vint un moment, où Roger, tenant le cornet, n'avait plus qu'une chance pour gagner: je crois qu'il fallait six quatre' (541). A brief mention that the other officer is asleep then eliminates the only clear witness. The Dutchman is drowsy, 'Roger seul était bien éveillé.' We see in succession the candle knocked over by Roger's throw, the Dutchman's trousers spattered with wax, then the dice, with an imperfect indicating that they have settled: 'Ils marquaient

---

12. Richard Hobbs has linked this with the contrast between the Restoration and the Napoleonic period (*From Balzac to Zola: Selected Short Stories* (Bristol Classical Press, 1992), 11).

six et quatre'; then Roger's face ('pâle comme la mort') as he receives his winnings. Is this what the Dutchman sees? or some (non-existent) witness who can watch both, like a camera, guess their state of mind, and follow their eyes; but a witness who is not allowed to look at the crucial moment? The reference to the Dutchman: 'Je crois le voir encore. C'était un grand blond, flegmatique, dont la figure semblait de cire' retrospectively implies the (impossible) presence of the Captain as witness.

It is difficult to arrive at one consistent narrative position and focalisation for the scene. It presents problems as omniscient narrative, in that Roger's cheating, is not recorded, and as something watched by the Captain, or reconstructed by him later from Roger's account, as he would by then know of Roger's cheating. What counts however is the effect: we do not worry about 'who is seeing' and feel we are watching the gripping events as they unfold. The two subsequent scenes with Gabrielle, when Roger reveals his cheating and they argue, likewise come over as if directly witnessed; but the Captain was not there either, and it is only later that he finally hears from Roger the truth about the game and his guilt.

Should this apparent inconsistency worry us? Mérimée's cheating enables the *récit*, the account of the Captain's narrative, to return three times to the crucial moment when Roger cheated: the initial ellipsis of the moment when it took place, the 'vide dans le récit'[13] is gradually filled in. At first Roger baldly admits that he has cheated: '"Oui, j'ai triché, Gabrielle; j'ai triché comme un misérable que je suis"' (543). After the second scene with Gabrielle, Roger relates to the Captain both the game and the scenes with Gabrielle in terms that imply that we now know everything: 'Alors il me raconta l'histoire de la partie de trictrac, et tout ce que vous savez déjà' (545). His final confession to the Captain, however, reveals that there was a double narrative ellipsis: not only of the act of cheating, but of his motives, which were not what the Captain (and we as readers) might have deduced. The full significance of events becomes clear only with this final confession.

The Captain had stressed initially Roger's need for the 'considération' of others in society and his 'désir continuel et violent de primer' (537). His wounded pride at being rejected by Gabrielle means

---

13. Mérimée, *Nouvelles*, ed. Crouzet, I, 387.

CHAPTER 3. SINGULAR THINGS							85

that he will not give up, and we see the impulsive and absurd reactions that the threat of losing prompts in him: offers of marriage, threats of suicide (539). When the Dutch ship anchors, Roger gambles, or so he imagines, to 'soutenir l'honneur de son pays' (540); but he is also responding to the challenge of high stakes. He fails to commit suicide, after his confession to Gabrielle. Although his self-esteem is shattered by what he has done, his pride needs the esteem of others. Unable to do anything that could affect his posthumous reputation, he remains alive despite the Captain's and Gabrielle's anxieties. His full revelation to the Captain reveals his shame and anger at being a 'friponneau' who has cheated for only twenty-five *napoléons*. This may be a paltry sum in comparison with his honour; but it is (the irony is clear) the same sum with which he attempted to buy Gabrielle, and it is reckless: as the Captain notes, it represents two months' pay (541). The Captain's rationalisation: that Roger cheated for love of Gabrielle, turns out to be inadequate. He suffers not from the dishonour of cheating, but from knowing that he he cheated for nothing of significance,[14] and it is this that plays on his susceptibility and insecurity.

In the frame, Mérimée warns us that 'telling a story' has a positive and a negative side. In can be an antidote to the boredom of journeys and limited company, and the first paragraph stresses the flat calm and stifling heat; in *Candide* the old woman had justified her narrative by saying that it was normal 'dans un vaisseau, de conter des histoires pour se désennuyer'.[15] The story is prompted by the Captain's knife, to which he is 'singulièrement' attached: conjuring up the promise both of a singular (extraordinary) tale to break the monotony,[16] and of a tale told *once*. On the negative side the tale is nothing but a last resort against this boredom, an amusement when other 'ressources

14. See also Pierre Trahard: 'Roger souffre moins de son crime que de la petitesse de son crime' (*La Jeunesse de Prosper Mérimée (1803-1834)*, 2 vols (Paris: Champion, 1925), II, 174).
15. *Candide*, Chapter xii, in Voltaire, *Romans et contes*, edited by Henri Bénac (Paris: Garnier, 1960), 163.
16. Compare the Marquis des Arcis in Diderot's *Jacques le fataliste* (edited by Jacques and Anne-Marie Chouillet, Paris: Librairie Générale Française, 1983): 'Si vous n'avez rien qui vous occupe plus utilement ou plus agréablement, je vous raconterai l'histoire de mon secrétaire, elle n'est pas commune' (201).

d'amusement' have been exhausted (534), on a par with the idle knife-throwing of the officers. And stories, however gripping, lose even this potential by retelling, become totally predictable, like the first lieutenant's tales of war (cut short, as the Captain's will be, with a perfunctory 'etc., etc.!' (535)), and the 'histoire bien intéressante' of the *commissaire de marine*. The Captain's tale itself grips the first narrator who has not heard it before; but as he senses, it has been often told: 'Je devinai qu'une histoire allait suivre' (536-7), and the other officers slip away. Over any narrative, however singular, hangs the threat of completion, knowledge, repetition. Any real event — here, the sighting of a whale — suffices for it to be abandoned.

The story remains interesting for the first Narrator, and for us, only as long as it remains 'singular', individual, new and incomplete; and any story risks losing its grip on the audience's curiosity, what Ross Chambers calls its 'narrative authority',[17] as it gradually unfolds and we know more. The Captain's story has two centres of interest. The motivation for Roger's cheating represents the pessimistic moral and psychological point; the techniques that Mérimée plays with (ambiguous focalisation, ellipsis of the moment of cheating, repetitive narrative which gives several accounts of it) all return us to this key moment. The second, more conventional centre of interest, the death of Roger, is constantly anticipated, repeatedly announced, notably by Roger's persistent suicide threats, but never recounted. It is linked teasingly with the dagger which never fulfils its expected narrative role. The interplay between the two centres of interest allows Mérimée to accomplish several effects at the same time.

While we follow events through (as we think) to Roger's death, sustained by narrative curiosity, we continue to to explore motive. The point that this exploration implies is typical of short fiction: human vulnerability to chance. For Mérimée, human life, constantly disrupted by impulses both uncontrollable and beyond rational analysis, 'n'a pas de sens humain', as Paul Bourget remarked.[18] His world is one of the fragility of human ambitions and resolutions, of the vanity of mankind's confidence in reason and foresight. In 'Le Vase étrusque', Saint-Clair's

17. Chambers, *Story and Situation*, 26.
18. Paul Bourget, *Nouvelle Pages de critique et de doctrine*, 2 vols (Paris: Plon, 1922), I, 3-25 (19).

susceptible vanity was central to his undoing. Roger's self-esteem cannot resign itself to the meaninglessness of his act. But this lack of significance is only gradually unveiled. Mérimée sustains the reader's interest by maintaining the red herring of the second climax, and by constantly leaving incomplete our knowlege of the first. The Captain seems unaware of the full implications of the tale he is telling. His indulgence glosses over Roger's faults, though the clues are there: suicide threats, obsession with honour, generosity to buy consideration, and he is finally carried away in narrating the heroic events of the sea battle. But the story will not add up to the martial or maritime tale that the Captain seems to want to tell. The narrative prompt (Roger's dagger) may promise a tale of nautical heroism to set against the military heroism of Mérimée's earlier 'L'Enlèvement de la Redoute';[19] but we never get there. All we have is a tale of vanity, infatuation, cheating, bravado, suicide threats; the heroic climax is missing, the one repeatedly told scene is of weakness and failure. The frame, mocking the potential boredom of story-telling and ending cavalierly, enables Mérimée to play his standard trick, also seen at the end of 'Carmen', of distancing himself from the events narrated by appearing not to take them too seriously. As Alan Raitt notes,[20] the devaluation of motivation in Roger is matched by a devaluation of story-telling and its tricks.

The second story in which the narrative prompt can guide us to the meaning of an enigmatic embedded tale is Barbey's 'La Vengeance d'une femme', the final tale of *Les Diaboliques*. It opens with a substantial discursive preamble by a heterodiegetic narrator which arouses specific expectations.[21] It makes two points: first, that contemporary literature, for all its self-proclaimed boldness and the shock expressed by prudish critics, does not deal adequately with the 'crimes que la société commet mystérieusement et impunément tous les

---

19. As Crouzet remarks (Mérimée, *Nouvelles*, ed. Crouzet, I, 385). As he notes, at the end of the tale, past, drama and heroism give way to present, fishing, and reality: a characteristic deflation (I, 388).
20. Raitt, *Prosper Mérimée*, 136.
21. Jacques Petit calls this *préface* 'presque trop claire', seeing the sense lying above all in Barbey's 'opposition vive à l'époque'; but he then suggests it might rather be a defence against anticipated criticism (*Œuvres romanesques complètes*, II, 1326), and later (in his notes to *Les Diaboliques* (Paris: Gallimard, 1973) remarks that 'ce prologue est bien curieux' (371).

jours' (229), such as incest. The second point is that these modern crimes are more interesting because of their greater refinement and 'intellectualité', a dimension the Inquisition would have been aware of since it judged 'la pensée' and viewed 'crimes spirituels' as the greatest ones (231). We expect a hidden crime with a spiritual dimension: but is this quite what we find at first reading?

The tale, just like 'La Partie de trictrac', seems at first inconclusive: the reader is frustrated at not finding the obvious ending. After the preamble, a rapid orientation evokes the setting and the protagonist, seen externally: 'Vers la fin du règne de Louis-Philippe, un jeune homme enfilait, un soir, la rue Basse-du-Rempart qui, dans ce temps-là [...]' (232); this description conventionally slides into a revelation of who he is (Robert de Tressignies, a dandy), what he is thinking, and from here on the narrative adopts his point of view, as he follows a prostitute to her room. There he learns, in a second-level narration, her identity and the reason for her prostitution. She is the duchesse de Sierra-Leone, married for dynastic reasons to 'le plus grand seigneur des Espagnes' (246). She had fallen in love with the duke's cousin, don Esteban, with 'un amour tout à la fois brûlant et chaste' (249). Her husband had had her platonic lover murdered in her presence, throwing his heart to his dogs. She seeks revenge by degrading what he was most proud of, his name, living with her full title as a 'fille à cent sous' and anticipating dying 'dans quelque honteux hôpital' (254). Tressignies leaves, broods on the story, but does not retell it. After a year-long absence from Paris, he hears from a chance conversation at the Spanish Ambassador's that a curious passer-by had seen, in the church of La Salpêtrière (then a women's hospice), her name and titles displayed on a catafalque, followed by 'fille repentie', the usual term for a repentant prostitute who had retired to a religious establishment. The next day he visits the hospital and hears the gruesome details of her death from the chaplain.[22]

As in 'Le Rideau cramoisi', and as often in *Les Diaboliques*, at the centre of the tale lies a secret event, glimpsed or revealed in one or

22. The time-scale is rather accelerated: the interval between her leaving Spain and her death of an unspecified disease is just under two years. On the nineteenth century's partial ignorance of the stages and time-scale of syphilis, see Roger L. Williams, *The Horror of Life* (Chicago University Press, 1980), esp. 106-9.

CHAPTER 3. SINGULAR THINGS

more second-level narrations: the duchess reveals the brutal murder of Esteban, and her plan of vengeance; the Ambassador's guest and the priest reveal the events that close the story: death, funeral, epitaph. Even more than in 'La Partie de trictrac', the characters seem concenred with narration as much with events:[23] the duchess's revenge seems to hinge on her telling of her prostitution, on Tressignies retelling this, on society and the arrogant duke learning how she has defiled his name. And she exclaims: '"Moi, je voudrais la dire [mon histoire] à tous ceux qui viennent ici! Je voudrais la raconter à toute la terre! J'en serais plus infâme, mais j'en serais mieux vengée"' (245). In other tales by Barbey, words are as powerful as actions. It has been often noted how the embedded tales affect their narratees, and how words exchanged within the tales can strike home. In 'A un dîner d'athées' la Rosalba taunts her lover Ydow,[24] telling him that he was not the father of her dead child, whose embalmed heart he has preserved like a relic in a crystal urn: these words provoke the violent dénouement. But here the trail of narration peters out. None of the duchess's previous clients wanted to listen to her. Tressignies points out the apparent flaw in her plan:

> 'Le sait-il, lui, le duc, ce que vous êtes devenue?...
> — S'il ne le sait pas, il le saura un jour,' — répondit-elle, avec la sécurité absolue d'une femme qui a pensé à tout. (253)

But she has not recruited anyone to tell him of her debauchery. Indeed, if we take the narrator's account of their conversation to be complete, she does not explicitly tell Tressignies to spread her story;[25] nor does he, just brooding on it. The revelation of her place of death and of the provocative inscription on her catafalque prompts a brief stir at the Ambassador's, but no details are known. The priest attenuates the

---

23. Eileen Sivert argues that in *Les Diaboliques*, 'narration is more important than what is narrated' ('Text, body and reader in Barbey d'Aurevilly's *Les Diaboliques*', *Symposium*, 31 (177), 151–64 (154)).
24. See, for example, the remarks of Crouzet (*Les Diaboliques*, ed. Crouzet, 17); Sivert, 'Text, body', 161–2. For 'A un dîner d'athées', see Chapter 6.
25. The narrator's account of Tressignies's thoughts later does say: 'La duchesse ne lui avait-elle pas demandé de raconter à tout venant son histoire?' (260). She may have implied it, but in the text she did not specifically do so.

inscription on the coffin, adding 'repentie' to the blunt 'fille'. Tressignies, who alone knows the full facts, does not tell him or anyone else. If we are to see, as some critics do, this final revelation as 'the accomplishing of her vengeance',[26] it seems incomplete. If the revenge is intended to work as a 'projet de vengeance' realised in the future,[27] it is disproportionately muted compared with the other *Diaboliques* and undramatic compared with the intensity of her narration to Tressignies.

What is the role of the narrative prompt, and can the object that triggers the embedded narrative again guide us to an understanding of the duchess's vengeance? Led by the prostitute to her room, Tressignies realises that her extreme reactions, during their love-making, are not caused by him. She is apostrophising a portrait on her bracelet. Jealously suspecting that she is thinking of some former lover, he provokes her into revealing her identity, and telling her tale. In this the portrait functions as a conventional narrative prompt. But the role of the bracelet on which her eyes are fixed turns out to be more complex.

Watching and seeing play a key role throughout *Les Diaboliques*: for instance in the interrogative gaze of Brassard, the 'mute', indifferent eyes of Alberte, the eyes of her parents who see nothing in 'Le Rideau cramoisi'. 'La Vengeance d'une femme' is no exception: *yeux*, *voir*, *regarder*, and similar indications occur more than sixty times. The narrative opens with Tressignies standing at his vantage point over the boulevard in order to 'guigner de là les femmes' (232); his successive reappraisals of the duchess in the 'maison aveugle' to which she leads him are always linked to a reference to seeing (238, 257). The duchess and Esteban express their love 'par le regard seul' (251).

But looking is above all linked to aggressiveness and the attempt to control. When Tressignies first sees the 'prostitute', she stops and 'lui campa les yeux dans les yeux': he is 'littéralement aveuglé' by the

26. B.G. Rogers, *The Novels and Tales of Barbey d'Aurevilly* (Geneva: Droz, 1967), 132; cf. Jacques Petit, *Essais de lecture des 'Diaboliques' de Barbey d'Aurevilly* (Paris: Minard, 1974), 63: 'étrange victoire, mais victoire quand même, que ce dénouement.'
27. See the argument of Patrick Dendale, 'Le saura-t-il? Le malaise du lecteur dans *La Vengeance d'une femme*', *Neophilologus*, 75 (1991), 56–65 (62–64); and also Nabih Kanbar, 'Evolution de la figure du témoin dans *Les Diaboliques*', in *Barbey d'Aurevilly cent ans après (1889–1989)*, edited by Philippe Berthier (Geneva: Droz, 1990), 293.

CHAPTER 3. SINGULAR THINGS 91

magnificence of her face (234). Looking can also punish the seer by what he sees: the happiness of the duchess with Esteban is too obvious for the duke not to see it, and when he does, '"cela creva enfin les yeux à son orgueil, cette splendeur d'amour!"' (250). When the duchess explains the nature of her revenge to Tressignies, she refers at length to the bracelet that prompted her narration, and stresses how important is her consciousness of her act. For her, *pensée* (a word insistently repeated) and what exists in the imagination give as much pleasure as the real: '"Est-ce que je ne jouis pas, à chaque minute, de la pensée de ce que je suis?"' She forcefully links the theme of looking to the bracelet, making it clear that she is using the bracelet symbolically to force don Christoval to watch her: '"J'ai emporté avec moi le portrait du duc, pour lui faire voir, à ce portrait, comme si ç'avait été à lui-même, les hontes de ma vie!"' She watches him (this gives her power) watching her (this humiliates him): '"C'était comme s'il nous voyait par ses yeux peints!"' (254–5) It does not matter that the duke does not really see her, or may not learn of what she is doing; her vengeance lies in *her* awareness of her actions. Such purely subjective experiences are as effective, as 'real' as what happens. Hence her reference at this point to her understanding of the age of witchcraft and '"le bonheur insensé de planter le couteau dans le cœur de l'image de celui qu'on eût voulu tuer!"' (255) The emotional satisfaction provided by symbolic reenactment is for her not just a necessary condition for carrying out her revenge, but also a sufficient one.

The preamble to the tale had led us to expect a crime with a spiritual dimension; the role of the bracelet shows that the duchess's vengeance lies in the deliberation of her prostitution, in her awareness of it rather than in the act or the telling of it. As the ambiguity of the title hints, the story concerns more than one type of vengeance. 'La vengeance d'une femme' (of a woman,[28] but also of a wife, against her husband) follows the initial revenge of a man, and a husband, against Esteban. The jealous Spanish duke's vengeance is gory but traditional (tearing out her lover's heart), and has many literary antecedents, which run from

---

28. Dendale comments on the ambiguity of the title ('Le saura-t-il?', 61), but only in terms of an alternative between the revenge of a particular woman, and the type of revenge a woman might take (which the probable earlier title, 'L'Honneur des femmes', would imply: see *Les Diaboliques*, ed. Crouzet, 8).

Boccaccio to Balzac.[29] Her vengeance is more interesting as residing in the mind; moreover, her 'betrayal' also was purely in the mind. The duchess's infidelity cannot simply be described as platonic love: pride and blasphemy play key roles in it. She admits that her pride is as great as her husband's. Pride drives her first from Esteban to the duke, when she feels that her involuntary attraction is giving Esteban power over her, then back to Esteban when the duke insultingly spurns her call for help. Her love for Esteban, moreover, represents more than emotional infidelity. Her lover had '"pris possession de moi comme un Dieu"' (248); after his killing, the desire to eat his heart prompts a blasphemous comparison: '"J'aurais communié avec ce cœur, comme avec une hostie. N'était-il pas mon Dieu?"' (252) The symbolic and subjective meaning of the act is again more important than the physical reality. Her idolatrous love has displaced God, as she acknowledges in another variant on the *cœur arraché*: '"Esteban [...] m'avait arraché Dieu de la poitrine pour s'y mettre à la place"' (257).

From the beginning, images of physical isolation make us see the duchess as self-enclosed in passions (love for Esteban, hatred for the duke) that are self-destructive. She is the last of the Turre-Cremata, *tour brûlée* (246), and lived isolated in the mountains (237-8); in Paris her room is in an isolated and decaying house. Her one idea both keeps her alive ('"cette vengeance qui est ma vie"' (257)) and kills her. She is curiously unconcerned by Tressignies's reaction to her love for Esteban, and even to her story, as if what she was relishing above all was her performance, a 'spectacle' (259) for which he is only a pretext. 'Les immorales glaces au fond et au plafond de l'alcôve' (236) in the prostitute's room that Tressignies first takes as a standard item of erotic equipment are another pointer to the self-absorbed nature of the duchess's revenge. She may tell Tressignies that her revenge lies in the future, but (like Brassard in 'Le rideau cramoisi') she does not fully grasp her own motives.[30] What we and Tressignies see is rather a ritual

---

29. Philippe Berthier has noted Boccacio (*Decameron*, IV, 1), Mme d'Aulnoy (recorded by Barbey in *Omnia*, 43), Scott (*Anne of Geierstein*), Balzac (the episode in 'Une conversation entre onze heures et minuit', originally in *Contes bruns*), as well as the tale of Gabrielle de Vergy that the duchess refers to (252; see also Tressignies's reaction, 254) (*Barbey d'Aurevilly et l'imagination* (Geneva: Droz, 1978), 206).

30. 'La duchesse de Sierra-Leone est incapable d'expliquer son besoin

CHAPTER 3. SINGULAR THINGS

of revenge enacted in the present in which she finds full satisfaction. The public side of her revenge may seem incomplete; the internal aspect of the vengeance, embodied in the bracelet, means that it has been accomplished. As she says, '"Je saurais ce que je fais chaque soir, — que je bois cette fange et que c'est du nectar, puisque c'est ma vengeance!"' (254). As the narrator suggested in the preamble, this remains a hidden crime, largely unrecognised by modern society.

What role is played by the witness who refuses to retell, Tressignies? Unlike 'Le Rideau cramoisi' and most of the other *Diaboliques*, the initial narration is not homodiegetic: we are being told Tressignies's story by an external narrator.[31] Like those of the Narrator of 'le Rideau cramoisi', Tressignies's anticipations of what is to come are frequently wrong, and highlight the surprising nature of what he encounters. He expects a 'très vulgaire aventure' (233), but finds the extraordinary. He is attracted by a resemblance, but is sure that the prostitute cannot be the person she reminds him of;[32] — which of course she is, as he had seen her at Saint-Jean-de-Luz. He does not read the name on the door 'qu'il n'avait pas besoin de savoir' (236), but which he would have recognised. What he takes to be transports of pleasure turn out to be those of hatred. In this way he can guide the responses of the reader, in his shock at her use of *putain* (242), at his discovery of her identity (242), at the form of her vengeance. His final sense of combined fascination and horror, and his silent meditation (260), are characteristic of Barbey. And as the character of the Captain in 'La Partie de trictrac' contrasts with that of Roger, so Tressignies's character serves as a foil for that of the duchess: both are pushed to opposite extremes, in a way typical of short fiction. Tressignies remains detached from his immoral actions, acting in a way that he despises 'en se moquant de lui-même' (233). Ironic and sceptical, he is shocked by the duchess who is a

---

d'autodestruction qui est la base même de son acte de vengeance' (Timothy Unwin, 'Barbey d'Aurevilly conteur', 358).
31. On the patterns of narration in *Les Diaboliques*, see notably Nabih Kanbar, 'Evolution de la figure'; Jacques Petit, *Essais de lecture*, 19–45; Anne Giard, 'Le Récit lacunaire'.
32. 'Elle lui rappelait une autre femme, vue ailleurs... Il était sûr, absolument sûr, que ce n'était pas elle, mais elle lui ressemblait à s'y méprendre, si se méprendre n'avait pas été impossible' (*Les Diaboliques*, ed. Petit, 299; ed. Crouzet, 314; the second sentence is missing in the Pléiade edition, 233).

sublime and terrible embodiment of 'énergie' (255) and 'volonté' (256). 'Un libertin déjà froidi' (233), he contrasts with the images of fire associated with the duchess, who is compared to a volcano (247), and for whom the bracelet is a 'cercle de feu' (254). The reactions of this observer, shaken in his detachment and forced to flee the room, highlight the intensity and unity of her character.

Tressignies does not recount what he hears, but just broods over it afterwards, and is aware of its exemplary force as a 'poème d'une hideuse énergie' (260), belonging to a world beyond normal psychology.[33] In both 'La Partie de trictrac' and 'La Vengeance d'une femme', the invitation to follow events — to the death of Roger, to the outcome of the duchess's plan of revenge on her husband — sustains our curiosity but is a red herring. The reader is led back to the centre: to Roger's cheating and its motivation, to the vengeance enacted in the duchess's mind.

The use of a narrative prompt seems a natural way to introduce a story: how many times have we heard a tale begin when someone remarks: 'That reminds me of a story'? This naturalness perhaps explains Maupassant's reliance on it. But Mérimée's 'La Partie de trictrac' in 1830 already shows a more mischievous attitude, as he both uses it to set the story going in a conventional way, and subverts it by leading the reader astray, as the climax we are expecting is eluded and we have to look elsewhere for the point of the story. Just as in oral narratives, a story-teller can exploit what has been termed 'script deviation'.[34] A disconcerting narrative reflects a disturbing world, where chance and impulse win over reason and planning. Gambling and duels are appropriate motifs in stories in which man is the loser. Mérimée's world, where chance and misunderstanding play a key destructive role, where mankind is unable to master its destiny, where a life can turn on a single moment, is very much the world of the short story.[35]

33. On this characterisation in Barbey, see Anne Giard, 'Le Récit lacunaire', 50.
34. Livia Polanyi, 'The Nature of meaning', 58. Umberto Eco has provided the most detailed analysis of the subversion of expectation based on narrative clues in his discussion of Alphonse Allais's 'Un drame bien parisien' (*Lector in fabula*, 255–86).
35. On this recurrent feature, see Jean-Pierre Blin, 'Enseigner la nouvelle: perspectives et limites d'une didactique', in Gratton and Imbert (eds), *La*

CHAPTER 3. SINGULAR THINGS

The irrational impulse, by definition, cannot be explained, which means, as we have seen, that it is an advantage for a writer seeking brevity. It is not so much that the form of the short story determines a certain view of life, as some critics have suggested;[36] it is rather that a certain pessimistic vision of life lends itself to short fiction. The negative vision of Mérimée and Maupassant works in the brief space of a short story and runs counter to the general nineteenth-century belief in Progress and perfectibility. Even the energetic protagonists of Barbey can remain self-destructively ignorant of themselves and what is driving them.

In different ways, both Barbey's proud and vengeful duchesse de Sierra-Leone and Mérimée's Roger with his insecurity and 'désir de primer' are not just singular, but also obsessive characters. The individual is not a character who develops, with an interest in his or her own right, a complex personality, but one existing for, explored in and exhausted by one particular situation.[37] When Maupassant asserts at the beginning of 'Décoré!' (I, 1065) — another tale about an obsessive character — that 'des gens naissent avec un instinct prédominant', one could agree that they do in short fiction. And in both tales the tendency of short fiction to intensification and polarisation can be found in the relationship between the narrating Captain and his protagonist, between the duchess and her narratee Tressignies.

As Barbey's use shows, the narrative prompt is important when it provides not just a convenient trigger but also something to give a focus to the elements of the story. In Maupassant's 'Une veuve' (I, 533) a young woman asks about a ring of hair worn by an elderly maiden aunt, who explains how in her youth, a young cousin had been infatuated with her, and when she became engaged, had committed suicide. The ring of hair which prompts the tale comes from the boy; her tale explains why she wears it as a 'widow'; it is recalled at the end of her narrative to round it off; neat, perhaps, but apart from being made of his hair, and the matrimonial association of rings, it does not have a more significant

Nouvelle hier et aujourd'hui, 187–96 (191–2).
36. For example, Bernard Bergonzi's statement that it 'filters down experience to the prime elements of defeat and alienation' (quoted by Reid, *Short Story*, 1-2).
37. On this tendency in the 'classical' *nouvelle*, see Goyet, *La Nouvelle*, 72–73 and 86.

role. In 'La Vengeance d'une femme' and 'La Partie de trictrac', the prompt not only provides coherence, but is linked to a meaning that is not immediately obvious. The Captain's knife, by not playing the final role that we expect, underlines the fact that it is not a tale of heroism. Barbey's use of the portrait leads us to realise the importance of the inner life, of the imagination.

4. Structure, Patterning and Point

Maupassant, 'Marroca', 'Promenade'; Villiers, 'Les Brigands', 'A s'y méprendre'; Schwob, 'Arachné'; Mérimée, 'Djoûmane'

In his essay on Hawthorne, which set the agenda for much later discussion of short fiction, Poe linked the brief prose tale to the short poem as the forms best able to 'fulfil the demands and serve the purposes of high genius'. Read 'at one sitting', it can avail itself of 'the immense force derivable from *totality*', and is constructed by the artist to achieve 'a certain unique or single *effect*'.[1] As we saw, Poe's argument is not unproblematic: how long is a sitting? Poe's 'half-hour to one or two hours' is wide, and how fast do you read? His aim in part is to give the dignity of literature to short fiction by coupling it with the well-established poem[2] and to present the author as controlling its structure and meaning, against the market realities of the nineteenth century.[3] But this does not prevent the parallel between tale and poem being suggestive, and it is one that has often been taken up by writers and critics, who have argued, for instance, that a misplaced word is fatal in both, that both demand rigour and concision, that poetry and short fiction call the reader's attention to stylistic artifice and metaphorical density, and that both *nouvelle* and sonnet exploit structure and antithesis.[4]

In literary narrative generally, structure and formal linguistic features can become sources of pleasure. As Barbara Herrnstein Smith notes, 'the listener's natural impulse to prod the speaker to "get to the point"

1. Poe, *Works*, IV, 215-6.
2. Monfort, 'La Nouvelle et son mode de publication', 166.
3. Grojnowski, 'De Baudelaire à Poe', 107-108.
4. Respectively V.S. Pritchett, quoted by Reid, *Short Story*, 54-55; Pierre Mertens, quoted by Godenne, *La Nouvelle*, 218; Gaëtan Brulotte, 'De l'écriture de la nouvelle', in Gratton and Imbert (eds), *La Nouvelle hier et aujourd'hui*, 199-225 (203); Goyet, *La Nouvelle*, 57.

is [...] characteristically countered by the "pleasures of getting there"'.[5] As well as effects of humour, as with Maupassant's inhibited narrators, or of suspense, the pleasures can be formal ones, as in the highly structured novels of Flaubert. But brevity makes it easier for the writer of short fiction to play on parallelisms and symmetries of structure, and on the verbal repetition and patterning that play a key role in the poem.

In oral tales too we are used to ways in which a storyteller can use onomatopoeia, rhyme, or ternary patterns to call attention to key features of the narrative, and know how they, together with gesture and intonation, can be evaluative features.[6] As Dennis Tedlock observed (I respect his presentation):

> Conversational narratives THEMSELVES
> traditionally classified as PROSE
> turn out, when listened to CLOSELY
> to have poetical qualities of their OWN.[7]

What I shall try to show is how, in literary tales, such formal features can operate unobtrusively as well as obviously, giving coherence and plausibility to the story and guiding us to its point, even becoming an end in themselves.

Maupassant provides the best starting-point, precisely because in his work plot seems to dominate at the expense of the formal or stylistic preoccupations of late nineteenth-century writers linked with Symbolism, such as Villiers and Schwob. He is a writer whose story seems to 'tell itself' naturally: even Mallarmé called it 'le vrai conte, qui se narre tout seul [...]. J'admire comme la main ne se voit pas arrangeant le site derrière les personnages.'[8] The initial response to a

5. Smith, *Margins*, 195.
6. See, for example, Livia Polanyi, 'What stories tell us about their teller's world', *Poetics Today* 2 (1981), 97-119 (99-100); Labov, *Language in the Inner City*, 373-9. 'Poetic' features like repetition, parallelism, symmetry are of course important features of story-telling in oral cultures, both for mnemonic purposes, for emphasis and for their own sake: see, for example, Walter Ong, *Orality and Literacy: the Technologizing of the Word* (London: Methuen, 1982), Chapter 3.
7. Tedlock, *Spoken Word*, 109.
8. Letter to Maupassant of 8 [7] June 1887; Bertrand Marchal, 'La

CHAPTER 4. STRUCTURE, PATTERNING AND POINT

query about a Maupassant story is often to give a rapid plot summary, rather than to refer to setting, theme or character: '"La Parure"? It's the one in which a woman borrows a necklace for a soirée'. Indeed here as often character is subordinated to plot: we are told little of Madame Loisel except that she lacks fine dresses and jewels, but 'elle n'aimait que cela' (I, 1199). The phrase 'la nudité de l'intrigue',[9] frequently used about Maupassant's stories, implies that their effect comes largely from the bare lines of the narrative. But it is frequently the elaboration of thematic and verbal patterns around these 'bones' that creates coherence and so renders the story compelling or even plausible.[10]

A typical example is 'Marroca', where elaboration succeeds in disguising the rather crude elements of male fantasy and a standard literary situation frequently exploited by Maupassant, to form a story that satisfies the reader because of its formal properties (its 'neatness') and its embodiment of a certain moral climate. It is a fictional letter written by a traveller in Algeria to a male friend in France, who wants to know the nature of love there. The opening section, like a conventional oral abstract, tells us that the story will be about the dominance of 'l'amour des sens'. Then a leisurely orientation establishes the setting, describing the scenery on the coast, then the 'petite maison mauresque' the Narrator has rented in Bougie, his adaptation to siesta after lunch, and the torment created by the lack of women. After this a conventional transition ('Or, voici qu'un jour') leads into an incident. Unable to rest one hot afternoon, he walks by the sea and sees a woman bathing naked; she seeks refuge behind a rock, to emerge only as he departs; but from this a liaison develops. This

Correspondance de Stéphane Mallarmé: compléments et suppléments, VII', *French Studies* 50 (1996), 35-53 (41).
9. For example, recently by Joseph Balsamo, in his edition of Maupassant, *Choses et autres* (Paris: Livre de poche, 1993), 33 ('la nudité des faits'); by Charlotte Schapira, 'Maupassant et le fait divers', *Hebrew University Studies in Litterature and the Arts*, 14 (1987), 23-32 (27).
10. On thematic elaboration, see notably G. Hainsworth, 'Pattern and Symbol in the Work of Maupassant', *French Studies*, 5 (1951), 1-17; Jean Paris, 'Maupassant et le contre-récit', in *Le Point aveugle* (Paris: Seuil, 1975), 135-222; and in short fiction generally, Judith Leibowitz, *Narrative Purpose in the Novella* (The Hague: Mouton, 1974), where she argues that a characteristic feature of the novella is exhaustive exploration of a thematic area.

singulative section (relating once a single event)[11] is followed by a central iterative section evoking their repeated afternoon meetings in his house, and in the evenings, on his roof. Two final singulative sequences describe her invitation, first resisted, then accepted, to sleep at her house during her husband's absence; the visit, during which his surprise return forces the Narrator to hide under the bed; and a final twist, as Marroca reveals that the axe she had got out was intended to kill her husband if he discovered her lover.

So far, so anecdotal, and the stages of the story map on to Labov's model of the oral tale. But the series of events is held together by firm thematic and verbal echoes. These begin with the obvious parallel between the hot climate and the winds which 'embrasent le sang, affolent la chair, embestialisent' (I, 367), and the *ardeurs* of Marroca ('d'un type un peu bestial') and her love-making (I, 371), and are developed in more complex ways. She is first seen naked and in water. This nakedness is not just there to titillate Maupassant's readership:[12] it becomes the centre of a network of references, linked to water, *fraîcheur* and transparency, to ideas of frankness and independence, and is set against a contrasting network of references to hiding, shame, and embarrassment. The theme is prepared when the Narrator adopts the local siesta 'avec aussi peu de vêtements que possible', and indicates, via an allusion to Musset's Hassan, 'nu comme Eve',[13] that he too is naked (I, 369). He compares the lack of a woman that tortures him to a lack of water: 'on commettrait toutes les infamies pour un verre d'eau claire et froide. Que ne ferait-on pas [...] pour une belle fille fraîche et saine?' (I, 369) On his walk he emphasises the heat and the discomfort of wearing clothes. Then he sees Marroca:

> J'aperçus, prenant son bain, se croyant bien seule à cette heure brûlante, une jeune fille nue, enfoncée jusqu'aux seins. [...] Rien de plus étonnant que ce tableau: cette belle femme dans cette eau transparente comme un verre, sous cette lumière aveuglante. (I, 370)

---

11. Genette, 'Discours du récit', 146.
12. The story was first published in the licentious *Gil Blas* (2 March 1882), and then in the volume *Mademoiselle Fifi* by a Belgian publisher (Kistemaeckers) noted for his 'audacious' catalogue (I, 1411).
13. Musset, *Namouna* (quoted by Forestier, I, 1403).

CHAPTER 4. STRUCTURE, PATTERNING AND POINT

Realising that she is being watched, she flees his gaze behind the rock, peeking out intermittently until, after her angry protests, he leaves. This first involuntary display of her nudity echoes her frankness when he becomes her lover: 'Elle avait en horreur les voiles les plus légers; et elle circulait, courait, gambadait dans ma maison avec une impudeur inconsciente et hardie' (I, 371). She even sleeps on the terrace 'nue encore sous les clairs rayons de la lune', as unconcerned by others who can see them (and whom they can see), as she is unrestrained in her 'longs cris vibrants' when making love (I, 372).

When the Narrator yields to her invitation, he is again driven by the pressures of abstinence, setting in parallel his first walk and the final rendezvous. In Marroca's house, he is *gêné*, and it is she who forcibly drags off his trousers. Made to hide beneath the bed when her husband returns, he hears her fetch 'un objet que je n'aperçus pas' (I, 374); but he does see the husband's feet, and hears his 'tape sur de la chair nue'. When he finally emerges from his 'retraite', hesitant like Marroca when he first saw her, she is 'toujours nue' (a nudity accompanied as usual with references to her laughter and eyes), and dancing. He discovers the axe when he inadvertently sits on it. The repeated nakedness thus serves as the outward sign of Marroca's animal frankness, and as a means of leading up to this shocked discovery (bare flesh/bare steel). It provides a final chilling echo of the heat/cold opposition: he had sought 'un verre d'eau claire et froide' (I, 369) in the heat of the day; he found Marroca in the sea, a woman whose *r*s roll 'avec un fracas de torrent sur des roches' (I, 372); he feels the axe as 'une chose froide' (I, 375); and he confesses after his narrow escape: 'J'en avais encore froid dans le dos' (I, 375).

These various forms of repetition give the story coherence: what is ultimately a stereotyped vision of North Africa, relying on a facile exoticism (a country of heat, water, sensuality) and standard settings (the terrace roof, the curved bay), works effectively in the rapid creation of a vivid image based on intensified and contrasted impressions.[14] This disguises the fact that the two key components,

---

14. Pierre Soubias has stressed the stereotyped nature of Maupassant's Africa in his stories ('La Place de l'Afrique dans l'imaginaire de Maupassant: une lecture des Nouvelles Africaines', in *Maupassant multiple* (Toulouse: Presses Universitaires du Mirail, 1995), 29-39); and Goyet the role of the stereotype in the *nouvelle* generally (*La Nouvelle*, 62-66).

namely the fantasy of a naked woman seen bathing, and the discovery of a couple *in flagrante delicto*, recur in other stories by Maupassant in very different contexts, geographically and emotionally, and have little to do with the announced theme of 'comment on aime dans un pays'.[15] Moreover, the insistent thematic contrasts and patterns: heat versus cold; nudity and water; nudity and *impudeur*; watching versus hiding, also create a structure based on a reversal between the bathing scene (i) and the scene in Marroca's bedroom (ii). He sees her naked and she hides (i) → she forces him to hide, naked (ii); naked, she seeks refuge from his gaze behind a rock, then peeps out (i) → naked, he seeks refuge from her husband's eyes under the bed, but cannot refrain from peeping out (ii). The Narrator loses his voyeuristic position of superiority, goes from his house to hers, and ends up discomfited under her bed. When he watches her bathing, she says: 'Ça n'est pas bien de rester là, monsieur' (I, 370); at the end it is she who looks at him, and he who now finds 'cette joie déplacée, inconvenante' (I, 375). Although her ruthlessness makes the end seem surprising and shocking, a series of verbal and structural pointers have led up to it. Rereading enables us to see the function of the proleptic details, and, as with a poem, all falls into place and the overall pattern becomes clear. In the same way *féroce* and *luisant* recur to describe Marroca's features: her mouth, teeth, smile have 'quelque chose de férocement sensuel'; her laugh shows 'ses dents luisantes', and 'ses yeux semblaient toujours luisants de passion' (I, 371). These prepare the final moment: 'Et son doigt tendu, le pli de sa joue, ses lèvres entrouvertes, ses dents pointues, claires et *féroces*, tout cela me montrait la petite hachette à fendre le bois, dont le tranchant aigu *luisait*' (I, 375; my emphasis).

The point of the story turns out to be not quite as simple as the abstract states: 'Comment on s'aime ici'. The Narrator has inhibitions which are both verbal and moral. He is unable to refer directly to his naked siesta. He clearly objects to Marroca's nakedness on the roof,

15. The naked woman bathing appears in the early poems 'Au bord de l'eau' (1876) and 'Vénus rustique' (1878), set in Normandy (*Œuvres complètes, Des vers* (Paris: Conard, 1928), 37–39, 132–3); in 'Mes vingt-cinq jours', at a spa at Châtelguyon (*Contes et nouvelles*, II, 531); and in the sombre tale of rape, murder and remorse also set in Normandy, 'La Petite Roque' (II, 618). The couple discovered *in flagrante delicto* is a recurrent motif in Maupassant: for such repetition, see Chapter 5.

CHAPTER 4. STRUCTURE, PATTERNING AND POINT

where she '*s'obstinait* à se mettre nue' (my emphasis), and to the cries of passion she utters there, 'malgré mes craintes et mes prières' (I, 372). He resists, until sexual deprivation overcomes caution, her invitation to her house. When there, he tries to retain his trousers, which he cannot even name without a coy periphrasis: 'certain vêtement sans lequel un homme surpris devient aussi gauche que ridicule' (I, 374). Her lack of inhibition, visual and vocal, is contrasted with his 'civilised' constraint, moral and linguistic. In this way Maupassant is able to suggest that one of the points of the story lies in this contrast. At the end, faced with the naked and dancing Marroca and the bare axe, he still can refer to his own nakedness only by euphemism, when evoking the awkwardness of possible discovery: 'J'étais propre, moi, dans ce *costume*' (I, 375; my emphasis).

If we are looking for patterning in the story, we can find it, then, operating on the level of style: frankness/periphrasis, as well as in the themes: animality/sentimentality, nakedness/clothing. As well as an illustration of 'comment on s'aime ici', we see a structure of reversal that leads to the discomfiture of the Narrator. The reader can simply enjoy it as a risqué anecdote summed up by the final ironic comment of the fictional Narrator: 'Et voilà, mon cher, comment on comprend ici les devoirs conjugaux, l'amour et l'hospitalité!' (I, 376), ironic in that we have been shown the opposite of what these 'civilised' terms normally imply, namely infidelity, lust, and the indulgence of caprice. At the same time we can also see it as a tale in which Maupassant undercuts his Narrator's male assurance. A singularly unadventurous traveller, he declines Marroca's initial invitation by saying: 'Mais tu est folle.[16] J'aime mieux rester chez moi' (I, 373). The tale reverses the initial position of male superiority and female vulnerability, and shows the triumph of frankness over inhibition, passion over convention. In both cases it is not so much the events but their elaboration through verbal echoes and thematic patterning that guides the reader.

This verbal repetition, frequent in Maupassant's stories, reinforces the thematic patterning much more obviously than, for instance, in

16. The recurrence of 'fou' characterizes the narrator's attitude to Marroca. It is anticipated in the hot winds that 'affolent la chair' (I, 368); Marroca welcomes him to her house 'folle de joie' (I, 373); he feels 'une envie folle, stupide, incompréhensible' to touch the husband's shoes (I, 375); afterwards, her 'rires fous me blessaient un peu' (I, 375).

'Carmen', where the reader senses the opposition between various forms of constraint (academic life, the army, the law) and freedom without specific words acquiring the importance of *luisant*, *féroce*, *froid*, and *nu* in 'Marroca'. The brevity of Maupassant's text enables the reader to pick up their repetition. But the repetitions and reversals do not call attention to themselves or undermine the apparent realism of the story. At almost exactly the same time ('Les Brigands' was first published in 1882, and collected in *Contes Cruels* in 1883), Villiers was demonstrating how a very self-conscious stylisation can create coherence and point.

'Les Brigands' (I, 674) is a tale of two neighbouring provincial towns, Nayrac and Pibrac. A misunderstanding one night, when the village fiddler of one, short of money, accosts the churchwarden of the other, and is taken in the dark for a brigand, is fanned by the bourgeoisie of the towns, inclined to 'exagérer les fautes des personnes qui font mine d'en vouloir à ses capitaux', and leads to a state of panic. The landowners of each town, convinced that the region has been overrun by brigands, set out to collect rent from their tenant farmers in the safety of a group, in a carriage, and heavily armed. When they encounter at nightfall the carriage of the other town, each group mistakes the other for brigands; an accidental shot leads to mutual annihilation. Meanwhile the real brigands, playing cards and drinking, hear the shooting and hasten to the scene of the massacre, and, horrified, flee the country. As their leader says: 'ILS VONT PROUVER ... QUE C'EST NOUS'

If looking for elements of stylisation and patterning in the story, the reader is immediately struck by two features which push to extremes what Michael Sheringham has termed the 'strip cartoon' effect of the short story.[17] The preparation and the rent-collecting trip are presented initially in just one town, Nayrac. Each landowner returns in the evening to his wife; Villiers uses *chacun* to suggest that they all do exactly the same thing, but at the same time the dialogue and actions that he reports are particular. The effect is to empty the bourgeois of individuality and reduce them to the level of identical, caricatural

---

17. Michael Sheringham, 'Nouvelle et poème en prose: "Mademoiselle Bistouri" de Baudelaire', in Gratton and Imbert (eds), *La Nouvelle hier et aujourd'hui*, 85–93 (87).

CHAPTER 4. STRUCTURE, PATTERNING AND POINT   105

figures: husbands and wives, farmers and their families all enact the
same routine like marionettes, motivated by avarice, bombast, and
pusillanimity:

> Chacun rentra dans son ménage d'un air plus crâne que de coutume et le
> chapeau, ma foi! sur l'oreille, si bien que son épouse, lui sautant aux
> favoris, l'appela 'mousquetaire', ce qui chatouilla doucement leurs cœurs
> réciproques. (I, 675)

Each husband reveals that he will leave at dawn, each wife anxiously
resists, then is reassured when she learns they are going in company:
'Tu dois faire comme les autres, murmura chaque épouse, soudain
calmée.' Each puts on his stockings to the same words the next day,
takes a last kiss; each dines with his tenant, 'pinça le menton de sa fille,
au dessert, empocha la sacoche de l'affermage' — and this caricatural
lack of individuality is echoed by the brigands.

The symmetry is accentuated by the fact that the two towns mirror
each other: their names rhyme (Nayrac, Pibrac), they react in the same
way to the rumours, adopt the same strategy. We follow the group from
Nayrac until they meet the 'troupe jumelle' of bourgeois from Pibrac,
'lesquels avaient eu, exactement, la même idée que ceux de Nayrac' (I,
677). Caricature is pushed to the point of implausibility (and 'une
histoire de brigands' can mean in French an implausible invention).
This is achieved by exaggeration of the boastfulness and the fear of the
bourgeois, and also by the understatement of black humour: the mutual
massacre is described as a 'malentendu', and outrageous incongruity:
the real brigands are 'les bons brigands' (I, 678). Domestic situations
are presented in an incongruously elevated style, as the husbands
reassure their wives: '"Ainsi, sèche tes larmes, et, Morphée invitant,
permets que je noue sur mon front les deux extrémités de mon
foulard."' The narrative jumps from heroic dreams to cough sweets:
'Les bourgeois rêvèrent assauts, carnage, abordages, tournois et lauriers
[...] . Les dames, dans l'admiration, regardaient ces modernes paladins
et leur bourraient les poches de pâtes pectorales, vu l'automne' (I, 675).

In 'Marroca', the patterning and thematic echoes are disguised by
local colour and details that offer an illusion of reality and an easily
moving narrative, in which iterative passages (Marroca's visit to the
Narrator's house) are set between the key singulative moments of the
drama (the first sight of Marroca and the final scene). For Villiers, as

Jean-Pierre Gourevitch has put it,[18] literature is a weapon, not a mirror: he is less interested in evoking a plausible image of the world than in shocking or springing surprises on the reader. And two sorts of reader are targeted simultaneously: the conventional bourgeois reader will be shocked, or baffled; the happy few on the same wavelength as Villiers will appreciate his point. The self-conscious oddity of the style calls attention to itself and serves to provoke the reader. Details — the hats slanting on the husbands' heads, the knotted scarves, the cough sweets, the proverbs trotted out to the farmers — do not contribute to an illusion of reality, but stand out as bizarre. Such stylistic effects, characteristic of Villiers, can be fatiguing at length: short fiction is arguably their best medium.

Villiers pushes narrative stylisation and symmetry even further in 'A s'y méprendre!' (I, 628). The orientation describing the Narrator walking beside the Seine on a rainy day seems conventional. Then he visits two buildings: first the Morgue, where he shelters before calling a cab, secondly a café where he has a business meeting. The two buildings and their inhabitants are described in five paragraphs with only minimal differences (two phrases inverted, an added 'et'). After the first visit, the Narrator realises that the mistress of the house is 'la Mort'; three paragraphs then complete his description of the occupants of the Morgue who had 'assassiné leurs corps'. When the description of the second visit reaches this point, the corresponding paragraphs show slight variations, creating the effect of those twin pictures where you have to 'spot the differences':[19] the 'corps' of the Morgue become their 'âmes' in the café, murdered not to escape 'l'existence tracassière', but 'l'insupportable conscience'. We may think that we are in a *conte fantastique*, where the everyday world gives way to inexplicable events,[20] and that the Narrator, going to a different place, has magically found himself back where he started — an impression reinforced by the gloomy weather and buildings, and the 'idées pâles [...] et brumeuses' of the preoccupied Narrator. Then comes the realisation that the repeated descriptions designate different referents: the 'robinets de cuivre [...] destinés à l'arrosage quotidien de ces restes mortels' refer in

18. Gourevitch, *Villiers de l'Isle-Adam*, 35.
19. The suggestion is Jean-Louis Dufays's, '"A s'y méprendre!" ou le second coup d'œil', *Poétique*, 24 (1993), 451–61 (455).
20. See Chapter 5.

the first instance to the taps for washing the corpses, in the second, to the taps that dispense beer. The symmetry in turn points to the deadening effects of life in business, and leads to the Narrator's final decision '*à ne jamais faire d'affaires*'. Once we realise that two different buildings with two very different associations (suicide and lifelessness versus entertainment and business) are being evoked by parallel phrases, we realise that things are not what they seem. The opening evocation of Paris is distorted by the Narrator's vision: in the rainy morning passers-by are 'obombrés de parapluies difformes', the barges on the Seine are 'pareils à des hannetons démesurés'; when travelling down the boulevards, his vision turns the shrubs into 'végétations squelettes', the passers-by into running water. The final disclosure is paradoxically that things *are* what they seem to the hallucinating Narrator, the only one able to see business as death, and the patterning becomes the key evaluative feature of the tale.

'Marroca' and these two tales by Villiers have what one could term 'poetic' features: effects of verbal patterning and echo, of symmetry, antithesis, and reversal. These features do not by themselves put the stories into the problematic category of 'prose poem'. A few of Villiers's *Contes cruels*, notably 'Vox populi' (I, 562), have been regarded as *poèmes en prose*[21] because of their stylisation and the way they invest everyday events with symbolic potential.[22] The four symmetrical sections of 'Vox populi' all show the public acclaiming with equal enthusiasm the parades of successive regimes. Each ends with the same refrain by a blind beggar (which is also an alexandrine): 'Prenez pitié d'un pauvre aveugle, s'il vous plaît', and verbal echoes and an incantatory style reinforce the 'poetic' effect. Villiers frequently breaks with what we conventionally expect of a tale: an anecdote, events and their resolution, and the reliance on individualised characters, and accentuates the 'poetic' features. Indeed the publisher Calmann Lévy originally rejected the collection on the grounds that 'les morceaux composant ce manuscrit sont moins des nouvelles que des *articles de genre*, ou des essais psychologiques et des fantaisies

21. It was included as such in Des Esseintes's anthology of prose poems. See J.-K. Huysmans, *A rebours* (Paris: Flammarion, 1978), chapter 14, 221.
22. See Suzanne Bernard, *Le Poème en prose de Baudelaire jusqu'à nos jours* (Paris: Nizet, 1959), 358–9; for her, 'Vox Populi' and 'souvenirs occultes' are the only *Contes cruels* to match her definition of the *poème en prose*.

littéraires'.[23] Scientific fantasies like 'La Machine à gloire' or 'L'Affichage céleste' that hyperbolically celebrate the inventions of the automatic applause machine or advertisements projected on to the heavens are almost devoid of the sequence of events that constitutes a story and exist on the borderline between fiction and the humorous article.

'Poème en prose' might equally have been a way of categorising 'A s'y méprendre' and 'Vox populi', as well as other brief narratives of the nineteenth century such as Xavier Forneret's 'Et la lune donnait, et la rosée tombait' or 'Le Diamant de l'herbe': these couple schematic narrative with poetic features and a dream-like atmosphere.[24] Conversely, certain works which present themselves as prose poems — for instance in Baudelaire's *Le Spleen de Paris* — are anecdotes or brief provocative narratives that bring into poetry features of prose that Poe categorised as 'antagonistical to the nature of the poem':[25] the analytical, the sarcastic, the humorous, and refuse the 'poetic' patterning found in 'Vox populi'. The poetic features of some stories, the deliberately prosaic tendency of some prose poems, make it difficult to establish a clear boundary between short story and prose poem.

The verbal patterns, antitheses, and structural effects I have been examining lead to a single unproblematic point. But need this always be the case, even with a writer so apparently straightforward as Maupassant? 'Promenade' (II, 127) has been taken as a typical, even model tale built on a recurrent pattern: an unreflecting life of routine is

23. Letter to Villiers of 30 October 1877, quoted in *Contes cruels*, ed. by Pierre-Georges Castex, Classiques Garnier (Paris: Bordas, 1989), xiii. Some of the *Contes cruels* were first published as 'poèmes en prose', 'variétés', or 'chroniques' (xvi-xvii).
24. Louis Forneret, *Contes et récits*, edited by Jacques Rémi Dahan (Paris: Corti, 1994), 99, 271; and see Helen H. Goldsmith, 'The Short Story encounters the prose poem: a work of Xavier Forneret', in *The French Short Story*, edited by Philip Crant, French Literature Series, II (Columbia: University of South Carolina, 1975), 77-88.
25. Poe, *Works*, IV, 217. On these links, see, for example, Sheringham, 'Nouvelle et poème en prose'; Sonya Stephens, 'Boundaries, limits and limitations: Baudelaire's *poèmes-boutades*', *French Studies*, 52 (1998), 28-41; and Marie Maclean's exploration of the narrative element of the *Petits poèmes en prose* in *Narrative as Performance: the Baudelairean experiment* (London and New York, Routledge, 1988).

broken, the barrenness of an individual existence is suddenly revealed, and catastrophe follows.[26] At the centre, as often in short fiction, is the significant moment on which an individual's life hinges. The conventional opening presents an elderly, staggeringly nondescript bookkeeper who emerges on a sunny summer evening from his day's work; a lengthy analepsis sketches in the uneventful last forty years of his life. After a dinner near the Arc de Triomphe the warm evening leads him to walk to the Bois de Boulogne, where he sees the flow of cabs with amorous couples and is accosted by a prostitute; he suddenly becomes aware of the irremediable emptiness of his own life; next morning a young couple find him hanged. If we pay attention to recurrent words and themes in the tale, we find a pattern of simple oppositions. On the one hand there are details, images and expressions of confinement that are linked to Leras (starting with his name, evoking a trapped rat): his small office, a 'prison'; the courtyard like a 'puits' and a 'fosse'; the 'bruit de chaîne' of the alarm that starts his day; his own 'petite chambre propre et triste'. These are linked to instances of monotony, such as the daily ritual: 'Les jours, les semaines, les mois, les saisons, les années s'étaient ressemblé.' On the other hand we find expressions, both literal and figurative, and events that evoke life: the spring evenings which 'troublent les cœurs d'une ivresse de vie', the 'énorme palpitation de vie' coming from Paris. These are linked to evocations of sexuality: the lovers evoked in a fragment of song Leras recalls, the 'fiacres chargés d'amour', the prostitutes, the couple who discover his body. A parallel series of oppositions contrasts the wet, cold and dark (his office, 'toujours humide et froid', the 'odeur moisie' of the courtyard) with notations of heat (it is 'une nuit d'étuve'; as the cabs pass, 'l'ombre chaude semblait pleine de baisers qui voletaient', and a 'fièvre' emerges from them) and of light (the sky which 'flambait' and leads him out; the 'yeux brillants' of the lights of the cabs, the 'ciel étoilé'). The sun provides a structuring motif: the story opens with Leras emerging from the office to the 'éclat du soleil couchant'; this is recalled after the analepsis, and leads him to dine out for once; and the 'soleil déjà haut' opens the final section in which his body is discovered.

---

26. Sullivan, *Maupassant: the Short Stories*, 32-33; Bury, 'Maupassant pessimiste?', 81.

These insistent oppositions increasingly adopt negative and positive values: entrapment — life, monotony/sexuality, wet and cold/heat, dark/light, corresponding to the opposition Leras/others. This clear pattern suggests that the point of the story is Leras's sudden realisation of the emptiness of his life in a moment of loneliness. This is reinforced by the presentation of his thoughts: both his explicitly reported thoughts and free indirect speech function as an embedded evaluation, pushing the reader to accept his judgement and interpretation:

> Il y a des êtres qui n'ont vraiment pas de chance. Et tout d'un coup, comme si un voile épais se fut déchiré, il aperçut la misère, l'infinie, la monotone misère de son existence: la misère passée, la misère présente, la misère future: les derniers jours pareils aux premiers, sans rien devant lui, rien derrière lui, rien autour de lui, rien dans le cœur, rien nulle part. (II, 131)

Read this way, the story is related to others where the sudden realisation of an intolerable reality leads Maupassant's characters to forms of madness ('Un cas de divorce'), to suicide ('Suicides' (I, 175)), to withdrawal from the world ('Garçon, un bock!' (I, 1123), or 'L'Ermite' (II, 685)).

But a second reading is possible which draws on the same patterning elements but sees in them something beyond Leras's purely individual despair. This reading reflects the general pessimism implicit in related stories by Maupassant. The procession of lovers in the passing cabs is presented as unceasing and repetitive: 'Il en venait toujours, toujours. Ils passaient, passaient, allongés dans les voitures. [...] Tous ces gens enlacés, tous ces gens grisés de la même attente, de la même pensée, faisaient courir une fièvre autour d'eux' (II, 130). Leras's idealisation of love and domesticity, from this angle, is an illusion, specifically the illusion of love that Schopenhauer denounced as a cover for the sexual instinct that ensures the continuation of the species.[27] Mankind is in the grip of a uniform instinct, which denies individuality just as much as Leras's office job does for him. The monotony and emptiness of the prostitute's job ('"Faut bien qu'on vive"', she replies, when Leras asks her why she follows that 'métier') echoes Leras's work; the prostitutes

---

27. On parallels between Schopenhauer and Maupassant, see Colin, *Schopenhauer en France*, Chapter 5.

CHAPTER 4. STRUCTURE, PATTERNING AND POINT

accost him with the regularity of the passing cabs, breaking down any distinction between venal sex and passionate love. If we read the text this way, we can interpret Leras's suicide as a gesture of general despair, while still seeing his awareness as limited: he is not fully conscious of the forces driving mankind. The general value of Leras's suicide is reinforced in the coda by an anonymous comment that attributes it to a sudden attack of madness. As usual, the desire not to know can lead narratees and witnesses in Maupassant to reject, censor, or dismiss the tales and truths they are told.

The patterning of 'Promenade' leads the reader to see two points in the story. A first reading grasps the oppositions as Leras does, emphasising the contrast between the emptiness of his individual existence and love and life all around him. A second reading realises that the references to sex and light show that Leras and the world of 'lovers' are both trapped in a universe governed by repetition and meaninglessness. The advantage of this second reading is that it corresponds to the way that we interpret literature, whereas natural storytellers tend to formulate their moral point explicitly, and 'do not leave this matter to be understood from the specifics of the story'.[28] In short fiction in particular, the singularity of the event can have general implications: here an office-worker's wasted life has universal meaning. Perhaps because of its brevity the discoveries in short fiction are unsettling and negative: they call into question an aspect of our reassuring but unthinking assumptions about the world and ourselves.

It is possible to have a story with more than one point. But is it possible to have a story with such elements of verbal patterning and structuring without a point? How far can patterning provide not just a pointer to meaning, but a substitute for it? Can it prevent that withering response to a story in real life: 'So what?'[29] An examination of two highly literary tales, in which the sense of structure is paramount, may suggest an answer.

At the beginning of Marcel Schwob's 'Arachné', included in his first collection of stories, *Cœur double* (1891),[30] there are no conventional

---

28. Ryave, 'Achievement of a series', 121.
29. As Labov argues, *Language in the Inner City*, 366; see also Smith, *Margins*, 194.
30. References in the text are to Marcel Schwob, *Cœur double* (Toulouse: Ombres, 1996).

orientational features: no date, no place, no name (67). But the homodiegetic Narrator's references to a cell, a trial, and medical reports enable us (on the model of more explicit tales by Poe, such as 'The Tell-Tale Heart' and 'The Black Cat') to assume that he is a madman locked up after a murder, and to expect an account of it. Indeed his fragmentary retrospective narrative enables us to reconstruct, behind the self-justification and omissions that we expect in this type of story, a plausible sequence of events: his passionate love for a young *brodeuse* whom he calls Ariane, and his jealous strangling of her in order to 'l'attach[er] tout entière dans la mort'. We also deduce the nature of his subsequent madness. He thinks that she is alive and still with him in the form of a spider, as the nymph Arachné.[31] He is convinced that he will 'escape' from his cell with her, leaving the lifeless shell of his body behind.

In the prototypes in Poe, and in other tales by Schwob modelled on them such as 'L'Homme voilé' and 'l'Homme double', the bulk of the tale is concerned with the crime and the revelation of the Narrator's guilt. In 'Arachné' however the *récit* consists largely of his account of the nightly visits of Arachné (nine of the sixteeen paragraphs). It is here that we become aware of repetitions. The spider-nymph Arachné, 'petite, brune et vive des pattes', is described in terms used to describe Ariane, 'petite, brune de peau et vive des doigts'. Through the 'real' and the 'mad' worlds of the Narrator run references to threads: Ariane's embroidering, the 'cordelettes' of hemp used by the Thugs that give him the idea of murder, the 'cordelette de soie' with which he strangles her, the threads of the spider's web on which Arachné visits him, and on which he will 'escape'. Both worlds refer to binding/strangling (Arachné 'm'a serré la gorge d'un fil sans fin'), and to swinging/hanging: 'Je me balancerai au fil d'Ariane par-delà les étoiles' (67); 'Il faut traverser cet enfer pour me balancer plus tard sous la lueur des étoiles' (70); 'Nous nous y balançons pendant des heures' [on Arachné's thread] (71). The patterning is itself echoed in the description of Arachné's web as 'parcouru de points brillants qui fuient et se jouent entre eux'.

31. Arachne was a young Lydian girl transformed into a spider, and not strictly a nymph, but 'la nymphe' is the intermediate state between larva and imago, the chrysalis state in lepidoptera; and the narrator has liberated Ariane from 'sa chrysalide humaine' (70).

CHAPTER 4. STRUCTURE, PATTERNING AND POINT

Mythological names can often serve as evaluative features. Here they reinforce the internal patterning by echoing the Narrator's demented imaginings: Ariadne (Ariane in French) guided Theseus out of the Minotaur's labyrinth with a thread; the weaver Arachne hanged herself and was turned into a spider by Athene. Words in the epigraph from *Romeo and Juliet* (I, iv) evoking Queen Mab's carriage are picked up at the end of the tale. On a more mundane level, the reader cannot forget that 'avoir une araignée dans le plafond' is the French equivalent of 'to have bats in the belfry', which brings us back to madness. Once we notice the echoes, we also see that they are accompanied, as in 'Marroca', by reversal. Ariane's kisses were 'des coups d'aiguille'; Arachné's needle-like probing of his chest is described as a kiss: 'Arachné fouille sans cesse de ses lèvres pointues'. Others think that the Narrator is mad and Ariane is dead; he knows that he is sane and she is alive; he strangles Ariane, but Arachné is encasing him in her threads ('emmailloté dans sa prison de fils blancs' — echoing his 'cellule blanche') and draining his life-blood; his bold assertions of freedom turn into entrapment, action into passivity; images of floating become ones of viscosity ('son fil gluant', 'des voiles visqueuses'); dreams becomes nightmares in the penultimate paragraph.

The sixteen paragraphs of the story (here (a) to (p)) fall into a clear pattern:

i	a	b	c	—
ii	d	e	f	g
iii	h	i	j	k
iv	l	m	n	o
i	—	—	—	p

(i) is set in the present and looks to his future escape, and is resumed in the final paragraph ('Maintenant je sens') where it becomes clear that escape is death; (ii) recalls Ariane and her murder; (iii) represents the first three nights, when he is visited by an 'Ariane' who reveals herself in (k) as Arachné; in (iv) it is he who visits her in the 'Royaume des Araignées', and dream turns to nightmare.

What does this extreme patterning achieve, and how does it relate to the 'point' of the story? The tale is not an exploration of a murderer's motive, or of madness; rather it relies on the reader's knowledge of set ideas of jealous love and of madness in order for us to see how the elements interrelate. We know that possessiveness can lead to jealousy and murder, and so can see the link between his references to her 'caprices' and his 'exaspération' at the young men waiting for her, and his strangling her in order to 'attach' her in death.

Symmetry has a key role in Schwob's aesthetic, as the preface to *Cœur double* shows. In a rapid survey of Western literature, he argues that it oscillates between periods of realism and psychological interest, where 'la vie humaine intéressera par son développement', and periods of symmetry, where the work is dominated by a crisis, and for which he finds an architectural equivalent in the figures and scenes balanced on either side of the pediment of a classical temple. 'Dans la Symétrie, la vie est assujettie à des règles artistiques conventionnelles; dans le Réalisme, la vie est reproduite avec toutes ses inflexions les plus inharmoniques' (15). Schwob sees the 1890s as the beginning of a new period of symmetry, and implicitly casts himself as a pioneer.

Now the nineteenth-century preface is notoriously as the place where writers of short fiction, bringing together texts previously published separately, attempted to establish the unity of the collection, as with a volume of poetry, and give it the literary cachet it might otherwise lack, as the tales originated in the world of journalism.[32] Schwob's prefaces to *Cœur double* and *Le Roi au masque d'or* impose retrospectively an artificial unity on a group of disparate stories, and it is sometimes difficult to take their argument at face value. But the preoccupation with symmetry goes back to an early essay, in which he analyses Aeschylus in terms of exchanges and oppositions between characters.[33] Symmetry is omnipresent in Schwob's tales: as an organising principle in the volume *Cœur double*, as a theme in tales that show a preoccupation with the double ('L'Homme double' or 'L'Homme voilé'), in the form of parallelisms and mirror images ('Le Train 081').[34]

---

32. See Monfort, 'La Nouvelle et son mode de publication', 164-5. There are exceptions, such as Schwob's *Vies imaginaires* or Barbey's *Les Diaboliques*, where a single conception guides the writing of the individual stories and is articulated in the preface.
33. 'Eschyle et Aristophane', in *Œuvres complètes*, edited by Pierre Champion, 10 vols (Paris: Bernouard, 1927-1930), I, *Ecrits de Jeunesse* (1927), 67-82.
34. See Christian Berg, 'Marcel Schwob, le récit bref et l'esprit de symétrie', *La Licorne*, 21 (1981), 103-14.

CHAPTER 4. STRUCTURE, PATTERNING AND POINT

In 'Arachné', however, the role of patterning and symmetry is pushed to extremes. The Narrator is mad, but he adduces his precision of recall and his 'logique lucide' as proof of his sanity (just as the narrator of 'The Tell-tale Heart' cites his caution and cunning),[35] and sets up a series of oppositions between his lucidity and the opaque 'fumée' of the really mad, between 'la symétrie de mes propres inventions' and the 'défauts de composition' of novels he has read. The paradox is that his madness lies in his patterning, in the links drawn between the spider and Ariane, in his logical construction of a totally coherent world, untroubled by any link with the untidy, 'inharmonic' real world. It is not clear exactly how he dies, but his death is linked to the threads of the network he is constructing. The recurrent verb *se balancer* and the omnipresent *fil* suggest suicide by hanging; but Arachné is also said to be draining his blood from a wound (a bite) in his chest, as well as strangling and binding him. The construction of patterns has become an end in itself; the implication is that where the patterning has become the point, this leads to or is madness.

There is another, equally nihilistic, use of extreme patterning, as Mérimée's tale 'Djoûmane' shows: it can be used to play a trick. In contrast to 'Arachné', the opening orientation could hardly be more conventional and reassuring, as the homodiegetic Narrator both situates his tale ('Le 21 mai 18.., nous rentrions à Tlemcen' (1091)) and indicates who he is: a French lieutenant in Algeria. The standard exotic details: the Moorish architecture, the Arabs' costume and music, serve a similar reassuring function: we know exactly where we are, literally and in terms of genre. We expect a military adventure in North Africa, and we recall that early in his career Mérimée had written the military episode set during Napoleon's Russian campaign, 'L'Enlèvement de la redoute'. The Lieutenant's narration is not motivated by any enquiry, unlike 'Marroca', but we can imagine it as proceeding from a statement like: 'Let me tell you about an exciting moment from my last campaign in Africa.' The Narrator reveals how his troop of *chasseurs*, returning exhausted from a thirty-seven day campaign, hear that they have to leave again the same evening, to block one of the escape routes of the

---

35. Poe, *Selected Writings*, 277. Robert Ziegler notes the similarities in his analysis of the story, 'Escaping the mortal web of time in Marcel Schwob's "Arachné"', *Nineteenth-Century French Studies*, 24 (1995–1996), 440–6.

rebel leader Sidi-Lala. The reader follows the Narrator's account of a spectacle at the Colonel's presented by a magician which culminates in a young girl being bitten by a snake (this turns out to have been part of the show), then dinner; the troop's departure and arrival at the ford they have to guard; the sudden appearance of Sidi-Lala on a white horse, and his pursuit by the Lieutenant; their fall over a precipice into a river; the Lieutenant's recovery and his following of a woman into a cave, where he witnesses a ceremony culminating in the sacrifice of the girl seen the previous day to a giant snake, and by the same magician; the Narrator's escape down a subterranean gallery, which leads to a room where a young woman offers him a cup of coffee.

On a first reading, this increasingly bizarre sequence of events is linear and chronological. Apart from brief details lines about their previous expedition, and some explanations about Sidi-Lala and the local terrain, we merely follow the actions and perceptions of the Narrator. Paragraphs typically start: 'Tout à coup, j'entendis' (1098); 'Bientôt je distinguai' (1099); 'J'aperçus alors' (1099), with adverbs underlining the sequence of events. Sustained at length, which is unusual,[36] this simple chronological succession creates an unsettling effect. This is abruptly terminated when the Lieutenant's sergeant, Wagner, awakens him with a cup of coffee, and we realise that the events since the arrival at the ford have been a dream. We have been lured into accepting them as real because of the imperceptible transition[37] which occurs as he symbolically crosses the river: Mérimée sought for the Arabic word for 'ford' as the original title of the story.[38]

The reader is struck by the way in which certain figures and features (young girls, the magician, snakes) recur without any apparent sense, since in a short story we expect such details to be relevant. With hindsight we see that the dream recycles his real experiences and preoccupations in distorted and dramatic form, while introducing the staple ingredients of literary dreams: abrupt disappearances and

---

36. Genette suggests that it is rare outside the *récit folklorique* (*Figures III*, 79–80); even there it is rare, and difficult to sustain for long (Smith, 'Narrative Versions', 226–7).
37. There is a similar blurring of the transition from reality to dream, but in a heterodiegetic narrative, in Ambrose Bierce's 'An Occurence at Owl Creek Bridge' (1891).
38. See Mérimée, *Correspondance générale*, XVII, 63.

CHAPTER 4. STRUCTURE, PATTERNING AND POINT   117

reappearances, falls, subterranean galleries.[39] There are from the outset references to the Narrator's tiredness: he looks forward to sleeping in a real bed, avoids sitting in his wing-chair after learning of the new expedition 'de peur de m'endormir', grows bored as they approach the ford listening to his sergeant's often-told tale of amorous misfortune, which 'semblait encore plus longue que de coutume' (1096). His sexual deprivation (he looks forward to a rendez-vous with Mademoiselle Concha, and alludes euphemistically to 'le grand fonds de tendresse qu'on rapporte du désert' (1091)) explains the dream's sexual content: the increasingly alluring girls and young women, culminating in the invitation from the 'vraie beauté' in her 'chemise de soie transparente'. Secondly, Wagner awakens him with a cup of coffee, which not only breaks the dream but explains its final moments, and is anticipated in the 'affreux liquide' of the well from which the giant snake emerges (1099–1100). We know from experience that the event which breaks a dream can also determine that dream (falling out of bed you have a dream that ends in a fall...).[40] So we see that it is Wagner's remark as he offers the coffee: 'Est-ce que nous ne tuons pas le ver, mon lieutenant?' — a colloquial idiom for having a stiff drink before breakfast — that triggers the (re)appearance in the dream of the snakes and his resolve, after the 'sacrifice' scene, to return to 'exterminer les abominables hôtes de ces lieux, hommes et serpents' (1100).

How, then, does patterning function in the trick that Mérimée has played? The revelation of the ending forces us to reread the story. On closer examination we see that the events of the dream recapitulate real events, but in *reverse* order. After the arrival at the ford, the pursuit of Sidi-Lala reflects the expedition to stop him; the snake seen in the river reflects the eel eaten at dinner; the subterranean river reflects the tales of troglodytes at that dinner; the sacrifice reflects the spectacle before dinner; the seductive woman and divan recall his tempting wing-chair; and her moustache (left by coffee?) reflects the officer's moustaches at the outset — and Wagner's, as he awakens. This overall structure is reinforced by details (as in 'Arachné') which cross from reality into dream: the 'cheveux longs' of the soldiers (1091) are echoed in the

39. See Mérimée, *Nouvelles*, ed. Crouzet, II, 400.
40. A story by Henri Mérimée of 1832 uses the same pattern: a kiss turns out to have been triggered by a dog licking the dreamer's face (Bryant, *Short Fiction*, 78).

woman's black hair, spreading over her shoulder and the divan; the colonel's Moorish house becomes the 'appartement somptueusement meublé dans le goût arabe' of the cave (1101); the 'sorte de prière ou d'incantation, appuyée par sa musique' (1092) reappears in the 'incantation' of the magician in the cavern (1099). This is especially true of costumes: the real 'veste de velours brodée' and 'pantalons courts en satin bleu' (1093) are echoed in the dream in the 'veste de velours soutachée d'or' and 'pantalons courts en satin bleu' (1102). The more we look, the more we find: do hopes that colonel R***'s infantry will 'culbuter' Sidi-Lala turn into the fall into the ravine? The girl in the real spectacle is bitten and falls, then recovers and reappears in a 'galerie' to collect money; is this echoed in the dream when she is swallowed, but in effect reappears when the Narrator follows a 'galerie latérale' and finds another woman (1101)?

At the beginning of the tale, the Narrator calls the previous campaign a 'chasse incessante' (1091), anticipating the dream sequence. And during the initial spectacle and dinner, there are hints of the trick that is to follow. The scene between the 'magician' and the young girl is a trick; the Narrator refers to it as 'la pièce qui allait se jouer' and, twice in one paragraph, a 'spectacle' (1093). The Narrator is taken in by this first trick, just as we are by the second, and is mocked by the doctor: 'Innocent! ... Ne voyez-vous donc pas que c'est dans le programme?' (1094). He shows contempt for the travelling troupe: 'Lorsque la fatigue et le vertige eurent fait perdre à ces gens le peu de cervelle qu'ils avaient' (1093); but he is duped by his own fatigue and imagination. And in the dream itself we are reminded that things are not always what they seem: climbing from the river, the lieutenant seizes a root, but it proves to be 'un énorme serpent'; it slides into the river, 'où il me sembla qu'il laissait comme une traînée de feu', but when he recovers his composure, this in turn proves to be only 'le reflet d'une torche' (1098).

No doubt the recurrent details could be read as referring to Mérimée's sexual preoccupations (Raoul Roche argued that the whole tale embodies Mérimée's repressed sexual desire for an under-age

CHAPTER 4. STRUCTURE, PATTERNING AND POINT   119

Jewish girl)[41] or to sexual and mythical associations (Anne Hiller).[42] But these patterns exist *inside* the story, in which the imagination of the sleep- and sex-deprived homodiegetic Narrator, not an expert on myths and symbols, but a simple French officer in Africa, transforms the exotic commonplace into the alarming and the sexual, all the more imperceptibly as it is precisely these elements that we expect from a tale set in North Africa. It unsettles us by calling into question the barrier between dream and reality, as a story like Gautier's 'La Morte amoureuse' does much more explicitly; but it does not really tell us anything about dreams. It relies rather on our knowledge of dreams to work out how Mérimée has constructed his trap, in much the same way that 'Arachné' relies on our common conceptions of jealousy and madness to put the elements of the tale into a coherent pattern.

Both stories remind us that in a fictional narrative, the 'real events' and their order (the *histoire*) are something constructed from the *récit* by the reader (imperfectly in the case of 'Arachné', mistakenly the first time round in 'Djoûmane').[43] Both offer self-contained worlds, with minimum evocation of previous events, and rely on familiar literary models, even stereotypes. Both are told by a homodiegetic Narrator, inside whose world (a mad world, a dream world) we are increasingly trapped — and in which, at the end, *he* is revealed to be trapped, although being woken allows Mérimée's Narrator to escape. Both are accompanied by structural reversals. Verbal echoes and structure become an end in themselves. The point in both is the enjoyment had by the reader in successive readings of the story; as with a poem, their formal pleasures are increased on rereading.

It is obvious that patterning can play a key role in the novel in the elaboration of coherence and meaning, from the careful constructions of Flaubert to the mad world of Humbert Humbert in *Lolita*. But it is in short fiction that the reader is most likely to be aware of these formal

41. Raoul Roche, 'Un rêve de Mérimée: *Djoûmane*', *La Grande Revue* (October 1928), 626–38. The tale may, nevertheless, allow Mérimée to indulge covertly his sexual curiosities, as Raitt argues (*Prosper Mérimée*, 335–6).
42. Anne Hiller, 'L'Enigme de "Djoûmane"', *Essays in French Literature*, 11 (1974), 14–34.
43. The point is made forcefully by Smith: any fictional *histoire* is a version constructed from the *récit* ('Narrative Versions', 229–30); and by Bauman, *Story, Performance and Event*, 5–6: 'Events are abstractions from narrative.'

elements, and that the author can exploit them. The more we reread, the more the elements interrelate and form patterns. But patterning in short fiction has a more complex relationship to point than in the natural oral tale. It can be used to lead to a fairly simple point, as in 'Marroca', but the apparently straightforward 'Promenade' shows how patterning can be used to imply the more general implications about life that we expect to find in literature. Barbara Herrnstein Smith suggests that a story is usually told 'because it exemplifies or indicates (or apparently contradicts) some general proposition — again, one that is presumably of some interest to the listener — which may or may not be explicitly stated'.[44] The parenthesis is important. If the implications are predominantly unsettling and negative, as they are overwhelmingly in the best French short fiction in the nineteenth century, it is the indirect way in which they are suggested that disturbs the confidence we have about the world and our place in it. The shift from illusion to reality has a destructive effect on the individual character (Leras in 'Promenade'), but the wider implications also disturb the reader. The patterns of reversal that are so frequent (in 'Marroca', in 'Arachné', in 'Djoûmane') not only exploit the simplified oppositions that short fiction relies on, but almost invariably lead to humiliation, defeat or entrapment of the protagonist, or even the reader.

The teller of a natural tale is discomfited if the response of his or her listener is: 'So what?' But to respond in that way to 'Djoûmane' or 'Arachné' would be both justifiable — and to miss the point, and the formal satisfaction. Both tales are essentially games; in Clare Hanson's terms, they are the types of short story that do not 'tell' us things, but 'are' things,[45] and bring us back to poetry, or at least to a certain view of poetry as a game with words. Schwob pushes to an extreme his conviction that the pursuit of symmetry and form is all that is left for the writer of short stories in the 1890s, but could also be seen as implying that to neglect reality is madness. Mérimée re-enacts his sceptical awareness that story-telling is a process of deception.

44. Smith, *Margins*, 195.
45. Hanson, *Re-reading the Short Story*, 28.

5. Playing with the Kaleidoscope: repetition and focalisation

Gautier, 'Le Roi Candaule', 'Avatar', 'Jettatura'

Anyone who reads in rapid succession a series of short stories by one author is likely to be struck by an element of repetitiveness. The repetitiveness is not just a question of technique, as with Barbey's elaboration of the role of conversation in the frame, or of types of character or setting, as with Maupassant's recurrent use of prostitutes, of Norman farmers, and of the Franco-Prussian war, but of types of situation. The climax of Mérimée's 'La Vénus d'Ille' of 1837, narrated by an archaeologist on tour, is a wedding and the unexplained death of the husband on the wedding night. It seems possible that he has been crushed to death by a statue of Venus recently unearthed nearby. Over thirty years later 'Lokis', in which the narrator is a professor undertaking linguistic research, culminates in a wedding; after the wedding night the wife is found with her throat torn open and the husband has vanished; his bizarre previous behaviour could be explained by his mother having been raped by a bear. The settings, the eastern Pyrenees and Lithuania, are different, but the improbable explanations of events are similar (statues do not come to life, bears cannot impregnate humans), especially if characters are considered in terms of their relationship and function in the plot.[1] Equally evident is the way that Mérimée has varied the situation in the two tales by

---

1. Such a view springs from Vladimir Propp's analysis of Russian fairy tales, in which he reduced the multiple characters and events to a limited number of 'functions' (*Morphologie du conte*); the process was pushed further in A.J. Greimas's analysis of 'actants' (including animals, objects, concepts) whose relationship underlies a narrative. Given the simplification of characterisation and importance of structure and plot in the *nouvelle*, Goyet has noted the tendency of characters not to leave their actantial role; they do not develop the complex and autonomous 'personality' of a novel's characters (*La Nouvelle*, 86).

reversing the sex of the victim: the bridegroom in 'La Vénus d'Ille', the bride in 'Lokis'.

Our perception of repetitiveness is heightened by the bringing together into collections of stories originally published separately. Mérimée collected his first stories under a title, *Mosaïque*, that indicated the diversity of the material in the volume. Maupassant's collections were governed largely by commercial opportunism,[2] and put together 'pour vider mon sac de chroniques'.[3] Although Barbey, Villiers and Schwob were concerned with the structure of their volumes, modern editorial practice, bringing together related stories or the entire output of the same author, has accentuated repetitiveness.

This is also explained by the circumstances of periodical publication: the success of an author or of a type of story is likely to lead to pressure to produce 'more of the same'.[4] The first translations of Hoffmann from 1828 led to a demand for *contes fantastiques* that writers were happy to satisfy. An author as prolific as Maupassant had inevitably to fall back on the model of stories he had written before, and by the end of his brief writing life, his irritation with the genre, increasingly a distraction from the novel, is related to the pressure of external demands, as well as to the lower status of the short story: 'C'est usé, fini, ridicule. J'en ai trop fait, d'ailleurs'.[5] Moreover, a writer of short fiction, producing work to short deadlines, has less time for stock-taking and renewal than a novelist. A second explanation for repetitiveness lies in the more or less conscious preoccupations or obsessions of a writer: it is not surprising that Antonia Fonyi, arguing from a Freudian perspective, should consider that 'un écrivain raconte toujours la même histoire', and that Jacques Chabot's psychoanalytic reading of Mérimée finds a recurrent pattern of three figures: the narrator, lucid and rational; the hero; and the double he has to confront.[6]

2. See Forestier's remarks in Maupassant, *Contes et nouvelles*, I, lxxxi.
3. Letter to his publisher Havard, quoted by Forestier, *Contes et nouvelles*, II, 1354. He was sufficiently careless not to notice publishing a story twice in different volumes (I, 1254). But in the case of 'Un cas de divorce', changes seem to have been made to avoid repetition of ideas (see Chapter 2).
4. This tendency was already present in the 1830s: see Roland Chollet, *Balzac journaliste: le tournant de 1830* (Paris: Klincksieck, 1983), 567.
5. Letter of October 1891, quoted in *Contes et nouvelles*, II, xxvi.
6. Antonia Fonyi, 'Un écrivain raconte toujours la même histoire', in *Fiction,*

The psychoanalytical approach, however, does not help pinpoint what might be specific to short fiction in this sort of repetitiveness. Moreover, both approaches see repetitiveness as a problematic feature that needs explaining, and both deny the author freedom and autonomy, as if the repetition were imposed or involuntary. But might repetition be deliberate?

Some cases of repetition in Maupassant show him trying to improve a story, returning to a situation to treat it in a less stereotyped way or to increase its ambiguity,[7] or to explore more fully its implications. This is clearly the case with the final version of 'Le Horla'. Here Maupassant reworks a briefer framed story (published in *Gil Blas*, 26 October 1886), in which a patient, at the request of his doctor, gives an account of a sequence of unnerving experiences to an audience of fellow doctors and scientists. At the end of this account, the doctor himself poses the alternative: is the patient mad, or does, as the patient has argued, some invisible agent really exist that can explain the events narrated? The first possibility would provide a reassuring way out for the doctor (although he confesses himself uncertain at the end), and for the reader; it is only the second that is disturbing. The patient himself is convinced that he is as lucid as his scientific audience, and that he has discovered the truth. In the final version of 'Le Horla' (published in volume form in 1887), there is no explicit frame. The use of a diary allows the 'madman' to narrate the successive stages of his experiences and reflections; it is a *récit intercalé* where the individual sections of the narrative occur between the stages of the *histoire* that they are recording. The tale maintains a balance between accounts of disturbing events (a carafe of water emptied at night, untouched by human hand; a rose plucked from

narratologie, texte, genre. Actes du symposium de l'Association internationale de littérature comparée, vol. II, edited by Jean Bessière (New York: Lang, 1989), 89–95; Jacques Chabot, *L'Autre Moi* (La Calade: Edisud, 1983). See a similar pattern in D.L. Gobert, 'Mérimée Revisited', *Symposium*, 26 (1972), 128–46; and on repetition in the *nouvelle*, Thierry Ozwald, *La Nouvelle* (Paris: Nathan, 1996), 26–27.

7. See Rachel Killick, 'Mock heroics? Narrative strategy in a Maupassant war story', *Modern Language Review*, 82 (1987), 313–60. The emphasis of Charlotte Schapira, 'L'Elaboration de l'histoire dans un conte de Maupassant: "Monsieur Parent"', *Studi Francesi*, 34 (1990), 43–59, is also on improvement, though she shows how elements of a situation can be recombined as in a kaleidoscope (44, 58).

a bush by someone or something) and discussion of their implications. Are there invisible forces and beings that we cannot see? can our organs be relied on? These questions rework the ideas of earlier stories like 'Un fou?' and 'Lettre d'un fou' (II, 308, 461), in the first of which the exploration of ideas had swamped the narrative. The Narrator in 1887 is no longer in the calm position of the patient in the first version, but is torn between disturbing possibilities, both now representing a loss of autonomy and control: either he is hallucinating, or there is an invisible threat out there. Consequently the second version is more effective in its integration of theoretical discussion and events and in its maximising of the anxiety in the Narrator's mind. Here repetition is a method of improving the story, and, significantly, Maupassant himself did not collect in volume form the earlier version of 'Le Horla' or the other stories that contributed to it.

Certain types of repetitiveness in Maupassant's stories seem to spring from the desire to exploit possibilities of a given situation. That of a married couple where the wife has an illegitimate child is a recurrent one. It can be portrayed, as André Vial has noted,[8] from different angles, and the restriction to one particular angle obviously suits the confined space of the short story.[9] It is seen from the point of view of the illegitimate child in 'Le Testament' (I, 620); from that of the mother seeking out the abandoned son in 'L'Abandonné' (II, 225); from that of the husband and supposed father in 'Le Petit' (I, 957) and 'Monsieur Parent' (II, 500). Maupassant's interest in the situation may, as has been frequently argued,[10] spring from a personal preoccupation with the problem of illegitimacy. But he is also turning to his advantage the narrative potential of a situation. The discovery of a couple *in flagrante delicto* was one familiar to Maupassant's readers: it could lead to imprisonment of the wife, and was the classic means of obtaining separation; it was the subject of numerous allusions in the literature of

---

8. André Vial, *Guy de Maupassant et l'art du roman* (Paris: Nizet, 1954), 503-504.
9. Maupassant's novel *Pierre et Jean* explores the situation largely from the point of view of the legitimate son, but also offers insights into the views of the mother and the illegitimate son.
10. For example, Maupassant, *Pierre et Jean*, edited by Pierre Cogny (Paris: Garnier, 1959), xiii; Forestier in Maupassant, *Contes et nouvelles*, I, 1480.

CHAPTER 5. PLAYING WITH THE KALEIDOSCOPE

the time.[11] At least a dozen ingenious variations occur in his stories, in which he plays with angle, tone and outcome. On the one hand we find lovers discovered together in stories that are generally comic: the young protagonist of 'Le Verrou' (I, 489) tells how he is found in bed with a *femme du monde* when he forgets to bolt his door, surprised by his landlord, his concierge, and the chimney sweep; in 'Sauvée' (II, 651) a wife sets up the discovery of her husband with the maid by the wife's parents, a lawyer, and the inevitable concierge. In 'L'Ivrogne' (II, 94), a rare serious treatment of the situation, the point of view is (as in 'Sauvée') that of the person discovering the couple, rather than the discomfited pair: the husband returns home from the bar to find his wife just after her lover has left, and beats her to death. The couple need not be adulterous: in 'Ma Femme' (I, 659) the Narrator, staying in the country, falls asleep, drunk and exhausted, in the room of the daughter of a fellow guest, and is forced to marry her. Other comic variants evoke surprising discoveries associated with amorous encounters: in 'La Chambre 11' (II, 393) an unfaithful wife who is expecting her lover discovers a dead man in bed in a hotel bedroom; in 'Le Lapin' (II, 967) the shepherd's wife has hidden her lover under her bed; he is discovered there by gendarmes who are looking for proof, not of adultery, but of the theft of a rabbit (found in a casserole under the bed as well). In another series of stories, lovers who are about to be caught in a compromising situation by husbands who return home inopportunely, manage to escape by diverse stratagems. The wife of 'Une ruse' (I, 560) smuggles out of the bedroom the body of her lover with the help of her doctor; the wife of 'Décoré!' (I, 1065) manages to conceal her lover, but not his coat with the ribbon of the Légion d'honneur, which she has to explain to her husband by 'revealing' that he is about to be decorated. The Narrator's explanation of why he first refused Marroca's invitation: 'Ce sont là [les rendez-vous sous un toit conjugal] des souricières où sont toujours pris les imbéciles' (I, 373), is a nod by Maupassant to the stereotyped nature of the situation, to which he repeatedly returns as the turning-point of a narrative.

This recurrent exploitation of the potential of a situation is clear in the short fiction of Théophile Gautier. When the *récits fantastiques*[12]

---

11. As Forestier notes in connection with 'La Bûche' (I, 1394).
12. References in the text are to Théophile Gautier, *Œuvres*, edited by Paolo

that he wrote intermittently from the 1830s to the 1860s and published initially in periodicals, and then with other works in heterogeneous volumes, are grouped together, one situation stands out. From 'La Cafetière' (1831) to 'Arria Marcella' (1852), via 'Omphale' (1834), 'La Morte amoureuse' (1836) and 'Le Pied de momie' (1840), we find 'une fable dont les articulations sont immuables':[13] a young man, enticed by some object or work of art (a tapestry representing a woman, a mummified foot, the imprint of a breast in volcanic ash) escapes to another time and experiences an amorous adventure with a woman whom his love has somehow brought back to life; following the intervention of a figure of paternal authority (an uncle, the woman's father, a monk), he is excluded from this other world (which might have been a dream) and returns abruptly to reality. Rather than lack of imagination, these embody 'l'une ou l'autre des grandes obsessions de l'auteur':[14] the desire to escape from the present world (commercialised, ugly, materialistic), the pursuit of an ideal love outside time, the sense of the inevitable triumph of the real world and of the fragmenting and destructive power of time. But they equally represent (as with Maupassant's variations on the *flagrant délit*) the exploitation of the potential of a single scenario.

A second series of tales, where the recurrent elements are less obvious, also shows a single underlying pattern. They also show how a key feature of narrative, focalisation or point of view,[15] can be exploited to involve the reader in the tale. 'Le Roi Candaule' dates from 1844, 'Avatar' and 'Jettatura' from 1856. All three are leisurely tales first published in serial form before reappearing in volume form alongside other works.[16] In all of them we find a heterodiegetic narrator who does

Tortonese (Paris: Laffont, 1995).
13. Théophile Gautier, *La Morte amoureuse, Avatar et autres récits fantastiques*, edited by Jean Gaudon (Paris: Gallimard, 1981), 27-28.
14. Marcel Voisin, *Le Soleil et la nuit: l'imaginaire de Théophile Gautier* (Université de Bruxelles, 1981), 171.
15. On the term, see Chapter 1, note 26.
16. 'Avatar' was the only one to be published (1857) in a volume on its own, before being reprinted in *Romans et contes* (1863). Chapters coincide with serialised episodes for all stories, except that the final chapter of 'Jettatura' was divided into two episodes (Théophile Gautier, *L'Œuvre fantastique*, ed. Michel Crouzet, 2 vols (Paris: Bordas, 1992), II, 382).

not seek to efface his presence as storyteller, but frequently addresses the reader directly. The narrator, according to the standard convention of narrative fiction, is *potentially* omniscient; but this is never fully exercised, and Gautier in the three stories increasingly restricts the focalisation, thus intensifying the emotional impact. All repeat a triangular situation in which we find a wife or fiancée who is modest and virtuous, but who is betrayed; a husband or legitimate lover, whose possession of the woman is threatened; and an illicit voyeur, linked to some magical power. All involve the 'double' frequent in the *conte fantastique*, who usurps the position of the protagonist, and causes him to doubt his own identity.[17]

'Le Roi Candaule' is the simplest of these tales, and the one which remains closest to a literary source: Baudelaire observed in an essay on Gautier that 'il était difficile de chosir un thème plus usé, un drame à dénoûment plus universellement prévu'.[18] Gautier opens his narrative with the wedding procession of Candaule, King of Lydia, to a Bactrian (Afghan) princess, Nyssia, daughter of the Persian satrap Mégabaze, whose 'barbarian' ideas do not allow her to be seen by any other man than her husband. A flashback reveals that Gygès, the Captain of Candaule's guards, had inadvertently seen her face when, in the course of a secret mission to her homeland, a gust of wind had blown aside her veil as she returned from gathering flowers with a group of girls. Suspecting whom he had seen, he had been 'ébloui, fasciné, foudroyé [...] par cette apparition surhumaine' (692). Candaule, an aesthete absorbed in architecture, painting, sculpture, persuades Nyssia reluctantly to pose for him, thereby treating her, in Nyssia's view, more as a mistress than as a wife; and then, unable to keep her beauty to

---

17. There is another type of double, the individual who is split, often into a good and an evil self, and who poses the question: what am I? — Stevenson's Jekyll and Hyde, or Romuald in Gautier's 'La Morte amoureuse'. The two types sometimes overlap, as in Poe's 'William Wilson'. See Peter Whyte, 'Gautier, Nerval et la hantise du double', *Bulletin de la Société Théophile Gautier*, 10 (1988), 17-31; Gautier, *L'Œuvre fantastique*, ed. Crouzet, I, cxvi-cxxxi; and Pierre Jourde and Paolo Tortonese, *Visages du double: un thème littéraire* (Paris: Nathan, 1996).
18. Published in 1859; Charles Baudelaire, *Œuvres complètes*, Bibliothèque de la Pléiade, edited by Y.G. Le Dantec, revised by Claude Pichois (Paris, Gallimard, 1961), 675-700 (694).

himself, calls on Gygès to witness it, concealed behind a door, as she undresses for bed. Candaule's plan backfires: Nyssia glimpses Gygès's eye and guesses what Candaule has done; having seen Nyssia's beauty, Gygès feels that she belongs to him. Overcome by shame and anger, and determined that only her husband shall see her beauty, Nyssia offers Gygès the alternative of death, or the throne if he kills Candaule. Gygès, forced to chose, hides behind the bedroom door a second time, then springs out to kill the King whom Nyssia has drugged.

The moral argument of the tale is more straightforward than a simple outline of events suggests. In one of Gautier's sources (Plato's *Republic*, Book II), Gygès is a simple shepherd who uses a magic ring that makes him invisible to enter the bedchamber, seduce the Queen, and kill the King: the tale illustrates how human egoism, if unrestrained by the law, fails to respect the rights of others. Gautier allows Gygès to keep the ring (a well-known element in the legend)[19] and it is alluded to in gossip about him (694); but he does not use it, and in all other respects Gautier stays close to Herodotus's version of the legend[20] where there is no ring and it is Candaule's foolish offer that leads to the act of voyeurism and the King's death. In spite of Gygès's womanising reputation which leads Candaule to choose him as confidant, he uses no dubious means to conquer the Queen and is an innocent pawn, trapped first by his master, then by Nyssia's ruthless alternative which makes him a 'complice passif' in the King's murder (724). Moreover, Gygès's dispossession of Candaule is made almost legitimate. Not only does Gautier shift responsibility to Candaule with his rash and insensitive proposition, but Gygès is made in a sense the true husband of Nyssia: he has seen her before Candaule, and the idea that, as Gygès reminds Candaule, 'chacun ne doit regarder que ce qui lui appartient' (707) has as its corollary that seeing proves possession. Whereas Candaule's attitude to Nyssia is aesthetic appreciation, Gygès shows the desire and jealousy of human love.

Given that we have a well-known tale, how does Gautier manage our interest in this triangle of characters? Although the title suggests that Candaule is the central figure, the opening chapter establishes Gygès in

19. In the *Grand Dictionnaire Universel* of Pierre Larousse of 1866–1876, 'L'anneau de Gygès' occupies a whole column, and four of the six nineteenth-century quotations refer to its power to confer invisibility.
20. *Histories*, I, 7–12; it is quoted in Gautier, *Œuvres*, 1621–2.

CHAPTER 5. PLAYING WITH THE KALEIDOSCOPE 129

that role by conventional narrative means, rather than by simply enlisting our approval or sympathy.[21] The heterodiegetic narrator could know everything and 'en [sa] qualité de poète' (698) even describes the face of Nyssia hidden beneath her veil, but what he chooses to show is crucial in determining our involvement. In the wedding procession, events and characters are portrayed externally, as if perceived by an invisible spectator. The conversation of the expectant crowd introduces key facts, such as the reported beauty and modesty of Nyssia, and Candaule's curiosity about her, but tells us nothing that is not common knowledge. Candaule and Nyssia are also evoked from outside: Nyssia's costume is described at length, but her feelings can only be guessed at: 'Nyssia *paraissait* gênée [...] de voir tant de regards fixés sur elle' (697: my emphasis). The presentation of Gygès is very different. A flashback tells how he first saw Nyssia, a scene known to no one else in Sardis; it is focalised through Gygès, and accompanied by the narrator's omniscient account of his reactions (in Dorrit Cohn's terms, psycho-narration):[22] 'Il songeait aux enivrements de la toute-puissance, au bonheur de fouler la pourpre sous une sandale d'or' (691), and emphasises his fascination and terror at seeing Nyssia's beauty. The end of the chapter reinforces Gygès's centrality. Nyssia descends from her elephant and enters the palace; this is presented through his reactions: 'Et Gygès poussa un soupir, lorsqu'il vit Nyssia [...] descendre sur les têtes inclinées des esclaves damascènes [...] jusque sur le seuil de la demeure royale' (698): we feel that we stay outside the palace with him.

Gygès remains the character who is present at events and whose thoughts and feelings the narrator describes through much of the remaining narrative. In the course of his conversations with Candaule, and later with Nyssia, we are told Gygès's thoughts, but observe others externally, as perceived by the Captain, who is baffled by Candaule (704) and cannot understand the instructions Nyssia gives in 'une langue inconnue' to her slaves (724). With Gygès, we are led into a series of secret or forbidden rooms: the inner courtyard of the palace, the bedroom, the apartment and the 'recoin obscur du palais' (724); and

---

21. On the defining of the 'hero' by consideration of frequency of appearance, information, function, rather than by a problematic sympathy of the reader, see Mieke Bal, *Narratology* (Toronto University Press, 1985), 90.
22. Cohn, *Transparent Minds*, 11-12.

when characters separate, the scene closes by describing Gygès and his thoughts (706, 710). This leads us to involve ourselves with Gygès and culminates in the climax when we follow Gygès's perceptions (here touch, not sight) as he is led by Nyssia to wait a second time at her bedchamber door:

> La main qui tenait celle de Gygès était froide, douce et petite; cependant ces doigts déliés la serraient à la meurtrir comme eussent pu le faire les doigts d'une statue d'airain animée par un prodige; la roideur d'une volonté inflexible se traduisait dans cette pression toujours égale, semblable à une tenaille, que nulle hésitation partie de la tête ou du cœur ne venaient faire varier. Gygès vaincu, subjugué, anéanti, cédait à cette traction impérieuse, comme s'il eût été entraîné par le bras puissant de la fatalité. (725)

But this focalisation is not maintained with total consistency. The narrator, in Chapter II, allows us to see the hidden beauty of Nyssia, and then Candaule's reaction to her beauty, mingling ecstasy and fear: 'Il se sentit pris d'éblouissements et de vertige, comme quelqu'un qui se penche sur l'abîme ou fixe ses yeux sur le soleil' (701). After Gygès has seen Nyssia's naked beauty, Chapter IV develops the feelings of all three characters: Gygès's jealous thoughts, Nyssia's anger and shame, and Candaule's complacent satisfaction.

Gautier develops his sources to show the conflicting emotions of the characters: Candaule, torn between admiration for Nyssia's beauty and frustration at not being able to share it; Nyssia, ashamed, furious and bent on revenge; Gygès fascinated and intimidated by Nyssia's beauty, ambitious but helpless. The emotional tension is centered above all on Gygès. Although his magic ring is not used, and the narrator mocks the populace's superstitious belief that Nyssia can see through walls (692), the emotional atmosphere has much in common with a *conte fantastique* like 'Le Horla' or 'Il Vicolo di Madama Lucrezia' in that it is a tale of a helpless individual in the grip of forces that he cannot control, which fill him with terror. Chance, or Fate as Gygès is tempted to believe,[23] has made him see Nyssia first; he cannot escape Candaule's proposition; after he has seen Nyssia naked,

---

23. 706, 708, 723.

CHAPTER 5. PLAYING WITH THE KALEIDOSCOPE

> Gygès n'était plus maître de lui, et il éprouvait ce désespoir morne d'un homme monté sur un char qui voit ses chevaux, effarés, insensibles au frein, courir avec l'essor d'un galop furieux vers un précipice hérissé de rocs. (715)

Nyssia's ruthless alternative fills him with 'le vertige de la fatalité' (723). Events repeat themselves ominously: first Candaule hides him behind the door to watch Nyssia undress; then Nyssia hides him behind this same door to kill her husband, setting desire and murder in parallel: 'Cette répétition des mêmes actes, dans une intention si différente, prenait un caractère lugubre et fatal' (725). When she loosens her hair, 'cette action si simple et si gracieuse prenait des choses terribles qui allaient se passer un caractère effrayant et fatal qui faisait frissonner de terreur l'assassin caché' (726). After Candaule's murder, the tension is resolved briskly with a happy ending: Nyssia's modesty is avenged, Gygès's dream fulfilled, Candaule dead and a new dynasty established. Gautier breaks with the centrality of Gygès's focalisation in order to explore Nyssia's equally powerful emotions of shame and rage, expressed in a long interior monologue (717-18), and also in order to show Candaule's thoughts. But compared to the conflict within the other two, the King's complacency and unawareness mean that his point of view remains less interesting.

Gautier's treatment of the traditional story in 'Le Roi Candaule' develops a series of atmospheric scenes of anxiety in a way that suits short fiction: what grips the reader is the moment of intense feeling and the apprehension of what is to come, rather than the gradual unfolding of a novelistic plot. At the same time the dispersal of interest among the three characters in the triangular situation deprives the tale of a clear centre of interest. In 'Avatar', a superficially very different plot develops a similar underlying situation in a more balanced manner. In Florence Octave de Saville sees and falls in love with the beautiful Prascovie Labinska; rejected by her (she loves her husband Olaf), he falls ill. In Paris he consults Dr Cherbonneau, who has learned in India the secret of moving souls from one body to another. The doctor realises that he is literally dying of love, and switches the souls of Octave and Olaf. Now in her husband's body, Octave is accepted as him in their mansion; but seeing 'le regard d'Octave' (824) in his eyes, Prascovie realises that something is wrong, and shuts him out of her bedroom. Meanwhile Olaf, in Octave's body, is excluded from his own house, but succeeds in challenging Octave to a duel. Octave wins and has Olaf at his mercy; but, realising that he will never succeed in winning Prascovie, he reveals his failure to Olaf, and the pair return to the doctor's. Olaf is reintegrated into his real body; Octave's soul however escapes, and the doctor rejuvenates himself by taking over Octave's vacant form.

The setting is contemporary Paris as opposed to Mediterranean antiquity; whereas the events of 'Le Roi Candaule' remain rationally explicable (only popular credulity saw magic power in Gygès's ring or Nyssia's eyes), in 'Avatar' the impossible moving of souls is central to the plot. But the same underlying pattern can be seen. Prascovie is the modest and virtuous wife. Octave is the illicit voyeur helped by the 'magician' Cherbonneau to see what is forbidden, invisible like the Gyges of legend. Olaf has the role of the legitimate and threatened husband.

Like Gygès glimpsing Nyssia in Bactria, Octave is seized by an impossible love for '"la seule femme qui ne peut m'aimer"' (817); just as the husband leads Gygès 'jusque sur le seuil de la chambre nuptiale' (711), Octave goes in the husband's body 'sur le seuil de la chambre conjugale' (836); the same importance is given to the male gaze and the woman's intuitive response; and just as Nyssia asked herself: '"En quoi Nyssia diffère-t-elle à présent de la courtisane la plus vile?"' (718), Prascovie feels degraded, 'désirée pour sa beauté comme une courtisane' (823). But if the verbal parallels underline a similar situation, Gautier develops it differently. Olaf, the legitimate possessor, is like Candaule threatened and collapses into 'un sommeil ... semblable à la mort' (813); his duel with Octave recalls the moment when Gygès leaps on Candaule with a dagger. But whereas Gygès was able to enter a series of secret places, in 'Avatar' the threshold serves as a barrier defended by the betrayed wife. Unlike Gygès's, Octave's desire is not made legitimate. It is not the husband's betrayal, but the doctor's intervention and 'un moyen horrible [...] qu'une passion délirante pouvait seule risquer' (836) which let him usurp Olaf's place. He has no priority in that he sees Prascovie only after her marriage to Olaf, when it is too late. As Florence Goyet has noted, in the *nouvelle*, 'il ne peut être que trop tard, sinon les forces mises en présence n'auraient pas

CHAPTER 5. PLAYING WITH THE KALEIDOSCOPE

dégagé la puissance maximale qu'elles peuvent produire'.[24] Gautier's reworking of the situation means that he can push to extremes the emotional predicament of both male characters. Octave's love may be 'involontaire', as Prascovie recognises (787), but it drives him to desire to possess her, and is ultimately frustrated; the husband Olaf is (unlike Candaule) innocent, but this does not spare him the anguish of dispossession.

The use of focalisation in 'Avatar' brings out these moments of intensified emotion. The heterodiegetic narrator could show us the feelings of all the characters. In the opening chapter this narrator observes Octave externally, as an intriguing enigma: 'Comment se faisait-il que, jeune, beau, riche, avec tant de raisons d'être heureux, un jeune homme se consumât si misérablement?' (777). Gradually décor and events are described as perceived by Octave, and his confession to the doctor of his love for Prascovie (Chapter II) seems to establish him as the protagonist. But Chapter III switches to Olaf, with a description of his mansion, his past, and his marriage. We then follow events as they are experienced by Octave in Chapters IV, VI and IX, and by Olaf in Chapters V, VII and VIII. We follow from Olaf's point of view his visit to Cherbonneau and the transposition of his soul into Octave's body. The narrator combines an objective account of Cherbonneau's magic with a subjective one of Olaf's perceptions as he comes to in Octave's body: 'Les objets vacillaient autour de lui [...]. Peu à peu cette fantasmagorie s'évapora; tout revint à son aspect naturel' (808). We continue to follow Olaf as he leaves, enters Octave's brougham, and is taken to the Labinski mansion to be humiliated by his own servants and by Octave:

> Le captif du suisse tourna les yeux vers le fond de la cour, et vit debout sous l'auvent de la marquise un jeune homme de taille élégante et svelte, à figure ovale, aux yeux noirs, au nez aquilin, à la moustache fine, qui n'était autre que lui-même, ou son spectre modelé par le diable, avec une ressemblance à faire illusion.
> Le suisse lâcha les mains qu'il tenait prisonnières. Les valets [...] rendaient à ce fantôme les honneurs qu'ils refusaient au comte. (810-11)

---

24. Goyet, La Nouvelle, 53.

He faints, then recovers in Octave's house. First using free indirect speech, then quoted interior monologue, Gautier develops his awareness of his predicament, dispossessed of his body, name and home, then gripped by the idea of Prascovie unwittingly yielding to his double:

> Il ne pouvait réclamer son titre de comte Labinski avec la forme dans laquelle il se trouvait emprisonné. Il passerait aux yeux de tout le monde pour un impudent imposteur, ou tout au moins pour un fou. [...] Comment prouver son identité? [...] Une idée affreuse lui mordit le cœur de ses crochets de vipère: 'Mais ce comte Labinski fictif [...] peut-être à cette heure met-il son pied fourchu sur le seuil ce cette chambre où je n'ai jamais pénétré que le cœur ému comme le premier soir, et Prascovie lui sourit-elle doucement.' (812-3)

Maintaining this focalisation, the following chapter allows Olaf's jealousy to reach a new peak when he is shocked to discover Octave's portrait of Prascovie:

> A la surprise succéda un furieux mouvement de jalousie. [...] Cette Prascovie si religieusement adorée serait-elle descendue de son ciel d'amour dans une intrigue vulgaire? Quelle raillerie infernale l'incarnait, lui, le mari, dans le corps de l'amant de cette femme, jusque-là crue si pure? (816)

Suspecting Prascovie, 'il sentait sa raison près de s'échapper' (816); although Octave's diary calms his doubts, he remains helpless, with Prascovie in Octave's power, and unable himself to persuade anyone who he really is.

These chapters alternate with ones that follow Octave and adopt his point of view. His arrival at Cherbonneau's house, his shock at seeing Olaf's apparently inanimate body ('Il crut d'abord à un assassinat' (802)), his fleeting guilt, his reawakening after the exchange of souls, his arrival at the Labinskis', are handled exactly like Olaf's parallel experiences. This restricted focalisation builds up to an emotional climax, using free indirect speech and psycho-narration:

> Il allait se trouver en présence de la belle créature adorée, et elle ne le repousserait pas! [...]

CHAPTER 5. PLAYING WITH THE KALEIDOSCOPE

> Près de ce moment suprême, son âme éprouvait des transes et des anxiétés affreuses: les timidités du véritable amour la faisaient défaillir. (820)

The internal focalisation continues as he enters her dressing-room. But at this point Prascovie senses something wrong in Olaf's kiss — 'un long, un ardent baiser' (822) — and the focalisation briefly switches to her, 'gênée et brûlée par ce regard'; and we follow her as she bolts herself in, seeks refuge in bed, and is tormented by 'des rêves incohérents et bizarres' (824).

After this brief interruption, the alternation between the experiences of the two men resumes: Octave frustrated by knowing that he can make no progress with Prascovie ('Quelle rage! être dans ce paradis […] et ne pouvoir tromper sa pudeur céleste […] !' (828)), Olaf unable to contain himself in the presence of Prascovie and Octave ('Une rage subite s'empara de lui en voyant son spectre animé par une autre âme installée dans sa propre maison' (831)), the perplexity of both faced with the prospect of wounding their own body in a duel. Thus though we are twice allowed to glimpse the thoughts of Prascovie, the wife is marginalised in comparison with Nyssia, and the narrative balances symmetrically the points of view of husband and lover. Cherbonneau, though crucial to the plot, remains a marginal figure as he lacks a strong inner life: when Gautier needs to portray his thoughts, he resorts not to psycho-narration or interior monologue, but to the conventions of the revealing expression: 'Un vague sourire de dédain erra sur le pli de ses lèvres' (802), and the soliloquy: '"Très bien!" fit M. Balthazar Cherbonneau, s'applaudissant lui-même de son ouvrage' (803). He also closes the story, returning us to normality with a touch of humour.

The dramatic interest in 'Avatar' is evenly balanced. Whereas Gygès feels helpless in face of the events confronting him, Candaule is the victim of his own plan rebounding on him, never realises this, and dies drugged and asleep. In contrast both the rivals in 'Avatar' are defenceless and aware of it: Octave helpless in face of his love, and in face of Prascovie's refusal; Olaf, initially a rather boring ideal husband, dispossessed of his body, his home and his wife: 'Il était bien réellement et bien absolument dépossédé de son moi' (813). The idea of doubles and mistaken identity is capable of comic development: as well as the myth of Amphitryon that Molière and others had reworked and which goes back to Plautus (Zeus takes on the appearance of

Amphitryon to seduce his wife Alcmene, and Mercury that of his servant Sosias), and Plautus's *Menaechmi* (reworked by Shakespeare in *The Comedy of Errors*),[25] Gautier drew elements of 'Avatar' from a contemporary *vaudeville* he had reviewed in 1844, in which an Indian magician exchanges his body with that of an Englishman in order to marry his fiancée. Gautier noted that this produced 'des quiproquos plus ou moins divertissants',[26] but added that the subject 'demandait ... à être moins légèrement traité, étant, au fond, beaucoup plus sérieux qu'on ne pense'. We find in 'Avatar' elements of this scenario used to rework the triangular situation of 'Le Roi Candaule' and to present moments of intensified emotion.

'Jettatura', also set in the present, offers a third variation on this triangular situation. The story opens with the arrival of Paul d'Aspremont in Naples and his visit to Alicia Ward and the Commodore, her guardian, at their rented villa. A flashback describes Paul and Alicia's previous acquaintance and growing love, but also the illness, seemingly consumption, that has brought her to Italy. Count Altavilla, with many of the local population, suspects Paul of possessing the 'evil eye', and asks for Alicia's hand, although her uncle has agreed to her marriage with Paul. Signs of Alicia's illness reappear, which Altavilla blames on the evil eye; he challenges Paul to a duel, in which the Count dies. Now convinced that he does have the evil eye, Paul pays a visit to Alicia, then blinds himself. Returning to the villa two days later, he finds Alicia dead, and throws himself from a rock into the sea.

We can recognise the same situation: a modest woman, Alicia; a voyeur whose gaze is linked to supernatural powers, Paul; and a rival who seeks to take his place, Altavilla, confronted in a duel (echoing the murder of Candaule and the duel in 'Avatar')[27] which leads to a death. But if the situation seems similar, Gautier has transposed the roles of the trio. Paul, the voyeur, is the legitimate owner: he has priority over

---

25. These are discussed by Jourde and Tortonese, *Visages du double*, 16–21.
26. *Histoire de l'art dramatique en France*, quoted by Peter Whyte, *Théophile Gautier, conteur fantastique et merveilleux* (University of Durham, 1996), 84; Gautier's debt to his various sources is outlined by Whyte, 83–84.
27. The duel with a double is, as Peter Whyte notes, one of the clichés of the *conte fantastique*, and is found also in Gautier's 'Le Chevalier double' (*Gautier, conteur*, 51), and in Poe's 'William Wilson'.

CHAPTER 5. PLAYING WITH THE KALEIDOSCOPE

his rival like Gygès, but as a potential husband his role is that of Candaule and Olaf. The rival who threatens his possession of Alicia is killed in the duel. And whereas Olaf's love is pure and contrasted with Octave's dangerous desire, Paul's love, though respectful, seems to provoke Alicia's death, and Paul sees himself as both innocent and destructive: 'Je suis innocent comme la foudre, comme l'avalanche, comme le mancenillier, comme toutes les forces destructives et inconscientes' (907-908).

In consequence of this redistribution of stock elements, Paul becomes unambiguously the emotional centre of the story. All the key tensions brought out in the other two versions — between pure love and desire, between justified possession and illicit voyeurism, between owning and the threat of dispossession — are embodied in him. This centrality is reinforced by the use of internal focalisation. The story begins with the conventional external observation: we watch the passengers on the steamer arriving in Naples. They are stereotypes — English tourists, artists — portrayed with a touch of humour; Paul is different, 'un passager qui ne s'était pas fait voir de toute la traversée' (849); our curiosity is aroused by this 'voyageur bizarre' (850) with a 'physionomie énigmatique' (849). We follow him from boat to hotel, but the viewpoint remains external: we learn his name only when he asks if a letter has been left for him. In general the subsequent action follows Paul's actions; characters (the Commodore, Alicia, the maid Vicè, Altavilla) are described when he first sees them; settings are described when he first enters them. In Chapter II the narrator starts to give insight into the thoughts of 'notre voyageur' (853) with brief hints of his impatience to see Alicia. In Chapter III these develop into lengthy psycho-narration as Paul returns to the hotel and has an ominous dream in which, still on the boat, he sees Alicia signalling to him not to land. This dream provides a pretext for an analepsis: to escape 'ce rêve pénible, Paul [...] se mit à penser' (859) and recalls the beginning of their relationship in England. From this point, Paul occupies a privileged position: the narrator rarely describes a scene at which he is not present, or after he has left; in conversations, we are given insight into his thoughts, but only infrequently into those of others, and even then, through what an observer could deduce.[28] But there are three

---

28. The Commodore's brief interior monologues in Chapter X (890) and XI,

major exceptions to this pattern, which play an important part in the effect of Gautier's narrative.

Many chapters end with a brief section in which the narrator shifts from the main scene evoked, generally Paul's actions, to a different character, and evokes their thoughts. Thus we have Vicè's gesture to ward off the evil eye, hidden from Paul (II); the porter's muttered distrustful phrase (III); the flowers and the giant horns sent by Altavilla (IV); Vicè's intervention to point suspicion at Paul (VI). These brief codas provide an element of variety, and round off each chapter as a self-contained unit. They also add a different note, sometimes optimistic (Alicia's letter in Chapter I), more often ominous and hinting at suspicions about Paul's supernatural powers.

Secondly, there are scenes (the term seems appropriate since Gautier himself uses it (855) and dialogue is important in them) from which Paul is absent: the scene in the hotel kitchen when the cook, the porter, the coachman and the maids discuss why they suspect Paul of possessing some undefined power (Chapter V); the scene where Altavilla explains the power of the evil eye and asks for Alicia's hand (Chapter VI); and the scene between Alicia and her uncle where they discuss the *jettatura* (Chapter XI). Thirdly, there is the scene where Alicia, ill, awaits Paul and recalls her dream of the previous night, in which she saw her mother:

> Une tendresse mêlée de terreur faisait palpiter le sein d'Alicia. Elle voulait tendre ses bras à l'ombre, mais ses bras, lourds comme du marbre, ne pouvaient se détacher de la couche sur laquelle ils reposaient. Elle essayait de parler, mais sa langue ne bégayait que des syllabes confuses. (900)

Otherwise the interest is concentrated on Paul. As his thoughts become more anguished, the narrator shifts from psycho-narration and the 'rêves bizarres' (878) which drive him to suspect the innocent Alicia, as Olaf does Prascovie, to the direct presentation that he terms 'monologue intérieur'.[29] From Chapter VII, 'la vague terreur superstitieuse qui commençait à s'emparer de lui' (879) crystallises into specific fears; fears of what he may have caused in the past (the death of a dancer),

---

recalling Alicia's mother, are exceptional in this respect.
29. The term is used of the porter (862) as well as of Paul (908, 911).

and of what he could be doing — notably, of course, causing Alicia's illness: '"N'est-ce pas moi qui la tue?"' (883). As this 'idée fixe' (879) grips him, 'il se reprochait son amour meurtrier' (879):

> Paul d'Aspremont se sentait pénétré d'une secrète horreur; il était donc, lui chrétien, en proie aux puissances de l'enfer, et le mauvais ange regardait par ses prunelles! il semait les catastrophes, son amour donnait la mort! Un instant sa raison tourbillonna dans son cerveau, et la folie battit de ses ailes les parois intérieures de son crâne. (898)

Even scenes when he cannot see: the duel, when he is blindfolded; his recovery after blinding himself (too late, of course); his final visit to the villa, are presented largely as perceived by Paul:

> Altavilla s'élança d'un bond de tigre et rencontra le stylet de M. d'Aspremont.
> Paul toucha la pointe de son arme et la sentit mouillée... des pas incertains résonnèrent lourdement sur les dalles; un soupir oppressé se fit entendre et un corps tomba tout d'une pièce à terre.
> Pénétré d'horreur, Paul abattit le bandeau qui lui couvrait les yeux, et il vit le comte d'Altavilla pâle, immobile, étendu sur le dos [...] (905)

> Il souleva ses paupières, et [...] il eut une sensation horrible. Ses yeux s'ouvraient sur le vide, sur le noir, sur le néant, comme si, enterré vivant, il se fût réveillé de léthargie dans un cercueil. (911; see also 913)

What is the nature of the effect created by Gautier? The interest of the story lies not in the leisurely descriptions, nor in the characters who are either idealised (Paul and Alicia) or caricatural (the Commodore and the Neapolitans), but rather in moments of intensified emotion dominated by a sense of passivity and helplessness, seen from the point of view of Paul. Alicia's dream breaks with this perspective, but it too is dominated by this sense of apprehension and inability to act. The scenes when Paul is not present serve to advance the plot, and in so doing build up anticipation: the dialogue in the kitchen shows superstitious fears about Paul, and is complemented by Altavilla's explanation of the *fascino*. They also underline the fundamental ambiguity that runs through the tale: does Paul have the evil eye, or is it just a local superstition and do events all have a rational explanation?

Such an ambiguity is at the heart of the *conte fantastique*. The term was used in the first translations of E.T.A. Hoffmann to designate a tale in which inexplicable events occur in an apparently normal world. But is the *fantastique* 'une intrusion brutale du mystère dans le cadre de la vie réelle', as Pierre-Georges Castex argues?[30] Or is, as Roger Caillois suggests, the crucial element the emotion of fear or uncertainty that this provokes, in a character or in the reader, distinguishing it from the world of fairy-tale where real and supernatural happily intermingle: 'Le fantastique [...] manifeste un scandale, une déchirure, une irruption insolite, presque insupportable dans le monde réel'?[31] Does it lie, as in Tzvetan Todorov's analysis, in the consequent hesitation about how this is to be explained, as something beyond the normal laws of nature ('merveilleux'), or as something 'étrange', bizarre perhaps but natural, like a dream, a hallucination, a coincidence?[32] Any attempt to give a rigid definition to a range of works by authors with different attitudes to life is doomed to failure. Nevertheless most definitions agree on the presence in the *conte fantastique* of a tension between an everyday world where normal explanations hold sway and a different order of things, not immediately accepted by a character, or by the reader. In 'Le Roi Candaule' only rumour, dismissed by the narrator, gave credence to the powers of Gygès's ring and Nyssia's eyes, and the events of the tale can be explained rationally. In 'Avatar', equally unambiguously, Cherbonneau's magical powers have to be accepted, and no rational explanation in terms of dreams or drugs is possible: as the narrator remarks, it is a 'conte invraisemblable et pourtant réel' (840). 'Jettatura', however, sustains the ambiguity.

To guide us in our interpretation in 'Jettatura', there are two sets of voices.[33] On the one hand Altavilla and the superstitious Neapolitans warn against Paul's supernatural powers. On the other hand is Alicia:

30. Pierre-Georges Castex, *Le Conte fantastique en France de Nodier à Maupassant* (Paris: Corti, 1951), 8.
31. Roger Caillois, *Images, images...* (Paris: Corti, 1966), 15. So too Louis Vax: 'La rupture d'une constance du monde rassurant [...] ne suffit pas pour que ce monde paraisse fantastique; il faut que cette rupture entraîne une menace, et pour l'univers, et pour nous' (*La Séduction de l'étrange: étude sur la littérature fantastique* (Paris: Presses Universitaires de France, 1965), 178).
32. Tzvetan Todorov, *Introduction à la littérature fantastique* (Paris: Seuil, 1970).
33. This duality is explored by Whyte, *Gautier, conteur*, 95–98.

CHAPTER 5. PLAYING WITH THE KALEIDOSCOPE 141

'Sa foi inébranlable en ce qu'il faut croire rejetait comme des contes de nourrice toutes ces histoires mystérieuses, et se riait des préjugés populaires' (888); she thinks that Paul has succumbed to a naïve local belief only 'par une inconcevable faiblesse d'esprit' (889). The narrator, who could give a definitive verdict, is at times sceptical: when Paul reads the book on the *jettatura* that crystallises his fears, he notes that Paul is 'préparé à la *crédulité* par une foule de petits incidents' (879; my emphasis), and he refers to Paul's 'fatale monomanie' (889). But on another occasion he turns away from this sceptical view:

L'esprit humain, même le plus éclairé, garde toujours un coin sombre, où s'acroupissent les hideuses chimères de la crédulité, où s'accrochent les chauves-souris de la superstition. La vie ordinaire est si pleine de problèmes insolubles, que l'impossible y devient probable. On peut croire ou nier tout: à un certain point de vue, le rêve existe autant que la réalité. (880-1)

Later the narrator seems ready to accept either the sceptical or the supernatural interpretation of events: 'Soit que cette scène eût déterminé chez elle quelque excitation fébrile, soit que Paul exerçât réellement sur la jeune fille l'influence que redoutait le commodore' (893). Paul's own position moves from unawareness to anxiety and then a horrified conviction of his 'powers'. The reader is unable to resolve the alternative: Paul's emotional conviction is set against the ironic detachment of the English tourists, indifferent to Neapolitan superstition, who treat even violent death (the discovery of Altavilla's body at Pompeii) as local colour, 'quelque chose d'italien, de pittoresque et de romantique à raconter à nos amies' (907).[34] The brief codas have the same ambivalence. The pirouette with which they round off the chapters, and their initial focus on Neapolitans whose superstition is coupled with gullibility, reinforce sceptical detachment; but their cumulative effect is to reinforce doubts about Paul.

Why *should* the reader hesitate between supernatural and rational explanations, and not immediately conclude that Alicia is dying of tuberculosis, that the other manifestations of the evil eye are coincidences, that the Neapolitans are credulous and have ulterior motives for discrediting the foreigner? It is not that there is any firm

---

34. On the effect of detachment created, see Whyte, *Gautier, conteur*, 93-94.

evidence to support the supernatural explanation, as there is in Mérimée's 'La Vénus d'Ille'. Two features of how we react to stories are important here. After outlining the power of the *fascino* to Alicia and the Commodore, Altavilla, instead of saying that he suspects Paul, abruptly asks for Alicia's hand. The lack of transition surprises the other two: as the Commodore remarks, '"Cela ne se suit pas"' (875). The reader has heard the Neapolitans' suspicions and sees that Altavilla is trying to save Alicia from Paul. Succession makes us look for a connection that we easily find. The narrative plays on this desire by constantly stressing Paul's scowl before the minor incidents in the early chapters that arouse the locals' suspicions: the boys falling from the boat, the sudden downpour preceded by 'ce regard étrange que nous avons remarqué' (861). So when the narrator uses an ambiguous turn of phrase, such as: 'Alicia pâlissait sous le regard de Paul' (860), we are only too ready to attribute a destructive power to his gaze.

This could, of course, merely be leading us up the garden path, as Mérimée does in 'Il Vicolo di Madama Lucrezia'. But the story becomes much more coherent if Paul does have the evil eye; if he does not, Altavilla's intervention is misguided, the duel and his death unnecessary, and Paul's self-blinding and suicide a ghastly mistake. The extremes of emotion expressed in Paul's thoughts and monologues make the reader expect coherence in the narrative. But if we can see that his death becomes meaningless if he is not a *jettatore*, in what way does it become more meaningful if he does have the evil eye? When a writer constructs a *conte fantastique*, it is not just to grip us with the eeriness of an inexplicable event, but to raise a question about the real world and the individual's position in it — as in 'Le Horla'. Characteristically the *conte fantastique* points to aspects of the world and the self we cannot fully control or understand, and highlights the inadequacies of a narrow rationalism. We toy with impossible explanations not because they are literally true, but because of their symbolic potential, the way they point to things that are irrational and destabilising.

One feature that links 'Le Roi Candaule' and 'Jettatura' are the pointers to half-understood motives. The narrator revealingly refers to the love aroused in Gygès by his first sight of Nyssia — a love which he had tried to dismiss because it inspired 'une secrète terreur' (692) — as 'cet amour souterrain, accroupi au bas de l'escalier de son âme' (708).

CHAPTER 5. PLAYING WITH THE KALEIDOSCOPE

Why does Gygès stay and watch Nyssia undress? As well as the reasons he gives himself (he cannot resist his King, his sense of fatality)[35] the narrator reminds us: 'On ne peut exiger d'un capitaine de vingt-cinq ans l'austérité d'un philosophe blanchi par l'âge' (712): in other words simple sexual curiosity. Why does Gygès kill Candaule? Again the motive he gives to Nyssia, 'l'instinct de sa propre conservation' (723), contrasts with 'd'autres plus nobles dont il ne parlait pas': the opportunity to realise his dream, jealousy; and the narrator reinforces our sense of ambition and desire in Gygès when he is described as leaping on Candaule like a 'tigre', urged on by Nyssia with 'un regard si humide, si lustré, si chargé de langueurs, si plein d'enivrantes promesses' (727). For Nyssia too, the alternative she offers Gygès springs from her outraged modesty; but the narrator suggests that she had been struck by Gygès, 'le plus beau jeune homme de l'Asie', on their first encounter, before claiming that 'la vraie pensée de Nyssia' is unrecoverable (174). At the moment of the murder, her sensual gaze suggests that more is at stake than just vengeance.

When Alicia takes Paul to her retreat in the garden, she wants him to look at her: on one level this embodies her explicit disbelief in the evil eye, her refusal to be frightened by 'de viles superstitions' (887). At the same time her love for Paul is such that she wants him to look at and desire her even if this should kill her: she is consenting to die for love, and as she says to him: 'Qui sait aimer, sait mourir' (887).[36] Paul too is aware of a gap between his conscious thoughts and deeper anxieties embodied in the dream 'dont il craignait de sonder le mystère'; and before he learns of the evil eye, 'son âme [...] semblait deviner ce que sa pensée éveillée ne pouvait comprendre, et tâchait de traduire ses pressentiments en images dans la chambre noire du rêve. [...] Il tournait autour du fatal secret, fermant les yeux pour ne pas voir et les oreilles pour ne pas entendre' (878). On one level Paul and Alicia's love is pure, respectful, idealised. The evil eye seems to point to the presence in love, as in 'La Roi Candaule' and 'Avatar', of elements that are

---

35. Marie-Claude Schapira comments that he is governed by a mixture of love and jealousy, disguised under the name of fatality 'pour sa bonne conscience' (*Le Regard de Narcisse: romans et nouvelles de Théophile Gautier* (Presses Universitaires de Lyon, 1984), 34).
36. As Crouzet notes (Gautier, *L'Œuvre fantastique*, II, 378).

passionate, possessive, jealous, and destructive, which are brought out when Paul and Alicia are alone in the garden:

> Paul, éperdu, fixait sur Alicia un long regard plein de passion et d'enthousiasme. — Tout à coup la jeune fille pâlit; une douleur lancinante lui traversa le cœur comme un fer de flèche: il sembla que quelque fibre se rompait dans sa poitrine, et elle porta vivement son mouchoir à ses lèvres. (888)

On his final visit his 'regard ardent' provokes in Alicia, 'fascinée et charmée', 'une sensation voluptueusement douloureuse, agréablement mortelle' (909): a desire he seeks to punish by his self-blinding.

The world of the short story is one in which the reader is conscious of artifice. We are aware, particularly in transitions ('Laissons M. d'Aspremont dans son immobilité douloureuse et occupons-nous un peu des autres personnages de notre histoire'(911)), of the presence of a narrator, undercutting the emotional tension and bringing us back to the sense that this is a story, that we should not take it too seriously.[37] This self-consciousness is sometimes accompanied by a humour which combines remarks on the implausibility of events. In 'Avatar' self-conscious allusions to other works of literature — Cherbonneau 'avait l'air d'une figure échappée d'un conte fantastique d'Hoffmann' (778)[38] — recall that this is one too. The narrator adopts a teasing attitude towards the reader: 'C'est là qu'habitent depuis quelque temps — le lecteur l'a sans doute déjà deviné — la comtesse Prascovie Labinska et son mari' (790). He mocks the conventionally idealised nature of his characters: 'Nous n'ajoutons pas que le comte possédait les dons de l'esprit comme ceux du corps' (791). The stories, however tragic or dramatic, end on a playful tone: 'Le Roi Candaule' with a brief paragraph slyly hinting that the oracle at Delphi had responded favourably to Gygès's succession because of a substantial offering by

---

37. On this narratological presence in the 'ludic mosaics' of Gautier, see Freeman G. Henry, 'Gautier / Baudelaire: *homo ludens* versus *homo duplex*', *Nineteenth-Century French Studies*, 25 (1996-1997), 60-77; Carmen Fernandez Sanchez, 'La Dialectique de l'humour et de la mort dans les récits fantastiques de Théophile Gautier', *Bulletin de la Société Théophile Gautier*, 18 (1996), 307-23 (314).
38. Other examples are noted by Whyte, *Gautier, conteur*, 84-85.

CHAPTER 5. PLAYING WITH THE KALEIDOSCOPE 145

the new King, and 'Jettatura' with humorous evocation of what could have been presented seriously, the transformation of Alicia's comic uncle:

> Son glorieux embonpoint a disparu. Il ne met plus de rhum dans son thé, mange du bout des dents, dit à peine deux paroles en un jour, le contraste de ses favoris blancs et de sa face cramoisie n'existe plus, — le commodore est devenu pâle! (915)

All three of Gautier's stories, like many of Mérimée's, have literary sources: 'Le Roi Candaule' draws not only on Plato and Herodotus, but on other versions, such as La Fontaine's (*Contes*, I, iv), in addition to those he ironically lists when pondering Nyssia's motives: 'Quoique nous ayons consulté Hérodote, Ephestion, Platon, Dosithée, Archiloque de Paros' (724). The impetus to 'Avatar' and 'Jettatura' comes from comic tales of doubles, and from contemporary works; the evil eye is a commonplace of the *roman noir* and *roman frénétique* of the Romantic period, but is also found in the literature of the time.[39] What is striking in all three is that Gautier is using these to develop variations on the underlying triangular situation.

The leisurely narration of Gautier's stories is a reminder that short fiction does not have to be economical to be effective. But how far do 'Avatar' and 'Jettatura', which Gautier himself referred to as both *contes* and *romans*,[40] still belong to short fiction? The real issue is not their length or serialised publication; Maupassant first published several of his longer tales, such as 'L'Héritage' and 'La Petite Roque', in instalments. What makes it useful to think of Gautier's tales in the same category as stories like 'Le Horla' is their handling of structure, characterisation and theme: their focus on a single situation and its resolution; the typical simplification of Nyssia's or Paul's motivation; the antithesis of modesty and desire, of respectful love and passion; the oppositions between East and West and their attitudes to the body, embodied in Candaule and Nyssia, between the soldier Gygès and his king; oppositions between the nature of Octave and Olaf's love for

---

39. Whyte, *Gautier, conteur*, 91–92.
40. Théophile Gautier, *Correspondance générale*, edited by Claudine Lacoste-Veyseyre, 12 vols (Geneva, Droz, 1985–2000), VI (1991), 246.

Prascovie, between Neapolitan superstition and English rationality in 'Jettatura'. The very different settings — classical antiquity, aristocratic Paris, tourist Italy — are not a social environment whose complexity can be explored, in the way the historical novel and the Realist novel do, but something stylised, decorative, exotic and remote.

If Gautier repeats the same situation in all three stories, it is not because he is recycling the same material, or even showing an inability to escape his obsessions. The recurrent pattern is as a way of rearranging the same elements to develop their potential. The characters are led to moments — one often has the impression of a static tableau — where intensity of emotion is coupled with helplessness, a threat to rationality and self-control: Gygès watching Nyssia undress before the murder of Candaule when 'tout dans cette chambre, qu'il trouvait la veille si riante et si splendide, lui semblait livide, obscur et menaçant' (727); Olaf confronted by his double: 'L'époux de Prascovie, quoique intrépide comme un Slave, c'est tout dire, ressentit un effroi indicible à l'approche de ce Ménechme' (811); Paul realising that his gaze can kill: 'Il était en proie aux puissances de l'enfer [...] son amour donnait la mort' (898). This sense of a threat to autonomy, identity and control, links Gautier's three tales, whether they are *fantastique* like 'Jettatura', *merveilleux* like 'Avatar', realistically explicable like 'Le Roi Candaule', to a tale like 'Le Horla', and to the disturbing sense in French nineteenth-century short fiction that man is a prey to chance, instinct, nature, and unknowable forces.

6. Closed Worlds

Maupassant, 'Le Signe'; Balzac, 'La Grande Bretèche'; Barbey, 'A un dîner d'athées'

The 'shortness' of short fiction in nineteenth-century France can be seen as a consequence of periodical publication, although this external constraint was seldom absolute, as a longer story could be published in serial form or in a volume. From this point of view, shortness is something that imposes on the writer of short fiction certain demands, and lies behind the formulation of 'requirements' for the short story that we find in manuals for authors, urging them, for example: 'Plunge right in'; 'Trim out flab, confusion, excess verbiage'; 'Everything you put in a story had better function in the story'; 'You can leave out most explanations'.[1] It is a difficulty to be overcome, for instance by the adoption of a self-designating, high-profile narratorial presence; as we saw in 'Le Garde', the voice of a homodiegetic narrator is particularly useful in cutting away unnecessary material. Ross Chambers has characterised all narration as 'violent' in that it imposes choices. 'A tout moment, mes options narratives se substituent à d'autres options que je ne retiens pas.' It sets the vision of the narrator over other possible visions, and by chosing one focalisation excludes others.[2] Significantly, though he does not mention it, the three instances of 'violent narrative' that Chambers examines are all from short fiction.

But if it is true that 'No story is the whole story' (Ian Reid),[3] one should not forget that when one uses phrases like: 'What Maupassant

---

1. The examples are from Jean M. Fredette (ed.), *The Writer's Digest Handbook of Short Story Writing* (Cincinnati: Writer's Digest Books, 1988), II, respectively by Roy Sorrels (91), Dwight D. Swain (102), Kit Reed (160, 162).
2. Ross Chambers, 'Violence du récit: Boccace, Mérimée, Cortazar', *Canadian Review of Comparative Literature*, 13 (1986), 159–86 (159–60).
3. Quoted by Chambers, 'Violence', 186.

leaves out is as much as what Maupassant puts in',[4] the elements left out do not have a verifiable existence. In real life what 'could be said' is more than any storyteller could manage and narration does become selection and omission, guided by a reason for telling and by the desire to tell a story effectively. In fiction, and especially in short fiction, the author may seek to foster in the reader's imagination the illusion of a wider context, but needs also to block too much curiosity. When the Narrator of Maupassant's 'Mouche' says: 'Je ne vous ferai pas le portrait de mes camarades' (before briskly characterising them in a couple of lines) (II, 1170), or of his heroine: 'Je ne sais lequel de nous la baptisa "Mouche" ni pourquoi ce nom lui fut donné' (II, 1171), this could be a statement of fact (the tale has strong autobiographical elements), economy of invention, saving space or focusing our interest.

What 'does not exist' is of course also what happens *after* the story. Abrupt closure (after a surprise revelation, a sudden reversal...) avoids the need for further explanation, or rather blocks further curiosity, and can send the reader back to the events just narrated, rather than forward to subsequent events.[5] In Maupassant's 'L'Aveu' (II, 192), a young woman has to explain to her mother how she became pregnant: they are from a family of well-off farmers, but the daughter confesses that she has saved on travel expenses on her twice-weekly visits to take produce to the town by giving herself to the coachman. The ending does not look forward to the problems that her pregnancy raises: the child, the impossibility of marriage, public opinion. It concentrates on the mother's reactions, as her anger suddenly gives way to calculation: she asks how much it has cost the coachman in lost fares, and works out how much time and money can still be gained by not yet revealing the pregnancy to him. These calculations, dominated by obsessive penny-pinching, send us back to the account the daughter has just given of the

---

4. Sean O'Faolain, *The Short Story* (Dublin and Cork: Mercier Press, 1972), 149.
5. On the effect in Maupassant's 'La Parure', see Goyet, *La Nouvelle*, 51, and Reid, *Short Story*, 60–61; and for the closure that throws the reader back to the story in Maupassant generally, Armine Kotin Mortimer, *La Clôture narrative* (Paris: Corti, 1985), 140; Richard Fusco, *Maupassant and the American Short Story: the Influence of Form at the Turn of the Century* (Pennsylvania State University Press, 1994), 26–33 (the 'surprise-inversion' story).

events which led to her pregnancy. She stressed her resentment of the cost of the journey ('Il lui en coûtait beaucoup à elle, de donner chaque fois ce demi-franc pour trois kilomètres de route' — a 'cost' retrospectively charged with extra meaning, when we see what her 'savings' have cost her), attempted to secure a lower rate as a regular, and 'elle calculait aussi que dans deux années encore elle aurait payé près de cent francs'. The daughter's response to her mother in the final sentence: 'Pour sûr que j'y dirai point', reverses the other main theme of the story, the 'confession' of the title: she may have told her mother, but she will not tell the coachman. The motive of peasant guile does not resolve problems, but provides a point for the story. It also contributes to its plausibility as it coincides with a commonplace about rural avarice and calculation that had replaced as orthodoxy a sentimental and idealising view of country life:[6] an earlier story, 'Le Petit Fût' (II, 77), had been introduced in a review as showing 'avec une étonnante vérité la nature cupide et madrée de ces roués qu'on appelle "nos bons paysans"' (II, 1337). Similarly in 'Le Retour' (II, 206), a fisherman, thought lost at sea, returns after thirteen years to find his wife remarried. Maupassant does not let the reader think of the problems this will raise in this tale of displacement by a double[7] —problems that are explored in longer fictions where similar situations occur, such as Balzac's *Le Colonel Chabert* (Chabert, supposedly dead on the battlefield, returns to find his wife remarried), or Zola's *L'Assommoir* (Gervaise's first lover reappears after her marriage).[8] Rather the story is developed in terms of the family's present fear of the mysterious stranger, of a conflict between the two men. This fear gives way abruptly to reconciliation as the two men go for a drink at the café, before calling on the curé, who will 'decide'; and the potential drama is over. The innkeeper's question and the husband's reply: '"Tiens! te voilà donc Martin?" [...] "Mé vlà!"' echo the words of his daughter near the beginning when the stranger appears: '"M'man, le r'vlà!"'. The abrupt reversal of the end and the verbal echo hide what is perhaps a rather sentimental evasion and the fact that nothing has been resolved;

6. Guy Robert, *'La Terre' d'Emile Zola* (Paris: Belles Lettres, 1952), 68–91.
7. Thierry Ozwald has noted the 'omnipresence' of this theme in short fiction (*La Nouvelle*, 87).
8. Parallels noted by Forestier in Maupassant, *Contes et nouvelles*, II, 1380.

but it also leaves a sense of what Edward Sullivan termed 'resonance',[9] an element of sympathy for the characters of a short story in their struggle to cope with the tricks of chance, and for once not overwhelmed by it.

The length of the short story can be thought of not as a problem to be solved but as a potential for constructing a narrative with an emphasis on point, structure, vivid and simple thematic opposition. The recurrent features of short fiction: the intensification, the cutting short of curiosity, and the reliance on stereotype, are not so much an elimination of nuance, of wider social background, of complexity, but the creation of something that will work in the brief span of the tale. In the same way, the simple and overriding fact that the story has to end soon can become an integral part of it, in terms both of its events, and of its telling.

There are various ways in which the author can make the reader keep the end in sight, either by making us aware that the act of narrating has a built-in deadline, or by relating events which themselves have such built-in deadlines. The train, for instance, provides (as Sullivan noted) 'a natural setting for the telling of tales much as the plague in Florence did for Boccaccio', to pass the time.[10] The train journey of 'La Peur' of 1884 (II, 198) provides Maupassant with a setting for a series of brief related anecdotes. Other journeys can alert us to the fact that the time for narration is limited. In 'Au printemps' (I, 284) the Narrator is travelling on a bateau-mouche down the Seine, and has been attracted by the sight of a young woman; a stranger accosts him, and tells him a cautionary story about the dangers of love in the spring. To fulfil its function as a warning, this tale must be over, not only before the end of the journey, but also before the attractive *ouvrière* leaves the boat; and it is just finished as they arrive at Saint-Cloud (which also figures in the embedded tale), where she disembarks. Other forms of frame enable interesting links to be set up between tellers and listeners and the embedded tale, but also alert the reader to limits to the narration, and Maupassant frequently uses a number of these: the letter, as in 'Marroca' (I, 367); the after-dinner story, as in 'Le Garde' (II, 347); the will that is read aloud to the heirs, as in 'La Confession' (II, 371);

9. Sullivan, *Maupassant: the Short Stories*, 23.
10. Ibid., 17.

the brief meeting, as in 'Rencontre' (I, 440) or 'Ça ira' (II, 572); the conversation in a café, as in 'Tombouctou' (I, 923), or in the street ('Mon oncles Jules', I, 931; 'L'Odyssée d'une fille', I, 997). We know that the end of the narration is approaching; and an enclosed setting, like the coach in Barbey's 'Le Rideau cramoisi', can reinforce this sense of confinement and enclosure. An extreme case is the narrative where narrator and reader are aware that the former will be executed the next day. The narrator of 'The Black Cat' observes in the opening paragraph: 'Tomorrow I die', and in 'Carmen' José alludes to his similar fate after relating his day with Carmen in the rue du Candilejo: 'Cette journée-là! ... quand j'y pense, j'oublie celle de demain' (967).

This limiting narrative situation is of course a convention, and not just of the short story. Prévost's novel *Manon Lescaut* is presented as a tale told orally by the hero, des Grieux, to a first Narrator in an inn in Calais: we accept this narrative situation as a means enabling him to recount 'l'histoire de [sa] vie'[11] and are not troubled by the length of the story or the implausibility of the Narrator's recalling it verbatim. The after-dinner frame can be used to introduce what are in no real sense stories at all, such as Maupassant's 'Rêves' (I, 449), which is a discussion by a doctor of the effects of ether, or 'Solitude' (I, 1255), a monologue on the isolation of the individual. At the same time the frame does provide frequent occasions for effective exploitation.

The disturbing 'Moiron' (II, 984) contains a doubly embedded oral tale. The initial frame sketchily suggests a social context in which the main tale is told by M. Maloureau, a former *procureur général* under the Second Empire, as his contribution to an ongoing discussion about a recently executed triple murderer. Maloureau relates the case of the school-teacher Moiron. After the early death of his own three children, Moiron apparently transfers his affection to the schoolchildren in his charge. When several of these die inexplicably, and sweets containing crushed glass and needle fragments are found at Moiron's, he is condemned to death, although his motive remains unknown. Maloureau is persuaded by a priest who has heard Moiron's confession that he may be innocent, and appeals to the Emperor, who reprieves him. Maloureau's narrative then jumps several years. He tells how, when

---

11. Antoine-François Prévost d'Exiles, *Histoire du chevalier des Grieux et de Manon Lescaut*, edited by Jean Sgard (Paris: Flammarion, 1995), 56.

visiting Lille, he was called by a priest to the deathbed of a man who turns out to be Moiron. In a third-level oral narration, Moiron reveals both his guilt and his motive. After the death of his own children, he had come to believe that God is evil, creating men and animals merely to kill them, and to let them kill each other. Moiron had in consequence chosen to kill children too: '"Je lui ai joué le tour"', and had lied in the confession that had obtained his reprieve so that God did not triumph too soon. Moiron's death-bed confession provides a way of avoiding awkward explanations of coincidence. When Maloureau discovers who has called for him, he asks:

> Comment êtes-vous ici?
> — Ce serait trop long. Je n'a pas le temps... J'allais mourir... on m'a amené ce curé-là. (II, 988)

After the confession, Moiron says: '"Maintenant, c'est fini"': he means that his life is over; but what is 'finished' is also his account of it, and Maupassant's story, and Maloureau can say to him:

> Vous n'avez plus rien à dire?
> — Non, monsieur.
> — Alors, adieu. (II, 990)

Maloureau leaves, and comments: 'J'en avais assez.' He has learned all he had to learn from Moiron and he wished to hear no more. Maloureau is an unwilling narratee, fleeing from an intolerable truth, since Moiron's views about the sadistic cruelty of 'God' correspond to Maupassant's. It is easier to escape from Moiron's presence than from his accusatory ideas. At the same time, Moiron is clearly mad in his vengeful attempt to rival God. Maloureau presents his limited narration in the salon as one of a 'bien curieuse affaire', but the tale he tells turns out to be disturbing; Moiron's embedded narration is a death-bed confession in a claustrophobic and wretched attic room, from which Maloureau flees.

The limitation of the narrative act is a convenient device, but in itself does not have the power to make the tale any more compelling. What is more interesting is the use of a story in which the presence of an approaching deadline is central to the actual events. From his first success, 'Boule de Suif', Maupassant uses journeys both to bring often

CHAPTER 6. CLOSED WORLDS

disparate people together, and to set a limit to their encounters, and also frequently links temporal constraint to physical confinement: in 'Boule de Suif', occupied Rouen, the coach, the inn at Tostes. 'Une partie de campagne' (I, 244) begins with the sentence: 'On avait projeté depuis cinq mois d'aller déjeuner aux environs de Paris.' Title and opening seem to set up the outing as a circumscribed event with a limited cast of characters: the Dufour couple, the grandmother, the daughter and the young man. They fall into conversation over lunch with two oarsmen, and we see the interest of the mother and the daughter in the two young men. As mother and daughter are taken by the oarsmen in their separate boats to a wooded island, where both are to be seduced, they leave the husband fishing and the young man asleep, activities that will not occupy them indefinitely: when the women return, M. Dufour is sober and impatient, the young man awake, the grandmother in the carriage and wanting to leave for fear of nightfall: a whole series of external constraints close the 'partie de campagne' and the amorous interlude. The tale is rounded off by a dual coda.[12] One oarsman, Henri, enters the Dufours' shop in Paris and learns that Henriette has married the young man; then Henri subsequently encounters Henriette and her sleeping husband in the wood, a meeting which ends again as the husband wakes up. Each episode closes with a loaded phrase which underlines that the events of the *partie de campagne* are now completed. The first ends with the mother's reference to the young husband: 'C'est lui qui prend la suite'; she means: taking over the shop, but we also understand: now taking Henriette over from Henri. The second closes with the husband's 'Il est temps de nous en aller': time for them to return to Paris; but also reminding us that time has now ended Henri and Henriette's fleeting idyll.

The more rigid constraints of railway travel can limit the events of a tale just as they do narrative acts. Alain Buisine has noted how the limitation of train journeys or stops can intervene in Maupassant,[13] notably in 'Un Duel' (I, 947), where events are punctuated by the stops and starts of the train: the duel between the Prussian officer and M.

12. On this double coda, see Grojnowski, *La Nouvelle*, 154–5.
13. Alain Buisine, 'Paris-Lyon-Maupassant', in *Maupassant miroir de la nouvelle*, edited by Jacques Lecarme and Bruno Vercier (Saint-Denis: Presses Universitaires de Vincennes, 1988), 17–38. See also 'En wagon' (II, 478), 'Idylle' (I, 1193), or 'Ce cochon de Morin' (I, 641).

Dubuis is fought during a stop at a station. But other means of travel provide forms of limitation. In 'Un fils' (I, 416) a respectable Academician tells his old friend, now a Senator, of two visits to an inn in Pont-Labbé. During the first, when he was 25, he had raped a young maid; on the second, thirty years later, researching a book, he had learned that the maid had subsequently died in childbirth; his unacknowledged son is now a lame and brutish servant in the inn. The first visit had been involuntarily extended because his travelling-companion was ill; the second one is curtailed because he cannot stay longer without arousing suspicion. In both cases he is trapped, not just by instinct and the unpredictable consequences of impulse, which form the obvious point of the story, but by constraints of time and place.

Such constraints of time and place suggest a parallel with the theatre, where the dramatist has the alternative of extending the action on stage in time and space, as convention allows, or (as in French Classical tragedy) of exploiting the unities of time and place and representing a limited action in which stage time and place approximate to the real time and single place of performance. Sartre's *Huis clos* is the obvious modern example, where the action is continuous and the three characters not only cannot leave the confining space of the scene — they are trapped in a room in Hell — but even when the door unexpectedly opens and provides them with the opportunity of escape, do not want to do so: they are trapped by their mutual interdependence, just as Vladimir and Estragon have to return to the same place in the road in *En attendant Godot*. And theatre, like film, is a form where the audience, like the reader of the short story, knows the temporal limit of the experience, and is more acutely aware than the reader of the novel of its essential artificiality. There is no need for the short story writer, any more than the dramatist, to respect such limitations of time or place, and a whole life can be encompassed, as in Flaubert's 'Un Cœur simple' and 'La Légende de Saint Julien l'Hospitalier'. But to do so can powerfully reinforce their impact.

An example of Maupassant exploiting both deadlines, those of the narration of an embedded tale and of the events of that tale, and simultaneously playing on constraints of place, can be found in 'Le Signe' (II, 725), which would otherwise be little more than a slight risqué anecdote. The frame establishes the baronne de Grangerie as the narrator of the embedded tale. She calls on the marquise de Rennedon before 9 a.m., anxious to tell her friend of 'la chose horrible' she

CHAPTER 6. CLOSED WORLDS 155

experienced the day before, and finds her still in bed. The baronne's embedded narrative relates how, sitting at her window, she had noticed a woman, also at a window across the street, who was obviously 'une vilaine fille', and who was using a discreet sign (left by Maupassant to the imagination or the experience of his readers)[14] to catch the attention of men passing in the street. Once the client is 'caught', she closes the window and disappears for twelve to twenty minutes, but never longer. The baronne gives in to the temptation to imitate the sign in front of a mirror, and finally to try it out herself 'pour voir. Qu'est-ce qui peut m'arriver? rien'. Something, however, does happen, as she is successful first time: a man comes into the house, and she dashes to the door of her flat to let him in before he can ring the bell and summon a servant. Unable to persuade him that she is not what she was pretending to be, and aware that her husband is due back in half an hour ('Et voilà la pendule qui se met à sonner cinq heures; et Raoul rentre tous les jours à cinq heures et demie!'), she yields, as this is the only means of getting rid of the man within twenty minutes and without bringing him to the attention of the servants.

The baronne's character is the stereotype that we have seen so often in short fiction: she is led to make the key gesture by a combination of 'feminine' qualities: curiosity ('Je me demandais: "Comment fait-elle pour se faire comprendre si bien, si vite, complètement?"'), vanity (she is 'enchantée' by her proficiency at making the sign), attraction for the passing men ('Il y en a qui ne sont pas mal, de ces hommes qu'on rencontre dans la rue') and the tendency to imitation.[15] But these are dominated by that key motive of short fiction: the impulse of the moment: 'Et voilà que je suis prise d'une envie folle de leur faire ce signe, [...] d'une envie épouvantable, tu sais, de ces envies... auxquelles on ne peut pas résister!' (II, 727–8). The story follows a typical schema. A chance idea leads to obsession, like the idea of murder in 'The Tell-Tale Heart': 'It is impossible to say how first the idea entered my brain; but once conceived, it haunted me day and night'.[16] Impulsive action springing from that obsession then leads to

14. As Anne Marmot Raim notes, *La Communication non-verbale chez Maupassant* (Paris: Nizet, 1986), 99.
15. Maupassant noted: 'Tous les philosophes affirment que la faculté dominante de nos compagnes c'est l'imitation' (*Chroniques*, II, 113–14).
16. Poe, *Selected Writings*, 277. Similarly, the remarks in 'The Black Cat' on the

disastrous consequences disproportionate to the initial impulse, as in 'A cheval' (I, 704) or 'La Petite Roque' (II, 610), and in Mérimée's 'Le Vase étrusque' or 'Carmen'. In a pattern of entrapment often noted in Maupassant,[17] the baronne is tempted, thinks that she is in control of the situation (just as the peasant gamblers in 'Le Petit Fût' (II, 77) and 'Le Diable' (II, 769) think that they have made the best deal), but the situation turns against her. The short story, as Goyet has noted,[18] is the world of antithesis and extreme reversal; and the position of being trapped, helpless, of a private space being invaded and violated, produces the same reaction as in other tales where protagonists feels they are being taken over by an external force. Olaf, dispossessed by his double in 'Avatar' feels it as the onset of madness: 'La folie allait submerger l'obscure conscience qu'il lui restait de lui-même' (813); so does the Narrator of 'Le Horla': 'Je ne suis plus rien en moi, rien qu'un spectateur esclave et terrifié de toutes les choses que j'accomplis' (II, 929). At the moment when she saw the man enter her house, says the baronne: 'J'ai cru que j'allais devenir folle'; at the door, she tries to persuade him to leave, stammering and 'tout à fait folle' (II, 728); describing how she finally solved the situation by giving in, she says: 'J'ai perdu la tête... tout à fait' (II, 729). The baronne's initial reference to the incident as 'la chose horrible' could be read as excited female overstatement, but the phrase also corresponds to the reality of an unclassifiable occurrence (as with the use of 'la chose' to preface the tale of 'Le Garde')[19] and to a real sense of horror. The implications of the mechanisms Maupassant has set up are as pessimistic in 'Le Signe' as in his serious tales: the individual is helpless; respectability and

    'spirit of perverseness': 'Who has not, a hundred times, found himself committing a vile or silly action, for no other reason than because he knows that he should *not*?' (322).
17. It has been defined in various ways: by Louis Forestier as the 'chasseur chassé' (*Contes et nouvelles*, I, 1449), by Régis Antoine as the temptation that sets a destructive process in motion ('Structure de la tentation dans les contes cauchois de Maupassant', *Amis de Flaubert* 38 (1971), 34–36), by Mary Donaldson-Evans as reversal (*Woman's Revenge*, 17), by Micheline Besnard-Coursodon as the trap (*Etude thématique et structurale de l'œuvre de Maupassant: le piège* (Paris: Nizet, 1973), especially 213).
18. Goyet, *La Nouvelle*, 28–47.
19. See Introduction.

social distinctions collapse in the face of instinct, imprudence, and chance; loss of control threatens the individual's reason. The baronne's narrative to her friend, separated from the framing narrative by a blank line, seems to end here, with the baronne suggestively pushing the bolt on the salon door: a line is drawn, the reader/listener is excluded from what follows, but the gesture also obviously evokes sexual intercourse.[20] But neither the embedded story nor the framing story is over. As the frame resumes, we discover why she has called on her friend so early. What worries her is not what she has done, but two consequent problems: the man had left promising — or as she sees it, threatening — to return the next day; and had left two *louis* (40 francs) on the mantelpiece. The marquise's solutions: report the man to the police for harassment, and buy her husband a present, may seem respectively practical and logical. But they leave an uncomfortable impression, underlined by her final remark: 'Ça n'est que justice': the baronne would be using the law against someone innocent whom she has enticed, and making her husband the pimp that the man had earlier taken him for. Even if the heroine here seems to have escaped the 'trap', the implications of Maupassant's story are disturbingly nihilistic. Distinctions between honesty and vice, between *femme du monde* and prostitute, are shown to be arbitrary; faced by a problem, the baronne's response: 'Que faire?' is always practical, not moral. Maupassant places us in a world from which just actions and moral responses seem to have been banished; where the individual is helpless, where no one is able to take responsibility for events, which are in the control of the 'malefic mechanisms' of the author[21] and of the world as he sees it.

In what way does this apparently slight but disquieting story help us understand how an awareness of 'deadlines' can be integrated into the events narrated and into their narration? The frame has the standard

20. The bolt often figures in Maupassant's tales of seduction: the young protagonist of 'Le Verrou' (I, 488) fails to push it, with disastrous consequences; the narrator of 'Ce cochon de Morin' (I, 641) pushes it before the seduction scene, where frequent candles fulfil a similar symbolic role (I, 649, 650). One recalls obviously Fragonard's painting *Le Verrou* (in the Louvre).
21. See A.S.G. Butler, 'Maupassant's Malefic Mechanisms', *New Zealand Journal of French Studies*, 5 (1984), 5–18.

function of concentrating on the one event. The baronne's breathless narration to her friend is obviously going to be limited in length; and the place of narration, the marquise's bedroom, reinforces (as in 'Moiron') this impression of confinement. The event she recounts is limited, not only in the sense that the baronne's narrative will concern 'une chose horrible' on the previous day, but also in that constraints of place and time are key elements of the problem and its solution. Both frame and embedded narration are full of references to time and timing. Time is the element with which the baronne opens her narrative: 'Ça m'est arrivé hier dans la journée... vers quatre heures... ou quatre heures et demie. Je ne sais pas au juste.' Initially we may relate the references to the activities of the 'vilaine fille' to the suggestive atmosphere of a tale destined for *Gil Blas*: the men who 'n'ont pas le temps' to accept the invitation of the woman opposite, the timing of the visits of those that do ('Je commençais à regarder ma montre'). But the references become more insistent: the man enters the house and will ring the bell 'dans une seconde'; the baronne begs him to go as her husband will be back 'dans un instant, c'est son heure'; it is clear that events will be resolved before or with the return of the husband at 5.30. The clock strikes five. The closing in of this deadline provokes the climax of the events narrated by the panic-striken baronne, just as another deadline, the threatened return visit at the same time the next day, causes her visit to her friend. It is because she has only half an hour, and because she knows that the visits observed opposite last a maximum of twelve to twenty minutes,[22] that time, essential to her problem, becomes its solution: if she yields now, he will be gone before Raoul returns. The restriction of space, a problem in that she has let the man in and he will not leave, similarly becomes a solution when she bolts the door to exclude the servants and to '[se] débarrasser de cet homme le... le plus vite possible'.

If a sense of deadlines characterises both the baronne's narration and the events she is recalling, the frame becomes part of the embedded narrative, not just because the baronne urgently needs a solution, but in its use of space. It sets up a pattern: there is a noise outside a room whose door is closed; a visitor bursts in, with repeated references to

---

22. Maupassant had originally written 'de douze à vingt-cinq minutes' (II, 1552), perhaps a rather narrow margin to allow the visitor to withdraw safely.

CHAPTER 6. CLOSED WORLDS 159

doors and bolts, and embraces follow; then the marquise encourages the stammering baronne to tell her tale, which she does: 'Il faut que je te parle'. The embedded tale repeats this pattern: a visitor comes in (doors are opened, later bolts will be drawn), he embraces the occupier, who resists and stammers, and encourages her: 'Allons montre-moi la route'; and again the baronne yields to 'necessity': 'puisqu'il le fallait... et il le fallait, ma chère...' At this point Maupassant returns to the frame, to the marquise's laugh, appropriately 'la tête dans l'oreiller, secouant le lit tout entier'. Frame and embedded story are linked by this pattern of events and by a network of verbal links: the word *entrer* is used eight times, *la porte* five times, *la fenêtre* eight times, at first innocently when the maid opens the windows, finally in the man's coarse colloquialism: 'Faut que tu sois rudement dans la dèche en ce moment-ci pour faire la fenêtre!' The words, like the inexorable logic of time and the constraints of space, seem to lead the baronne to 'faire la fenêtre' and to the inevitable consequences of her act. The confined space of the short story becomes the ideal form for the representation of a cruel world and an impotent humanity.

The use of the framing narrative and a deadline are not the only way of exploiting positively the reader's sense that a story will end soon. It is interesting to see Flaubert, when turning from the novel to shorter fiction in *Trois Contes*, exploiting in each of them three very different ways of setting up a situation with in-built limitation, even though they were in many respects unlike most short stories in the relative unimportance of the action and in their lack of guidance towards a point.[23] In 'Hérodias' events are limited in time to the twenty-four hours between dawn at the beginning, as Hérode watches fom the terrace of his citadel, the banquet of that evening, and the brief coda the next morning when the messengers and Phanuel depart with Iaokanann's head. We are constantly reminded of spatial restriction too. Within the enclosed fortress of Machaerous there are further confining spaces, in which forces of energy and violence are contained: the cistern that serves as a prison cell for Iaokanann, the underground rooms hiding Hérode's horses.[24] The attention is focused on one individual (Hérode)

23. A.W. Raitt, 'Flaubert and the art of the short story', *Essays by Divers Hands*, N.S., 38 (1975), 112–26 (112–15).
24. This contrast is explored by Michael Issacharoff, *L'Espace et la nouvelle* (Paris: Corti, 1976), 21–27.

facing a key decision at the centre of a network of pressures. The other two stories deal with the entire life of their protagonists, but in both Flaubert finds an approach that creates a sense of limitation. 'La Légende de Saint Julien l'Hospitalier' provides a self-consciously literary variant of one of the prototypical short prose forms, the saint's life, and exploits much more overtly than the other two effects of symmetry that have been frequently noted: the contrast between the military and hunting world of Julien's father and the piety of his mother, the twin predictions of the Hermit and the Gypsy, the two hunts, the contrasting journeys undertaken by Julien (warlike and penitential), the parental castle and his palace. This sense of stylisation and patterning is strengthened by verbal echoes and a dense network of symbols. 'Un cœur simple' follows the life of the servant Félicité from her childhood. Not only is she an isolated figure, but as the tale progresses, events are increasingly presented from her limited point of view, as a person of 'no culture, no imagination, no real intelligence'.[25] As she grows deaf, 'le petit cercle de ses idées se rétrécit encore';[26] the tale closes at the moment of her death on a purely private vision of her stuffed parrot — a parrot which provides the memorable singular thing on which the emotions and the meaning of the story are increasingly focused.

In short fiction, what is important is not just a sense of spatial or temporal constraint, but the sense that this exists in a state of tension with something unrestrained or limitless. Baudelaire argued for the effectiveness of the sonnet in terms which set the limiting form against a wider vision:

> Parce que la forme est contraignante, l'idée jaillit plus intense. [...] Avez-vous observé qu'un morceau du ciel, aperçu par un soupirail, ou entre deux cheminées, deux rochers, ou par une arcade etc..., donnait une idée plus profonde de l'infini qu'un grand panorama vu du haut d'une montagne?[27]

---

25. A.W. Raitt, *Flaubert: 'Trois Contes'* (London: Grant & Cutler, 1991), 14.
26. Gustave Flaubert, *Trois contes*, edited by Édouard Maynial (Paris: Garnier, 1961), 56.
27. Charles Baudelaire, letter to Armand Fraisse, 18 February 1860, *Correspondance*, edited by Claude Pichois, 2 vols (Paris: Gallimard, 1973), I, 676.

CHAPTER 6. CLOSED WORLDS

Barbey expresses a similar idea, using the same image, but significantly the partially glimpsed 'infinite' that he wants to show is infernal rather than celestial. An unnamed Narrator is preparing his audience, in an aristocratic salon, for the tale he is to tell, 'un de ces drames cruels, terribles, qui ne se jouent pas en public, [...] une de ces *sanglantes comédies*, comme disait Pascal, mais représentées à huis clos':

> Ce qui sort de ces drames cachés, étouffés, [...] est plus sinistre, et d'un effet plus poignant sur l'imagination et sur le souvenir, que si le drame tout entier s'était déroulé sous vos yeux. Ce qu'on ne sait pas centuple l'impression de ce qu'on sait. Me trompé-je? Mais je me figure que l'enfer, vu par un soupirail, devrait être plus effrayant que si, d'un seul et planant regard, on pouvait l'embrasser tout entier. (132-3)

This 'short glimpse of hell',[28] the combination of confining form and the limitless that leaves implications resonating in the reader's mind, is at one with the recurrent emphasis in short fiction on inexplicable and violent passion, on the irrational and the impulsive, and in the *conte fantastique* on forces at work that cannot be fully explained.

As so often, this combination can be seen at its most schematic in Maupassant, with both stories and enclosing objects in them offering a glimpse of reality as Maupassant sees it.[29] Old letters from a drawer reveal the mother's past affair to her children in 'La Veillée' (I, 445); the cupboard behind the bed conceals the prostitute's son in 'L'Armoire' (II, 401); the farming couple of 'Un réveillon' (I, 336) are forced to reveal that they have put their grandfather's body in the bread-chest. In 'La Confession' (II, 371), the will reveals the respected father's responsibility for the death of his illegitimate infant son. Here Maupassant multiplies examples of enclosure: room, coffin, burial, sealed will, before the secret is let out:

> Aussitôt la cérémonie terminée, ils rentrèrent à la maison du mort, et s'étant enfermés tous trois, le fils, la fille et le gendre, ils ouvrirent le testament qui devait être décacheté par eux seuls, et seulement après que son cercueil

---

28. Byron, *Don Juan*, V, 135.
29. For the importance of containment and control in Maupassant generally, see Bryant, *Rhetoric of Pessimism*, especially Chapter V.

aurait été mis en terre. Une annotation sur l'enveloppe indiquait cette volonté.

And at the end of the story, another series of details returns to the theme of containment. The intolerable truth has been let out momentarily, but it can still be suppressed by the family: 'Les pages qui contenaient la dangereuse confession' are put in the hearth to burn, the daughter crushes the few visible words with her foot, the family watches the hearth 'comme s'ils eussent craint que le secret brûlé ne s'envolât de la cheminée'.

Two tales, by Balzac and Barbey, show how the technique that Maupassant uses schematically to reveal or repress a truth, can be exploited more elaborately. 'La Grande Bretèche' is a tale that Balzac moved from one work to another[30] without significantly altering its events or narrative structure, before finally placing it in *Autre Etude de femme*.[31] Here it forms the last of a series of stories told, in the small hours, in an aristocratic salon. It is told by Bianchon, the doctor who is one of Balzac's recurrent narrators, who grows in stature as he crosses the *Comédie humaine*, becoming the incarnation of curiosity and objective observation. It is a triangular drama, which he learned about when staying in Vendôme. During the Napoleonic wars, Madame de Merret deceives her husband with a Spanish nobleman who is a prisoner on parole in the town; her husband discovers the affair, and is responsible for the lover's death; Monsieur and Madame de Merret separate and die.

This seems to be a simple tale of passion and revenge. Balzac, however, presents the events through a series of narrators. Bianchon tells his audience not the story he has discovered, but how he discovered it. He begins with his stay in Vendôme and his fascination with an isolated and deserted house, la Grande Bretèche. The garden is neglected and overgrown and gives an impression of mystery: 'une immense énigme dont le mot n'est connu de personne' (711). The property arouses his curiosity as something that 'renfermait un secret, une pensée inconnue' (712). In stages a succession of characters reveals

---

30. See the comments by Nicole Mozet, Balzac, *Comédie humaine*, III, 662-3.
31. References in the text to 'La Grande Bretèche' are to Balzac, *Comédie humaine* (1976), III.

the secret to him. First Regnault, a notary, calls on him at his inn to warn him that he should not be going into the garden, even if it is only protected by a hedge: 'Une haie vaut un mur' (713). Regnault explains how he became the executor of Mme de Merret's will, under the terms of which la Grande Bretèche was to remain empty and untouched for fifty years, but adds two further mysteries: M. de Merret's abrupt departure for Paris, dissipation and early death, and Mme de Merret's abandonment of la Grande Bretèche for a life of seclusion. The innkeeper, Madame Lepas, is then persuaded by Bianchon to tell him of Mme de Merret's marriage and the sojourn of a handsome Spanish aristocrat, Bagos de Férédia, at her inn. Férédia behaved oddly: he came in late, was annoyed at being seen swimming in the river; he disappeared abruptly, leaving money and diamonds in a drawer; his clothes were discovered on the river bank. Finally Bianchon turns to Mme de Merret's former maid, now working at the inn, who reveals the drama behind the mysterious events. M. de Merret had returned home late from his club in town; entering his wife's room, he had suspected that someone was in the closet. She threatened to leave him if he looked; when, at his request, she swore on her crucifix that no one was inside, he had it walled up.

Bianchon's *récit* begins with the recent past, which provides a starting-point for three analepses which fill in the events at la Grande Bretèche, but not in chronological order. First, from Regnault, comes the end: Mme de Merret's death and her will, then, from Mme Lepas, her marriage, and the beginning and the aftermath of her affair with Férédia; and finally, from Rosalie, the key scene between husband and wife and the walling-up: 'Rosalie me paraissait située dans cette histoire romanesque comme la case qui se trouve au milieu d'un damier; elle était au centre même de l'intérêt et de la vérité' (723).[32] The *récit* progresses to the walling-up of the Spaniard and M. de Merret imposing silence on the wife, 'sans lui permettre de dire un seul mot' (729); it is a gradual unearthing of a secret that is seen more in terms of its dramatic and horrific consequences than as a fully developed domestic drama.

---

32. On the order of narration in 'La Grande Bretèche' and closure, see Mortimer, *Clôture narrative*, 142–50.

Bianchon reports in direct speech his conversations with Regnault and Madame Lepas, neither of whom makes any attempt to keep rigidly to the point in their narratives. The self-important Regnault is only too happy to talk about the 'bizarrerie' (714) surrounding la Grande Bretèche, describes in detail his arrival in Vendôme, and gives a graphic account of his visit to the dying Mme de Merret; Bianchon has to summarise his digressive explanations, which are 'si contradictoires, si diffuses, que je faillis m'endormir, malgré l'intérêt que je prenais à cette histoire authentique' (719). With Mme Lepas, he is obliged to interrupt 'le flux de ses paroles' (720), as what preoccupies her is the need to justify keeping the money and diamonds. But when Bianchon comes to Rosalie's account, he alters his mode of presentation, and summarises its content ('J'abrège donc'), because 'un volume entier suffirait à peine' to 'reproduire fidèlement la diffuse éloquence de Rosalie' (724), and also because we already know the beginning and end of the story. The narrative voice and focalisation change entirely. Regnault and Mme Lepas were witnesses who presented in their own words things as they discovered them, and they stressed their ignorance of key facts: why the Merrets separated, what happened to Férédia. Both have ulterior motives: Regnault's self-aggrandisement, Mme Lepas's guilt. Although Rosalie is purportedly the source of the information for the final scene, and was present or nearby for some of the events related, they are recounted as if by an omniscient narrator whose sole interest is the dramatic climax, and who can see into the minds of both M. de Merret ('Ce *non* navra M. de Merret, il n'y croyait pas; et pourtant jamais sa femme ne lui avait paru ni plus pure ni plus religieuse' (725)) and also of his wife ('Elle devina quelque malheur au seul aspect de la figure de son mari, et voulut être seule avec lui' (725)).

The information in the diffuse accounts given by Regnault and Mme Lepas in the earlier stages of the narrative intensifies the mystery that surrounds la Grande Bretèche.[33] But the understanding they offer of the main characters, whom they observed from the outside, is schematic and simplified: all we know of Merret is that he is quick-tempered ('vif') and proud, of Férédia, that he is young, handsome, and elegant; we know practically nothing of the circumstances and the nature of the

---

33. See Mortimer, *Clôture narrative*, 143.

CHAPTER 6. CLOSED WORLDS

affair between Mme de Merret and the Spaniard. What is important in the story is not social background or psychological development, but the drama of confrontation in the final scene and the glimpsed horror which is summed up effectively when the mason, walling up the closet, responds to a furtive request from Rosalie and, while M. de Merret's back is turned, cracks a pane in the door to leave a breathing hole: 'Cette action fit comprendre à madame de Merret que Rosalie avait parlé à Gorenflot. Tous trois virent alors une figure d'homme sombre et brune, des cheveux noirs, un regard de feu' (728).

This confrontation between the couple, the gap between their surface self-possession: his cold manner and orders, her calm denial that anyone is there, and their inner feelings: his jealous rage, her panic and despair, and the final explanation, all demand a narrator who knows more than any individual present at the scene. The desire for drama and understanding leads in effect to a heterodiegetic narrative giving insight into the minds of the characters. The reader accepts the paralepsis[34] whereby Bianchon knows more than Rosalie could have told him; Rosalie herself, although Bianchon's informant, figures in the scene as a participant rather than as a witness.

Representations of confinement run through this tale of illicit passion and violent revenge, linked to the themes of hiding and partial or reluctant revelation by verbal echoes (*secret, mur, clos; ouvrir, fouiller*).[35] Mme de Merret draws the sealed will which discloses her bizarre dispositions from beneath her bolster, and dies. Bianchon guesses that Mme Lepas's eyes are 'gros d'un secret' (719); when she is finally persuaded to reveal all, she claims: 'Jusqu'à présent, je n'ai point osé m'ouvrir aux gens de ce pays-ci' (720). Férédia has hidden a letter, diamonds and money in the drawer of his table which Mme Lepas finds 'à force de fouiller partout' (721); clothes are found by the river, then burned. Mme Lepas tells Bianchon that she has failed to make Rosalie talk, using an image that is by now loaded with associations: 'Cette fille-là, c'est un mur' (722). At this point, Bianchon sees in his mind's eye the house as an embodiment of enclosure:

---

34. Genette, *Figures III*, 211-13. For instances in Maupassant, see, for example, 'Le Rosier de Madame Husson' (II, 950) and 'Madame Parisse' (II, 703).
35. On this antithetical patterning of key words, see also Mortimer, *Clôture narrative*, 149.

> La Grande Bretèche et ses hautes herbes, ses fenêtres condamnées, ses ferrements rouillés, ses portes closes, ses appartements déserts, se montra tout à coup fantastiquement devant moi. J'essayai de pénétrer dans cette mystérieuse demeure en y cherchant le nœud de cette solennelle histoire, le drame qui avait tué trois personnes. (722)

He senses in Rosalie a hidden 'pensée intime': 'Son attitude annonçait un secret' (722); she tells him, but does not want the story passed on: 'Gardez-moi bien le secret' (723). The final dramatic scene takes place in Madame de Merret's ground-floor bedroom, with the central role played by the four-foot deep closet. Threats and bribes ensure the silence of Rosalie and the mason. Throughout the story we find a series of physical features: the house, the will, Férédia's drawer, the walled-up closet, which serve to enclose and to reveal. The intense emotions are only glimpsed, the eye serving as a conventional but nevertheless effective *soupirail*: the husband's 'regard de tigre' when his wife's lie about the crucifix is confirmed (729), the Spaniard's 'regard de feu' seen behind the door, Mme de Merret's 'œil hagard' when her husband proposes the oath. Their exterior otherwise remains controlled and impassive:

> Elle répéta la phrase sans se troubler. 'C'est bien', dit froidement monsieur de Merret. Après un moment de silence: 'Vous avez une bien belle chose que je ne connaissais pas, dit-il en examinant ce crucifix en ébène incrusté d'argent.' (726)

And the crucifix serves as the 'singular object' that links all three embedded narratives, plays a key role in the climax, and becomes a focus of emotion and meaning. It appears in the final sinister line of Bianchon's tale, summoning up the key moments of the story. After the walling-up of the wardrobe, M. de Merret stays close to his wife for twenty days; whenever a noise seems to come from the closet, he silences any potential appeal with the words: 'Vous avez juré sur la croix qu'il n'y avait là personne' (729).[36]

---

36. A crucifix plays a similar role in Stendhal's tale 'Le Coffre et le revenant' (published in the *Revue de Paris* in 1830) as a symbol of love between hero and heroine and as a means of identification, and the plot hinges on elements similar to 'La Grande Bretèche': a closed room, a lover hiding in a chest. But

CHAPTER 6. CLOSED WORLDS

The effectiveness of such a combination of effects can be seen in the tale that is in several respects the most extreme of Barbey's *Les Diaboliques*, 'A un dîner d'athées'. The basic situation is again triangular, with Ydow, his mistress, known as la Rosalba, and her former lover Mesnilgrand; Mesnilgrand tells their tale to his circle of friends. The events of the tale hinge on the discovery of infidelity. Ydow surprises la Rosalba writing a letter to an unnamed lover; his jealousy provokes her into disclosing her multiple lovers, that she never loved him, and that their infant son, now dead, was not his but (she alleges) Mesnilgrand's. His violent attempt to punish her is halted when Mesnilgrand emerges from the cupboard where he has been hiding and kills him. What provoked Mesnilgrand to tell this tale at the atheists' dinner is that another diner, Rançonnet, had seen him entering the confessional on the previous Sunday evening, and now challenges him to explain his surprising presence in church. Mesnilgrand reveals that he had been handing over for burial the embalmed heart of la Rosalba's child, which is, in effect, a concealed narrative prompt, as it lies behind Mesnilgrad's visit to the church.

Several features of the story are characteristic of Barbey's tales. The extreme climax inspires horror and fascination in both Mesnilgrand's audience and the reader. The settings — the atheists' dinner in the isolated provincial town, and the military milieu of Mesnilgrand's embedded tale, set during the Napoleonic campaign in Spain, — are cut off from the world, as is Mesnilgrand himself, anachronistic in his energy and misanthropy and aloof. Barbey (through Mesnilgrand's narration) repeatedly refuses to fill in details: we are left uncertain about Ydow's background, his character, whether he was a spy, even about how much he knows of la Rosalba's infidelities; all we know of la Rosalba's past is that Ydow had brought her with him from Italy. Barbey's psychology is simplified and intensified: Mesnilgrand's love echoes that of Brassard in 'Le Rideau cramoisi':[37] 'Je n'avais pas d'amour pour elle dans le sens élevé et romanesque qu'on donne à ce mot. [...] Ce fut la plus profonde des sensualités' (215). The characters are extreme and paradoxical: Ydow, impassive but inwardly possessive

the episodic development and lack of a sense of direction and control show Stendhal ill at ease in short fiction.
37. See Chapter 3, and Barbey, *Œuvres romanesques*, II, 47-48.

and violent; la Rosalba, known as la Pudica, constantly blushing but sensual, a 'monstre d'impudicité' (211) who selects her lovers, and asserts: 'Je les ai eus, [...] mais ils ne m'ont pas eue, eux!' (224), and remains 'un sphinx qui dévorait le plaisir silencieusement et gardait son secret' (217); Mesnilgrand, the cynical atheist ('Qu'ai-je à respecter?' (215)) who returns the child's heart to the priest.

The climax of the tale is a shocking scene where Ydow and la Rosalba hurl insults at each other before throwing, then stamping on the child's heart. Ydow attempts to 'seal' the promiscuous Rosalba using his sabre and the sealing-wax with which she had just closed a letter to her current lover, and Mesnilgrand, springing out from the cupboard, runs him through from behind. Short fiction of the nineteenth century abounds with acts that are literally or symbolically shocking. In Mérimée for instance, we find literal horror when Szémioth tears his bride's throat open to drink her blood in 'Lokis', or Mateo Falcone shoots his own son; but also acts that are transgressive because of their symbolic force: the fiancé in 'La Vénus d'Ille' puts his wedding ring on the statue of Venus; Iwinska humiliates Szémioth by leading him, blindfolded, to put his finger in a pot of honey (childish prank or, like the door-bolt in 'Le Signe', sexually charged symbol?). The climax of 'A un dîner d'athées' combines acts that are violent both literally and symbolically, in that they are visited on things that the characters hold sacred. The child's heart, 'ce cœur qu'il avait adoré' (225), has been kept 'pieusement' by Ydow (225); its desecration is anticipated when la Rosalba shouts at Ydow that she never loved him 'comme si elle lui eût dansé des entrechats sur le cœur' (223), and becomes literal when Mesnilgrand hears Ydow 'piétiner le cœur de l'enfant qu'il avait cru son fils' (225). It was la Rosalba's sexuality that fascinated Mesnilgrand; Ydow's brutal punishment is symbolically a refusal of her sexual autonomy, and is done with a sabre, the symbol of male authority in this military environment.

The preparation of this climax is also characteristic of Barbey in its length: the frame occupies over half of the story, and Mesnilgrand's preparation of the final scene two thirds of his narrative. This scene appears like a series of horrifying frozen moments glimpsed in succession, whose rapidity makes us overlook the implausibilities

CHAPTER 6. CLOSED WORLDS 169

(Chekhov said: 'You must give the reader no time to recover'):[38] the exchange of insults between la Rosalba and Ydow; the desecration of the heart; Ydow's act, seen by Mesnilgrand as he breaks down the cupboard door. The repeated imperfects add to the freeze-frame effect:

> Je vis... ce que je ne reverrai jamais! La Pudica, terrassée, était tombée sur la table où elle avait écrit, et le major l'y retenait d'un poignet de fer, tous voiles relevés, son beau corps à nud [sic], tordu, comme un serpent coupé, sous son étreinte [...] et il était dans l'acharnement de ce monstrueux cachetage, de cet effroyable vengeance d'amant perversement jaloux! (226)

Though the preparation may seem disproportionately long, the effect is not just to create suspense by delaying the climax, but also that of a jigsaw, as pieces are gradually assembled. The opening of the story, Mesnilgrand's visit to the church at dusk, brings in a series of objects and words that are to be taken up again in the climax. The 'sealing' of la Rosalba, 'ouverte au plaisir seule' (217), is anticipated in references to church doors, open in the evening, and to candles and wax. References to confession lead both to Mesnilgrand's 'confession' of why he went to the church, and la Rosalba's revelation of her secret to Ydow. References to sabres encompass the obvious literal uses: la Pudica is amidst men 'qui avaient toujours le sabre à la main' (214), and Rançonnet exclaims: 'Par mon sabre!' (202), and figurative uses of sabres to refer to things as varied as Mesnilgrand's rapid narrative transitions (215), his painting technique, 'sabrant la toile avec son pinceau' (181), and to the way Rançonnet clutches his glass 'comme la poignée d'un sabre' (219). La Rosalba's allegation of Mesnilgrand's paternity is 'un coup de poignard', plunged in 'comme on enfonce un couteau jusqu'à la manche' (224), prefigurant Mesnilgrand's literal act: 'Je lui plongeai mon sabre jusqu'à la garde dans le dos' (226). The final events pull together a series of words that have figured earlier,[39] reinforcing the central theme of violation and profanation, which

---

38. Quoted in Eugene Current-Garciá and Walton R. Patrick, *What is the Short Story?* (Glenview: Scott, Foresman, 1974), 21.
39. Ydow's act is also anticipated in acts of disfigurement: la Tesson scarring for life the soldier who takes liberties with her (199); the sabre wound that Sélune bears on his face, 'horrible, mais, après tout, grandiose' (205), which is evoked in terms that suggest a vulva.

connects Mesnilgrand's presence in the church, the atheists' dinner and its insistence on transgression in both food and conversation, Reniant's tale of the host scattered before the pigs, and Mesnilgrand's narrative of the desecration of the child's heart and of la Rosalba's body.

For all its length, the tale shows the convergent aesthetic of the short story. The story opens in an atmosphere of literal confinement and growing darkness: Mesnilgrand entering the chuch at nightfall, having to bend to enter through 'une petite porte basse'; the church itself has an 'aspect presque tombal' (175), and resembles a crypt; inside, the priest has retreated into the 'espèce de cellule en bois' of the confessional, where Mesnilgrand hands him an 'un objet indiscernable' (177). As a character, Mesnilgrand 'ce violent' (180), 'ce monstre de fureur' (182), embodies pent-up energies, 'endigu[ées]' by military discipline (180); after the end of the Empire, he is trapped in a world where they have no outlet, 'ses bras croisés et l'épée clouée au fourreau' (180). In his tale, Ydow intially keeps an 'attitude sobrement impassible' (214), and though Mesnilgrand thinks he sees flashes of jealousy in his eyes, 'il se contenait' (214). In the climactic scene, literal confinement plays a key role. Mesnilgrand calls on la Rosalba to find her writing a letter; she closes and seals it; Ydow is heard approaching, and she hurriedly shuts Mesnilgrand in a cupboard, where he witnesses the scene between the couple: 'Je ne les voyais pas, mais je les entendais; et les entendre, pour moi, c'était les voir' (222). Now confinement and repression give way to violence. When she refuses to reveal what is in the letter, Ydow tears it open: his act will reveal her infidelities, the parentage of 'his' child, and lead him to break the crystal vase with the embalmed heart. La Rosalba's appearance of modesty and secretiveness similarly gives way to fury and cruelty; and in turn, Mesnilgrand, controlling himself in the cupboard, breaks out to kill Ydow when he hears la Rosalba scream.

Both Mesnilgrand's tale and Barbey's framing one begin with an accumulation of reinforcing detail. This is not so much digressing, in that the material is relevant, but frustratingly stalling the key moment, like the *bavardage* of Regnault and Mme Lepas in 'La Grande Bretèche'. In a short story it may not necessarily be a good thing to get to the point as fast as possible, just as a joke can derive effect from delaying the punchline.[40] Mesnilgrand justifies his delaying tactics to the impatient Rançonnet, who cannot see the 'rapport' between Ydow and Mesnilgrand's visit to the church: 'Laissez-moi manœuvrer, comme je l'entends, mon histoire' (208). But once the secret is out, Barbey abruptly cuts the narrative short, leaving us with the key scene and its implications, rather than its consequences, just as Bianchon and Balzac do at the end of 'La Grande Bretèche'.

Barbey's tale creates, even more than Balzac's, a stylised world in which violent passions are constrained and then released to destructive effect. It is not in any sense realistic; the characters are cut off from society, lacking psychological complexity, pushed to extremes, and the events of the embedded story are abruptly and implausibly curtailed by a surprise Spanish attack, leaving Mesnilgrand (and the reader) uncertain of the final fate of la Rosalba. But within this closed world, stylisation works because of the coherent linking of motifs of control and confinement (the cupboard, the letter, the church) with a sense of passions unbounded and uncontrollable.

Constraint can work effectively in short fiction when built into the narration and the actual events narrated. It can be found in bets that must be won or lost within a deadline, plans set in motion (but these often rebound on their initiator), impulsive acts that set off an irreversible chain of events. And this constraint works most effectively when coupled with emotions and events that are boundless, undefined, or unpredictable: these are also things that the author can invoke without having to explain them in detail. We see their consequences, frequently disastrous (a life destroyed), or, even when they are comic, humiliating; the interest of the writer of short fiction lies in intensifying effect rather than exploring causes.

The tension between constraint (the limited duration of the story, or of its action, the tight control kept on details, construction, patterning) and the unbounded is often embodied in the innumerable confining rooms that figure in short fiction, from those of 'La Grande Bretèche' or the pavilion of the Narrator of Gautier's 'Omphale' to Maupassant's 'La Chambre 11' or the cell in Schwob's 'Arachné';[41] and in its

---

40. Daniel Grojnowski, 'Comique et brièveté', *La Licorne*, 21 (1991), 57–66 (58).
41. On the recurrence of the 'thème de la claustration' in particular, see Ozwald, *La Nouvelle*, 134.

recurrent boxes, courtrooms, cupboards, sealed letters, wills, and closed spaces. It is not that the choice of a confining space leads to brevity, but that our sense of the limited length of the tale is echoed in the sense of entrapment and claustrophobia. There are also comic variations: Alphonse Allais's blackly humorous 'Une mauvaise farce' tells of a wealthy prankster who hires two rather stupid masons to wall up a door — the only exit to the room they are in; the rich *rentier* of 'Le Mur' has the Prussians billeted on him in the war of 1870 walled up in the wine-cellar.[42] But the linking of closed space to destructive basic urges is more frequent. The railway compartment of Schwob's 'L'Homme voilé' (*Cœur double*) is the scene of brutal murder; in the carriage of Darcy in Mérimée's 'La Double Méprise' adultery takes place that will lead to death; in the private dining room in Villiers's 'Le Convive des dernières fêtes' an urbane guest turns out to be a madman and an executioner. In these confining spaces, elements which are antisocial and primitive break free. 'La Grande Bretèche' and 'A un dîner d'athées' represent two sides of the same coin: passion contained by an act of controlled violence, and passion unleashed; and the coda of Mesnilgrand's tale effectively closes this violent outburst as he recalls how he has returned the child's heart to the church and to burial.

42. Alphonse Allais, *Œuvres anthumes*, edited by François Caradec (Paris: Laffont, 1989), 202; *Œuvres posthumes*, edited by François Caradec (Paris: Laffont, 1990), 68-70.

Conclusion

Villiers, 'Le Convive des dernières fêtes'

Getting to grips with any text is to see what questions one can profitably ask about it. Who is talking, a character telling his own story like Don José, or one he or she has witnessed, or an external narrator like those of 'Avatar' or 'Jettatura'? To whom are they talking, and what effect does the narrative have on its audience, the audience on the tale and its telling? From whose point of view is it told, and how much does the teller let us know? 'Avatar' would be a very different tale if we had no insight into the motives of the dispossessed Olaf, as would 'Carmen' if we were sure what she really felt. Why are they talking and listening? We can usefully inquire into their motives: the archaeologist's reasons for his interest in José, José's for his confession, and into the vanity of the notary Regnault, the anxieties of the inkeeper in 'La Grande Bretèche'. We also sense the evasions or inhibitions of narrators or of narratees: Brassard's reluctance to face his past, the lawyer's censoring distaste at the arguments of the husband in 'Un cas de divorce'. What is the point of the narrative? How is it structured in terms of patterning of antithetical themes as in 'Carmen', of verbal echoes in Maupassant, and of symmetry or reversal? What elements serve to give it coherence and reinforce the meaning (and here we see the part played in the short story by the singular object that provides such a focus: 'Le Vase étrusque', the medallion in 'la Vengeance d'une femme')? The questions I have been asking of a short story are those one could ask of other types of narrative. They relate to issues of technique, rather than to plot, character, setting. Perhaps because we are always aware, in a short story, that is a tale being told (whether or not it uses a framing narrative and a homodiegetic narrator), and only for a brief period of time, and is not a slice of life into which we comfortably relax, these questions are central to our appreciation of the effect of short fiction. The essentially novelistic experience of entering a new world or of meeting new people assumes second place.

Baudelaire (talking of Gautier, but taking his cue from Poe), contrasted the freer novel, 'genre bâtard dont le domaine est sans limite', with the *nouvelle* to argue that 'la nouvelle, plus resserrée, plus condensée, jouit des bénéfices éternels de la contrainte.'[1] Constraint is not essentially a question of brevity, a limitation often imposed by publisher or newspaper editor, but lies in the controlling voice of the narrator, heterodiegetic as well as homodiegetic, taking charge of the narrative ('Or, un jour'), setting the pace, imposing an ending, bringing us back to the present. The playful narrator is also one who is in control, teasing us in Maupassant's manipulation of focalisation and ellipsis in 'La Serre', or trapping us as in Mérimée's 'Djoûmane'. Contrasting Maupassant's short stories with his novels, David Bryant has noted 'the dominant and manipulative role of the narrator'.[2] This is a characteristic of much nineteenth-century short fiction in France. A revealing example can be found in Barbey. In the course of Mesnilgrand's narration in 'A un dîner d'athées', Barbey (through Mesnilgrand) calls attention to the element of violence that can lie in abrupt transitions in narration. After characterising Major Ydow and his mistress Rosalba, Mesnilgrand is about to reveal his affair with the latter:

> Il y a des femmes qui aiment... ce n'est pas leur amant que je veux dire, quoique ce soit leur amant aussi. Les carpes regrettent leur bourbe, disait Mme de Maintenon. La Rosalba ne voulut pas regretter la sienne. Elle n'en sortit pas, et moi j'y entrai.
> — Tu coupes les transitions avec ton sabre! —fit le capitaine Mautravers.
> — Parbleu! —repartit Mesnilgrand, —qu'ai-je à respecter? (215)

The remark is reminds us that a narrative, especially in short fiction, is always an imposition of pattern and shape. But the remark is also revealing in the way that Barbey links the violence and abruptness of the narrative technique to his narrator's view of mankind. His lack of respect goes hand in hand with an attitude of defiance towards the conventional: not only is Mesnilgrand a member of the group of atheists who provocatively mock religion and the conformity of the provincial

---

1. Baudelaire, *Œuvres complètes* (ed. Le Dantec/Pichois), 691.
2. Bryant, *Rhetoric of Pessimism*, 141.

town where the story is set, but he sets himself apart from that group in so far as it falls into an unthinking orthodoxy of its own. Above all it is a reminder of the negative thrust of short fiction, of its tendency to attack, disturb, destabilise. Mesnilgrand goes on to characterise his narrative technique in opposition to that of the novelist: 'Je ne m'en vais pas vous faire des analyses à la façon d'un romancier' (215) — a remark that a twentieth-century writer of short fiction, Daniel Boulanger, echoes: 'La nouvelle n'essaie pas de comprendre, de soulager ou d'expliquer, elle viole et livre.'[3] Boulanger here links technique to a certain vision of the world: in the short story things are presented without being explained; the writer is more interested in effects that in causes.[4]

In a successful short story form and view of life are linked. In the short fiction of the nineteenth century, with all its diversity, certain points recur: the subordination of the individual to fate; the sense of time as an enemy, the tricks played by both characters and circumstances; the role of forces that cannot be pinned down, and whose consequences cannot be anticipated; the fragility of those things that represent the nineteenth century's control of the world, and the autonomy of the individual: reason, civilisation, science. Control may characterise the narrator of a tale, but it lies beyond the individual within it.

Some authors did have firm beliefs. Villiers, notably, insists on the value of the spiritual and the ideal in contrast to the narrow materialism and positivism of his age. In his short stories, however, this comes out most effectively when the ideal is only glimpsed, and in a way that serves to undercut our confidence in the significance of this world. In 'L'Intersigne' the initial frame presents a discussion between friends on 'ces coïncidences extraordinaires, stupéfiantes, mystérieuses, qui surviennent dans l'existence de quelques personnes' (695). In an embedded tale Xavier de La V*** relates how ill-health and spleen prompt him to leave Paris for the country and exercise; coincidentally he thinks of an old friend, abbé Maucombe, now a priest in Brittany whom he has not seen since before Maucombe left on a pilgrimage to

3. Daniel Boulanger, 'De la nouvelle,' *Nouvelle Revue Française* no. 265 (January, 1975), 67–73 (68).
4. The observation has been made about Mérimée by Raitt (*Prosper Mérimée*, 122), but clearly has a more general validity.

Palestine, and decides to visit him. He stays overnight with the priest: a letter from his father recalls him to Paris. On the way to the station, Maucombe lends him his old travelling coat to protect him from the rain. On his return to Paris, he learns of the death of the priest from a chill caught in the rain, and that the coat (in which Maucombe was buried) had accompanied him to Palestine '*et avait touché* LE TOMBEAU'. Xavier's narrative is unaccompanied by any commentary. It unsettling effect comes not from direct awareness of a spiritual world, but from moments (premonitions? coincidences?) when the familiar appearances of the 'real' world become unfamiliar, unstable, and suggest another reality behind, reminding Xavier, caught up in 'les affaires', that (as Maucombe remarks) 'la grande affaire, c'est le salut'. Such moments are the first sight of the priest's house at sunset, peaceful and reassuring, which unaccountably gives way (as if in a hallucination) to one dominated by images of ageing and death; the glimpse of the priest, when he accompanies Xavier to his bedroom, as 'un agonisant', no longer the healthy figure seen at supper; a dream (but is it a dream?) in which the priest offers him a travelling coat; the ominous atmosphere of the return journey to the station.

But if the world of the short story is a negative one, expressing 'a sense of alienation from dominant culture and ideology which may be frightening in its intensity' (Clare Hanson),[5] how does this square with the fact that short fiction, in the nineteenth century, is predominantly a phenomenon of periodicals seeking to entertain, rather than disconcert, its audience and masters? Florence Goyet has stressed how the *nouvelle* at its apogee between 1870 and 1925 (and she is talking of works that have stood the test of time, not just those that could be thought to pander to public taste) sets at a distance its characters, presents a world that is exotic, to provide reassurance for its readers and a sense of shared values between the author (and those reliable narrators who share his values) and the public.[6] In so far as short fiction undercuts the reader's expectation, it could be argued that it does this in ways that are metaphysical rather than social. It is true that one can see a vein of criticism of the faults of a 'bourgeois' society: for instance in Maupassant's 'Boule de Suif', of its complacency and hypocrisy; in

5. Clare Hanson, *Rereading the Short Story*, 5.
6. Goyet, *La Nouvelle*, especially 197, 219–20.

Villiers's 'Les Brigands', of its materialism, cowardice and unthinking routine, and of its egoism in both. But the essential thrust is general, striking not so much at the organisation of society, but at mankind's place in the world. This is why Sartre missed the point in his sweeping characterisation of Maupassant's use of the after-dinner frame as a means of distancing himself from society and its problems:

> La structure de ses nouvelles est preque immuable: on nous y présente d'abord l'auditoire, en général société brillante et mondaine qui s'est réunie dans un salon, à l'issue d'un dîner. [...] Tout concourt à symboliser la bourgeoisie stabilisée de la fin du siècle, qui pense que rien n'arrivera plus et qui croit à l'éternité de l'organisation capitaliste. Là-dedans, le narrateur est introduit: c'est un homme d'âge, qui a 'beaucoup vu, beaucoup lu et beaucoup retenu', un professionnel de l'expérience, médecin, militaire, artiste ou Don Juan. [...] Son cœur est calme comme la nuit; l'histoire qu'il raconte, il en est dégagé; s'il en a souffert, il a fait du miel avec sa souffrance, il se retourne sur elle et la considère en vérité, c'est-à-dire *sub specie aeternitatis*. Il y a eu trouble, c'est vrai, mais ce trouble a pris fin depuis longtemps: les acteurs sont morts ou mariés ou consolés. Ainsi l'aventure est un bref désordre qui s'est annulé. Elle est racontée du point de vue de l'expérience et de la sagesse, elle est écoutée du point de vue de l'ordre. [...] D'ailleurs y eût-il jamais trouble? L'évocation d'un brusque changement effrayerait cette société bourgeoise.[7]

There are indeed stock narrative situations that Maupassant relies on;[8] but in stories like 'Le Garde' or 'Le Bécasses', their conventional nature does not prevent them from creating interesting tensions between narrator and narratees in the frame. More often than not (and here Sartre's analysis is certainly misleading), the singular event recalled is a turning-point and has marked the narrator for life, just as much in realistic tales as in ones of *folie* that Sartre exempted from his criticism. In 'Apparition' (I, 780), the Narrator of the embedded tale, at the end of a 'soirée intime', introduces it as 'une chose étrange, tellement

7. J.-P. Sartre, *Qu'est-ce que la littérature?*, Idées (Paris: Gallimard, 1964), 172–4.
8. Discussing Sartre's criticism, Sullivan notes that such cases are in the minority; in general the frame reinforces the story (*Maupassant: the Short Stories*, 13–15).

étrange, qu'elle a été l'obsession de ma vie', so much so that he has never told it before: 'Oui, j'ai subi l'horrible épouvante, pendant dix minutes, d'une telle façon que depuis cette heure une sorte de terreur constante m'est restée dans l'âme.' In 'Un fils' (I, 418), in which a Senator tells an Academician — both, as he says, '[des] hommes dits *comme il faut*' — of his discovery of his illegitimate son: 'C'est pour moi un remords incessant, plus que cela, c'est un doute continuel, une inapaisable incertitude qui, parfois, me torture horriblement' (I, 418). Even in the essentially comic 'Nuit de Noël' (I, 695), in which Henri Templier relates how the prostitute whom he had brought home gave birth to a child after dinner, the adventure leaves an indelible mark: 'J'ai gardé une insurmontable horreur pour cette nuit stupide de gaieté imbécile', and leaves him encumbered both with the child ('Ayant payé dans le début, me voici forcé de payer jusqu'à ma mort') and with the gratitude and devotion of the mother. Indeed the turning-point that haunts a whole life becomes a predictable pattern in Maupassant. Nor is the audience untroubled: the implied silence that we noted at the end of 'Le Garde' is frequently underlined in Barbey's stories, where he insists on the disquieting effect of the embedded narratives on the social gatherings that provide a recurrent frame, expressed in the reflective silence of the audience. At the end of 'Le Dessous de cartes d'une partie de whist', 'l'émotion prolongeait le silence' (170); even the cynical atheists of 'A un dîner d'athées' are affected by Mesnilgrand's tale: 'Un silence plus expressif que toutes les réflexions leur pesait sur la bouche à tous' (228).

No doubt Maupassant's pessimism and somewhat anarchistic attitude to politics in his society[9] are conservative, but that does not prevent him writing stories that unsettle the reader. Indeed the nineteenth-century short story works as a gadfly, not weighty, not too long, not to be taken too seriously, but something that prompts us to think about our assumptions and our place in the world. To criticise Maupassant for lacking the specific social engagement that Sartre wants obscures the point that the embedded tales frequently do disturb audience, Narrator, and reader, even in a comic tale like 'Le Signe'. When we are returned to the comforting known world at the end of 'Djoûmane' or 'Il Vicolo

---

9. This comes out most clearly in his journalism; see 'Va t'asseoir!' (Maupassant, *Chroniques*, I, 274).

di Madama Lucrezia', when the baronne's panic is over and her problems solved at the end of 'Le Signe', even if Gygès finishes married and King of Lydia, the 'happy end' does not invalidate the emotions conjured up in the tales and the basic fears that they played on — a stable world giving way to an alluring but threatening nightmare, the past coming back to life, entrapment and violation, being caught up helpless in events beyond our control. And here again short fiction establishes an identity that contrasts with the stability and security of the knowable world offered by the novel.

A final example can illustrate three aspects of this apparent negativity. Villiers's 'Le Convive des dernières fêtes' appears fairly conventional, and in structural terms very similar to Maupassant's 'Promenade': in both reality is suddenly stripped of illusion to reveal a shocking truth. The story tells how a group of revellers, the Narrator and his friend C***, together with three young women whom they have joined for supper on a carnival night, discover that the urbane guest they have invited to complete their party is a madman whose obsession is participating in executions. But Villiers's account of events does not hinge on a single shock of discovery, an enigma (who is the stranger, where has the Narrator seen him before?) and its resolution. The homodiegetic Narrator relates the events of the evening, leading up to a first, partial discovery: the guest they have invited is a 'simple exécuteur' (I, 620). This is followed by the arrival of their friend Les Eglisottes, a doctor, who provides an embedded narrative; he tells of the baron's past, then offers them all a front-row view of that morning's execution, or at least of the executioner. They decline, and the narrative of the evening continues with the judgement on the stranger made by the Narrator's friend C***, and concludes with the departure of the group at the hour of the execution.

Events follow a simple chronological sequence, but our discoveries, in the series of flashbacks that punctuate the evening, do not. Before the main analepsis, Les Eglisottes's account of the past of the stranger, there have been other analepses: the Narrator's fragmentary memories of his previous meetings with 'mon inconnu de Wiesbaden' (I, 608), whom he had met in a purely social context; then the recollection, in two stages, of an earlier encounter at Lyons. The Narrator's memories form a mosaic from which he gradually builds up a fuller yet contradictory picture; they also move backwards in time, from the

recent encounter to the original one (forgotten at Wiesbaden) five or six
years previously; Les Eglisottes will take us further back still.
   Certain allusions in 'Le Convive' to real characters and events of the
1860s, such as the date, the conducting of Johann Strauss, the railway
murderer Jud, situate the events in a contemporary setting. The effect,
however, is not one of everyday reality, but of an artificial world,
peopled by women of exceptional beauty and wit, symmetrically
dressed in contrasting colours of velvet, on a carnival night when
implausible pseudonyms are accepted. All this contributes to a *récit* of
whose artifice we are very conscious, and Villiers does not seek to
disguise the impression of unreal neatness, of characters caught up in a
closed world: three women invite two men to a meal, so a third man is
invited 'pour la symétrie désirable', as Annah Jackson says (I, 609).
The frequent references to time likewise emphasise this closed world, as
well as being crucial for a short story turning on an execution at 6 a.m.,
and ending with the departure of all as this hour strikes.
   The structuring is obvious, but the implications of the discovery
about the baron are at first unclear. Can we find any formal features
that would guide us beyond the simple discovery of an indidivual's
identity? We can pick out recurrent motifs that operate both on the
literal and the metaphorical level. The most obvious of these are the
mask and madness. The story begins at the *bal de l'Opéra* with C***
and the Narrator watching 'la mosaïque tumultueuse des masques' (I,
607, recalled I, 610, 611); the girls enter and take off their masks. The
Narrator observes, referring to himself as a *convive*: 'Je portais aussi un
masque; moins apparent, voilà tout' (I, 616), in that his detached
enjoyment of the scintillating but superficial pleasures of society is only
apparent. We can link the masks with other forms of disguised identity.
C*** shrouded in cigar-smoke, like a demi-god in a cloud, recalls the
Classical divinities who appeared in disguise to mortals. The baron is
not the only one to take a false name: Antonie Chantilly's *nom de
guerre* is Yseult (I, 610); the executioner of Paris visits his café
'incognito' (I, 620). There is not just an opposition between disguised
Saturne and the others, between the baron's cruel nature and glittering
society, an incongruous juxtaposition of execution with love and
badinage. Numerous parallels are being set up between the two, in the
same way that in 'Promenade' the opposition between Leras's empty
life and the procession of lovers gave way to our awareness that
monotony and repetition linked the two. In 'Le Convive', masks, real

and metaphorical, and false names proliferate. The three women, as their pasts reveal, are not what they first seem. But at the end they resume their masks; and the baron leaves 'enveloppé d'un grand manteau noir, [...] l'air officiel' (I, 619).

A second recurrent pattern is of words evoking madness and hallucination, and these are not exclusively linked to Saturne any more than the mask is. The carnival evening is characterised as one of 'folie générale' (I, 608). The 'folies étincelantes' (I, 611) of the party's conversation and the Narrator's 'innocente manie d'observation' (I, 611) use words in a weak sense which take on full force later, when *folie, monomanie, maniaque* are applied to Saturne (I, 625-6). It is not just he, but everyone who is mad that evening. 'Est-ce que j'ai la berlue, ce soir?', says the Narrator on his first involuntary recollection of the Lyons encounter, wondering if he is going mad (I, 612). The apparently real world he perceives is constantly put into doubt. The carnival outside evokes the 'hallucinations' of nineteenth-century artists (Gavarni, Deveria, Gustave Doré). The three women belong to the world of the *fantastique*, and will vanish at dawn 'comme des visions' (I, 611). During the supper, C*** and the Narrator abandon themselves to 'le rêve' (I, 613), which magically transforms the ugly modern restaurant décor. The first memory of Lyons, though real, is presented as a vivid hallucination before being dismissed by the Narrator 'comme une sorte de perversion visuelle née de la fièvre et de la nuit' (I, 613). When Les Eglisottes begins his account, it gives 'a sensation d'un cauchemar' and prolongs the Narrator's sense that he is dreaming (I, 622). Everyone, especially the Narrator, is tempted to see the world through the distorting effect of the imagination; so can Saturne's obsession be dismissed that easily as a *perversion* that makes him different from them?

Both mask and madness suggest that several disturbing parallels exist between Saturne and the revellers. Nor does the discovery about the baron finally dissipate his mystery. The structure of the story and its gradual regression in time through successive partial revelations do not correspond to a simple pattern of unmasking. What lies beneath the surface in Saturne is not animal instinct but a warped, 'civilised' fantasy.[10] And the key issue is not who the mysterious guest is, or even

---

10. The sense of a secret hidden behind a respectable façade, of an underlying

what he is (an executioner, a madman), but *why* he is what he is. Saturne's cruelty —'les instincts d'une cruauté qui dépasse les capacités de conception connues' (I, 623) — has been stimulated by his experience of the tortures of the East, but ultimately they do not explain it. For Villiers, positivism and medical science, embodied in the figure of the doctor, prove inadequate, and can only say tautologically: 'Un fol est un fol, rien de plus' (I, 625).[11] Saturne's case is both incurable and inexplicable: Les Eglisottes refers to 'le mystère épais qui cache l'origine de son accident' (I, 622). Though the analepses take us further into Saturne's past: Wiesbaden, Lyons, the East, we never reach this origin, and at the end of the doctor's account, C*** observes: 'Vous aurez beau l'appeler fol, cela n'explique pas sa nature originelle' (I, 626).

The complex foregrounded structure undercuts the simple story of discovery and revelation; what can be read as a macabre anecdote acquires a wider meaning. The revelation of a hidden reality does not disclose something about which one can 'faire des analyses à la façon d'un romancier', and thereby control. The narrative takes us progressively back towards an origin that we never reach. At the end of the story the baron resumes his 'official' appearance, and the women put on their masks: all people have a secret, and that this secret remains ultimately unknowable.

This is a second, more disturbing, implication: the initial difference between the group and the mad baron gives way to the sense that they are linked. The parallels made through the motif of the mask and the words suggesting madness and hallucination imply complicity in the sanguinary monomania of the baron. This point is reinforced by hints in

---

reality that is not a simple instinct, but an aspect of the imagination, 'civilised' and perverted, is a recurrent theme in Villiers's other stories connected with the guillotine. See notably 'L'Etonnant Couple Moutonnet' (*Chez les passants*), 'Ce Mahoin!' and 'Les Phantasmes de M. Redoux' (*Histoires insolites*).

11. The point is made by Jean Decottignies, *Villiers le taciturne* (Presses Universitaires de Lille, 1983), 82. This is only one aspect of Villiers's criticism of science: other stories call into question its certainty (which invalidates any sacrifice of the present to the future and to 'knowledge': 'L'Héroïsme du docteur Hallidonhill') and its exploitation (the scientific fantasies in the *Contes cruels*).

the story that those present, because of their acceptance of capital punishment, cannot dissociate themselves from the the baron's *folie*, and the hypocrisy of civilisation. The 'civilised' French invented the guillotine. The issue is first raised by Les Eglisottes, and his rhetorical question about Oriental tortures functions as an embedded evaluation: 'Simple question: quel est le plus insensé de celui qui ordonne de tels supplices, ou de celui qui les exécute?' (I, 623). The idea is recalled as the clock chimes 6 a.m.: 'Voici une heure qui nous rend tous un peu complices de la folie de cet homme. [...] Ne sommes-nous pas, en ce moment même, implicitement, d'une barbarie à peu près aussi morne que la sienne?' (I, 627). A final reminder of the mask motif ('Susannah me regarda sous son masque') is coupled with a description of the setting and those present whose details evoke decapitation: the 'lueur d'acier' of Susannah's gaze, and two mentions of 'la tête'.

Thirdly, the point being made by this singular anecdote in a seemingly closed world is not about a particular group or society, but about mankind. Things and people are not what they seem: *fous* are everywhere, unnoticed. We all wear masks. The parallelisms of the story cause us to examine the secrets of the characters and by implication our own. In 'Promenade', we cannot dissociate ourselves from Maupassant's pessimistic vision of mankind. Society can complacently dismiss the logic of Leras's act of suicide, we cannot. Nor can we dissociate ourselves from Villiers's questioning of civilisation. The effectiveness of short fiction often lies in this leap from an unusual incident or character to a general and disconcerting truth implied by the way the story has been structured. When Maupassant, in 'Boule de Suif', compares an invading army to the earthquake or flood that 'déconcertent toute croyance à la justice éternelle, toute la confiance qu'on nous enseigne en la protection du ciel et la raison de l'homme' (I, 85), he is also highlighting explicitly (it is his first notable published story) a major tendency in the nineteenth-century French short story. It is as if the genre lacked confidence in its identity, reminding us now of poetry in its patterning, now of theatre with its sense of deadlines and enclosure, and of both in its inherent artificiality, reinforced by the presence of a narrating voice. But above all it situates itself as a pole of disquiet against the confident desire to explain of the nineteenth-century novel, disconcerting faith in an ordered and protected universe and in human rationality by the way the tale is told.

Glossary

This is a list of some key terms used; fuller explanations can be found in the works of the authors indicated or in Gerald Prince's invaluable *A Dictionary of Narratology*, to which I am indebted.

Abstract (Labov). The initial summary of an oral tale; answers the question: 'What is the story about?'

Actants. Characters or objects considered in terms of their role and relationships in the events narrated.

Analepsis (Genette). Discordance between order in which events occur and order in which they are related, which takes us back to the past with respect to the 'present' moment; flashback.

Aposiopesis. 'A rhetorical figure in which the speaker suddenly halts, as if unable or unwilling to proceed' (*OED*); interruption of a sentence (for instance, a threat), which the listener's imagination can complete.

Coda (Labov). In an oral tale, indicates that the narrative is over and restores the listeners to the present of narration; answers the questions: 'And since then?', 'And now?' Often marked by transition from past historic to perfect or present tense.

Complicating action (Labov). The series of events in an oral tale; answers the question: 'Then what happened?' Frequently marked by the transition from the imperfect of the **orientation** to the past historic: 'Or, voici qu'un jour il trouva.'

Diegesis (Genette). The (fictional) story world in which the situations and events narrated occur.

Embedded narrative. A narrative within a narrative, for instance a story told by a character within another story or **frame**.

Evaluation (Labov). The features of an oral tale (images, comments, interpolations), generally spread throughout the story, that guide the listener to the point; answers the question: 'So what?' These can be **embedded** (comments by characters or thoughts by the narrator at the time of events related), or **external** (added at the moment of narration).

Focalisation (Genette). The perspective in terms of which the narrated events are perceived.

Frame. A narrative serving to provide a setting for the telling of a tale.
Framed narrative. See **Embedded narrative.**
Free indirect discourse (or **free indirect speech / style indirect libre**). Reporting in indirect form of a character's speech or thoughts ('He was unhappy' representing 'I am unhappy') without explicit indication ('she said that', 'he thought that') of their status as speech or thoughts.
Hero (as opposed to **narrator**). (Genette) The character in a **homodiegetic** narrative insofar as he presents himself as living through and experiencing the events of his tale.
Heterodiegetic narrator (Genette). A narrator not part of the **diegesis** s/he presents; a 'third-person' narrator.
Histoire (Genette). The events that occur in a storyworld.
Homodiegetic narrator (Genette). A narrator who is part of the storyworld (**diegesis**) s/he presents and a character (protagonist, minor character, witness) in the events s/he recounts.
Interior monologue see *monologue intérieur*.
Iterative (narrative) (Genette). A single account of more than one event, e.g. of a series of repeated events.
Monologue intérieur (Gautier). The reporting in direct form of a character's thoughts; 'direct thought' as the counterpart to 'direct speech'.
Narratee. The person to whom a narrative is addressed, located at the same **diegetic** level as the narrator addressing him or her.
Narration (Genette). The act of narrating (e.g. by a fictional character).
Narrator (as opposed to **hero**) (Genette). The character in a **homodiegetic** narrative insofar as he looking back with hindsight on the events of his tale and his younger self.
Narrator (capitalised). An initial unnamed character telling a tale who is distinct from the author.
Orientation (Labov). The elements of an oral tale, usually near the beginning, that identify time, place, characters, and situation; answers the questions: 'When? Where? Who? Doing what?' Usually in the imperfect.
Paralepsis (Genette). Giving more information than should be available given the narrator and focalisation of the narrative.
Prolepsis (Genette). Discordance between order in which events occur and order in which they are related which takes us forward with respect to the 'present' moment; flashforward.

Psychonarration (Cohn). A heterodiegetic narrator's omniscient account of a character's thoughts or feelings.

Recipient design (Sacks). The tendency to make a story target the knowledge, ignorance, prejudices etc. of an audience.

Récit intercalé (Genette). One in which the individual sections of the narrative (*récit*) occur between the events (*histoire*) they are recording, as in the successive entries of a diary.

Récit (Genette). The account or narrative given of events (*histoire*) in the text.

Resolution (Labov). In an oral tale, concludes the complicating action; answers the question: 'So what finally happened?'

***Singulative* (narrative)** (Genette). The relating once of a single event.

Bibliography

(i) Authors of Short Fiction

References in the text are to the editions marked with an asterisk.

Allais, Alphonse. *Œuvres anthumes*, edited by François Caradec (Paris: Laffont, 1989).
____, *Œuvres posthumes*, edited by François Caradec (Paris: Laffont, 1990).
Balzac, Honoré de, *Correspondance*, edited by Roger Pierrot. 5 vols (Paris, Garnier, 1960-1969).
____, *La Comédie humaine*, edited by Pierre-Georges Castex and others. Bibliothèque de la Pléiade, 12 vols (Paris: Gallimard, 1976-1981).*
Barbey d'Aurevilly, *Œuvres romanesques complètes*, edited by Jacques Petit. 2 vols, Bibliothèque de la Pléiade (Paris: Gallimard, 1964-1965).*
____, *Les Diaboliques*, edited by Jacques Petit (Paris: Gallimard, 1973).
____, *Les Diaboliques*, edited by Michel Crouzet (Paris: Imprimerie Nationale, 1989).
Baudelaire, Charles. *Œuvres complètes*, edited by Y.G. Le Dantec, revised by Claude Pichois. Bibliothèque de la Pléiade (Paris: Gallimard, 1961).
____, *Correspondance*, edited by Claude Pichois. 2 vols (Paris: Gallimard, 1973).
Boccaccio, Giovanni. *The Decameron*, trans. by G.H. McWilliam (Harmondsworth: Penguin, 1972).
Champfleury. *Le Violon de faïence*, edited by Michael Wetherilt (Geneva: Droz, 1985).
Diderot. *Jacques le fataliste*, edited by Jacques and Anne-Marie Chouillet (Paris: Librairie Générale Française, 1983).
Flaubert, Gustave. *Trois contes*, edited by Edouard Maynial (Paris: Garnier, 1961).
Flaubert, Gustave and Guy de Maupassant. *Correspondance*, edited by Yvan Leclerc (Paris: Flammarion 1993).

Forneret, Louis. *Contes et récits*, edited by Jacques Rémi Dahan (Paris: Corti, 1994).
Gautier, Théophile. *La Morte amoureuse, Avatar et autres récits fantastiques*, edited by Jean Gaudon (Paris: Gallimard, 1981).
____, *Correspondance générale*, edited by Claudine Lacoste-Veyseyre. 12 vols (Geneva: Droz, 1985-2000).
____, *L'Œuvre fantastique*, ed. Michel Crouzet. 2 vols (Paris: Bordas, 1992).
____, *Œuvres*, edited by Paolo Tortonese (Paris: Laffont, 1995).*
Marguerite de Navarre. *L'Heptaméron* (Paris: Garnier, n.d.).
Maupassant, Guy de. *Œuvres complètes, Des vers* (Paris: Conard, 1928).
____, *Correspondance inédite*, edited by A. Artinian and E. Maynial (Paris: Wapler, 1951).
____, *Pierre et Jean*, edited by Pierre Cogny (Paris: Garnier, 1959).
____, *Chroniques*, edited by Hubert Juin. 3 vols (Paris: Union Générale d'Editions, 1980).
____, *A la feuille de rose, maison turque*, edited by Alexandre Grenier (Paris: Encre, 1984).
____, *Apparition et autres contes d'angoisse*, edited by Antonia Fonyi (Paris: Flammarion, 1987).
____, *Contes et nouvelles*, edited by Louis Forestier. 2 vols, Bibliothèque de la Pléiade (Paris: Gallimard, 1988-1989 (first edition, 1974-1979).*
____, *Choses et autres*, edited by Joseph Balsamo (Paris: Livre de poche, 1993).
Mérimée, Prosper, *Correspondance générale*, edited by Maurice Parturier. 17 vols (Paris: Divan, 1942-1947 (vols I-VI); Toulouse: Privat, 1953-1964 (vols VII-XVII)).
____, *Romans et nouvelles*, edited by Maurice Parturier. 2 vols (Paris: Garnier, 1967).
____, *Théâtre de Clara Gazul, Romans et nouvelles*, edited by Jean Mallion and Pierre Salomon. Bibliothèque de la Pléiade (Paris: Gallimard, 1978).*
____, *Carmen, et autres nouvelles choisies*, edited by M.J. Tilby (London: Harrap, 1981).
____, *Nouvelles*, edited by Michel Crouzet (Paris: Imprimerie Nationale, 1987).

Poe, Edgar Allan. *The Works of Edgar Allan Poe*, edited by John H. Ingram. 4 vols (Edinburgh: Black, 1874-1875).
_____, *Selected Works*, edited by David Galloway (Harmonsworth: Penguin, 1967).
Prévost d'Exiles, Antoine-François. *Histoire du chevalier des Grieux et de Manon Lescaut*, edited by Jean Sgard (Paris: Flammarion, 1995).
Schwob, Marcel, *Œuvres complètes*, edited by Pierre Champion. 10 vols (Paris: Bernouard, 1927-1930).
_____, *Cœur double* (Toulouse: Ombres, 1996).*
Villiers de l'Isle-Adam, *Correspondance générale*, edited by Joseph Bollery. 2 vols (Paris: Mercure de France, 1962).
_____, *Contes cruels*, edited by Pierre Citron (Paris: Garnier-Flammarion, 1980).
_____, *Œuvres complètes*, edited by Alan Raitt and Pierre-Georges Castex with Jean-Marie Bellefroid. 2 vols, Bibliothèque de la Pléiade (Paris: Gallimard, 1986).*
_____, *Contes cruels*, edited by Pierre-Georges Castex, Classiques Garnier (Paris: Bordas, 1989).
Voltaire. *Romans et contes*, edited by Henri Bénac (Paris: Garnier, 1960).

(ii) Critical Works Cited

Antoine, Régis, 'Structure de la tentation dans les contes cauchois de Maupassant', *Amis de Flaubert*, 38 (1971), 34-36.
Bal, Mieke, *Narratology* (Toronto University Press, 1985).
Bauman, Richard, *Story, Performance and Event*, Cambridge Studies in Oral and Literary Culture, 10, Cambridge University Press, 1986.
Bellenger, Claude, and others, *Histoire générale de la presse française*, 5 vols (Paris: Presses Universitaires de France, 1969-1976).
Bennett, E.K., *A History of the German 'Novelle'* (1st edition 1934; Cambridge University Press, 1938).
Berg, Christian, 'Marcel Schwob, le récit bref et l'esprit de symétrie', *La Licorne*, 21 (1981), 103-14.
Bernard, Suzanne, *Le Poème en prose de Baudelaire jusqu'à nos jours* (Paris: Nizet, 1959).
Berthier, Philippe, *Barbey d'Aurevilly et l'imagination* (Geneva: Droz, 1978).

Besnard-Coursodon, Micheline, *Etude thématique et structurale de l'œuvre de Maupassant: le piège* (Paris: Nizet, 1973).
Bonheim, Helmut, *The Narrative Modes: Techniques of the Short Story* (Cambridge: Brewer, 1982).
Boulanger, Daniel, 'De la nouvelle', *Nouvelle Revue Française*, 265 (January 1975), 67-73.
Bourget, Paul, *Nouvelle Pages de critique et de doctrine*, 2 vols (Paris: Plon, 1922).
Bowman, Frank Paul, *Prosper Mérimée: Heroism, Pessimism, and Irony* (Berkeley: University of California Press, 1962).
_____, 'La Nouvelle en 1832', *Cahiers de l'Association Internationale des Etudes Françaises*, 27 (1975), 189-208.
Brooks, Peter, 'Le Conteur: réflexions à partir de Walter Benjamin', in *Maupassant miroir de la nouvelle*, edited by Jacques Lecarme and Bruno Vercier (Saint-Denis: Presses Universitaires de Vincennes, 1988), 225-42.
Brooks, Peter, *Reading for the Plot: Design and Intention in Narrative* (Cambridge, Mass.: Harvard University Press, 1992).
Bryant, David, *The Rhetoric of Pessimism and Strategies of Containment in the Short Stories of Guy de Maupassant* (Lewiston: Mellen, 1993).
_____, *Short Fiction and the Press in France 1829-1841* (Lewiston: Mellon, 1995).
Buisine, Alain, 'Paris-Lyon-Maupassant', in *Maupassant miroir de la nouvelle*, edited by Jacques Lecarme and Bruno Vercier (Saint-Denis: Presses Universitaires de Vincennes, 1988), 17-38.
Bury, Mariane, 'Maupassant pessimiste?', *Romantisme*, 61 (1988), 75-83.
Butler, A.S.G., 'Maupassant's Malefic Mechanisms', *New Zealand Journal of French Studies*, 5 (1984), 5-18.
Caillois, Roger, *Images, images* (Paris: Corti, 1966).
Calí, Andrea, 'Histoire encadrante et histoire encadrée, ou de la réception du conte maupassantien', in *La Narration et le sens* (Lecce: Milella, 1986), 101-29.
Carter, Ronald, and Paul Simpson, 'The Sociolinguistic Analysis of Narrative', *Belfast Working Papers in Linguistics*, 6 (1982), 123-52.
Castex, Pierre-Georges, *Le Conte fantastique en France de Nodier à Maupassant* (Paris: Corti, 1951).
Cazauran, Nicole, 'Les Devisants de l'*Heptaméron* et leurs nouvelles', *Revue d'Histoire Littéraire de la France*, 96 (1996), 879-93.

Chabot, Jacques, *L'Autre Moi* (La Calade: Edisud, 1983).

Chambers, Ross, *Story and Situation: Narrative Seduction and the Power of Fiction* (Manchester University Press, 1984).

_____, 'Violence du récit: Boccace, Mérimée, Cortazar', *Canadian Review of Comparative Literature*, 13 (1986), 159-86.

Chollet, Roland, *Balzac journaliste: le tournant de 1830* (Paris: Klincksieck, 1983).

Cohn, Dorrit, *Transparent Minds: Narrative Modes for Presenting Consciousness in Fiction* (Princeton University Press, 1978).

Colin, René-Pierre. *Schopenhauer en France: un mythe naturaliste* (Lyon: Presses Universitaires, 1979).

Current-Garciá, Eugene, and Walton R. Patrick, *What is the Short Story?* (Glenview: Scott, Foresman, 1974).

Daireaux, Max, *Villiers de l'Isle-Adam* (Paris: Desclée de Brouwer, 1936).

Dällenbach, Lucien, *Le Récit spéculaire: Essai sur la mise en abyme* (Paris: Seuil, 1977).

Decottignies, Jean, *Villiers le taciturne* (Presses Universitaires de Lille, 1983).

Demers, Jeanne, and Lise Gauvin, 'Le Conte écrit, forme savante', *Etudes françaises*, 12 (1976), 3-24.

Dendale, Patrick, 'Le saura-t-il? Le malaise du lecteur dans *La Vengeance d'une femme*', *Neophilologus*, 75 (1991), 56-65.

Donaldson-Evans, Mary, 'Beginnings to understand: the narrative "Come-on" in Maupassant's stories', *Neophilologus*, 68 (1974), 37-47.

_____, *A Woman's Revenge: the Chronology of Dispossession in Maupassant's Fiction* (Lexington: French Forum, 1986).

Dubois, Claude-Gilbert, 'Métamorphoses de *Carmen*: un cas de réalisme mythologique', *Eidôlon*, 25 (October 1984), 9-62.

Dufays, Jean-Louis, '"A s'y méprendre!" ou le second coup d'œil', *Poétique*, 24 (1993), 451-61.

Dupouy, Auguste, *'Carmen' de Mérimée*. Les Grands Evénements littéraires (Paris: Malfère, 1930).

Eco, Umberto, *Lector in fabula: le rôle du lecteur*, trans. by Myriem Bouzaher (Paris: Livre de poche, 1990).

Ellis, John M., *Narration in the German Novelle: theory and interpretation* (Cambridge University Press, 1974).

Etiemble, 'Problématique de la nouvelle', in *Essais de littérature (vraiment) générale* (Paris: Gallimard, 1974), 192-208.

Fernandez Sanchez, Carmen, 'La Dialectique de l'humour et de la mort dans les récits fantastiques de Théophile Gautier', *Bulletin de la Société Théophile Gautier*, 18 (1996), 307-23.

Fonyi, Antonia, 'Nouvelle, objectivité, structure: un chapitre de l'histoire de la théorie de la nouvelle et une tentative de description structurale', *Revue de Littérature Comparée*, 50 (1970), 355-75.

____, 'Un écrivain raconte toujours la même histoire', in *Fiction, narratologie, texte, genre*, Actes du symposium de l'Association internationale de littérature comparée, vol. II, edited by Jean Bessière (New York: Lang, 1989), 89-95.

Fredette, Jean M. (ed.), *The Writer's Digest Handbook of Short Story Writing* (Cincinnati: Writer's Digest Books, 1988), II.

Friedman, Norman, 'Recent Short Story Theories', in *Short Story Theory at the Crossroads*, edited by Susan Lohafer and Jo Ellyn Clarey (Baton Rouge: Lousiana State University Press, 1989), 13-31.

Fusco, Richard, *Maupassant and the American Short Story: the Influence of Form at the Turn of the Century* (Pennsylvania State University Press, 1994).

Genette, Gérard, *Figures III* (Paris: Seuil, 1972).

George, Albert J., *Short Fiction in France 1800-1850* (New York: Syracuse University Press, 1964).

Giard, Anne, 'Le Récit lacunaire dans les *Diaboliques*', *Poétique*, 11 (1980), 39-50.

Gobert, D.L., 'Mérimée revisited', *Symposium*, 26 (1972), 128-46.

Goldsmith, Helen H., 'The Short Story encounters the prose poem: a work of Xavier Forneret', in *The French Short Story*, edited by Philip Crant. French Literature Series, II (Columbia: University of South Carolina, 1975), 77-88.

Gourevitch, Jean-Paul, *Villiers de l'Isle-Adam et l'univers de la transgression* (Paris: Seghers, 1971).

Goyet, Florence, *La Nouvelle 1870-1925: histoire d'un genre à son apogée* (Paris: Presses Universitaires de France, 1993).

Godenne, René, *La Nouvelle* (Paris: Champion, 1995).

Gratton, Johnnie and Jean-Philippe Imbert (eds), *La Nouvelle hier et aujourd'hui* (Paris: L'Harmattan, 1997).

Grojnowski, Daniel. 'Comique et brièveté', *La Licorne*, 21 (1991), 57-66.

_____, *Lire la nouvelle* (Paris: Dunod, 1993).

_____, 'De Baudelaire à Poe: l'"effet de totalité"', *Poétique*, 27 (1996), 101-109).

Haezewindt, Bernard P.R., *Guy de Maupassant: de l'anecdote au conte littéraire*. Faux Titre, 70 (Amsterdam: Rodopi, 1993).

Hainsworth, G., 'Pattern and Symbol in the Work of Maupassant', *French Studies*, 5 (1951), 1-17.

Hanson, Clare (ed.), *Re-reading the Short Story* (New York: St Martin's Press, 1989).

Henry, Freeman G., 'Gautier / Baudelaire: *homo ludens* versus *homo duplex*', *Nineteenth-Century French Studies*, 25 (1996-1997), 60-77.

Hiller, Anne, 'L'Enigme de "Djoûmane"', *Essays in French Literature*, 11 (1974), 14-34.

Hobbs, Richard (ed.), *From Balzac to Zola: Selected Short Stories* (Bristol Classical Press, 1992).

Issacharoff, Michael, *L'Espace et la nouvelle* (Paris: Corti, 1976).

Jeay, Madeleine, *Donner la parole: l'histoire-cadre dans les recueils de nouvelles du XVe-XVIe siècle* (Montréal: Ceres, 1992).

Jourde, Pierre, and Paolo Tortonese, *Visages du double: un thème littéraire* (Paris: Nathan, 1996).

Kanbar, Nabih, 'Evolution de la figure du témoin dans *Les Diaboliques*', in *Barbey d'Aurevilly cent ans après (1889-1989)*, edited by Philippe Berthier (Geneva: Droz, 1990).

Killick, Rachel, 'Mock heroics? Narrative strategy in a Maupassant war story', *Modern Language Review*, 82 (1987), 313-60.

Kunz, Josef (ed.), *Novelle* (Darmstadt: Wissenschaftliche Buchgesellschaft, 1973).

Labov, William, *Language in the Inner City. Studies in Black English Vernacular* (Oxford: Blackwell, 1972).

Labov, William, and Joshua Waletzky, 'Narrative Analysis: Oral Versions of Personal Experience', *Essays on the Visual and Verbal Arts*, edited by June Helm (Seattle and London: University of Washington Press, 1967), 12-44.

Lehman, Tuula, *Transitions savantes et dissimulées: une étude structurelle des contes et nouvelles de Guy de Maupassant* (Helsinki: Societas Scientiarum Fennica, 1990).

Leibowitz, Judith, *Narrative Purpose in the Novella* (The Hague: Mouton, 1974).

Levy, Andrew, *The Culture and the Commerce of the American Short Story* (Cambridge University Press, 1993).
Licari, Carmen, 'Le Lecteur des contes de Maupassant', *Francofonia*, 3 (1982), 91-103.
Lintveldt, Jaap, 'Pour une analyse narratologique des *Contes et nouvelles* de Guy de Maupassant', in *Fiction, narratologie, texte, genre*, edited by Jean Bessière (New York: Lang, 1989).
_____, 'La Polyphonie de l'encadrement dans les contes de Maupassant', in *Maupassant et l'écriture*, edited by Louis Forestier (Paris: Nathan, 1993), 173-85.
Lloyd, Christopher, 'Maupassant trichologue: histoires de poils', in *Maupassant conteur et romancier*, edited by C. Lloyd and R. Lethbridge (Durham: DMLS, 1994), 161-72.
Maclean, Marie, *Narrative as Performance: the Baudelairean experiment* (London and New York: Routledge, 1988).
McCormick, Diana Festa, *Les Nouvelles de Balzac* (Paris: Nizet, 1973).
Maingueneau, Dominique, *Carmen: les racines d'un mythe* (Paris: Sorbier, 1984).
Marchal, Bertrand, 'La Correspondance de Stéphane Mallarmé: compléments et suppléments, VII', *French Studies*, 50 (1996), 35-53.
Martin, Angus (ed.), *Anthologie du conte en France 1750-1799* (Paris: Union Générale d'Editions, 1981).
Martin, Henri-Jean, and Roger Chartier (eds), *Histoire de l'édition française*, 4 vols (Paris: Promodis, 1983-1986).
May, Charles E. (ed.), *Short Story Theories* (Athens: Ohio University Press, 1976).
Mihram, Danielle, '*La Partie de trictrac*, nouvelle aux résonances tragiques', *Nineteenth-Century French Studies*, 8 (1979-1980), 53-61.
Moger, Angela, 'Narrative structure in Maupassant: frames of desire', *PMLA*, 100 (1985), 315-27.
_____, 'That obscure object of narration', *Yale French Studies*, 63 (1982), 129-38.
Monfort, Bruno, 'La Nouvelle et son mode de publication: le cas américain', *Poétique*, 23 (1992), 153-71.
Mortimer, Armine Kotin, *La Clôture narrative* (Paris: Corti, 1985).
_____, 'Second Stories', in *Short Story Theory at a Crossroads*, edited by Susan Lohafer and Jo Ellyn Clarey (Baton Rouge: Louisiana State University Press, 1989), 276-98.

Mylne, Vivienne G., *Le Dialogue dans le roman français de Sorel à Sarraute* (Paris: Universitas, 1994).

O'Faolain, Sean, *The Short Story* (Dublin and Cork: Mercier Press, 1972).

Ong, Walter, *Orality and Literacy: the Technologizing of the Word* (London: Methuen, 1982).

Ozwald, Thierry, 'La Nouvelle mériméenne: entre atticisme et mutisme', *La Licorne*, 21 (1991), 91-102.

____, *La Nouvelle* (Paris: Nathan, 1996).

Paris, Jean, 'Maupassant et le contre-récit', in *Le Point aveugle* (Paris: Seuil, 1975), 135-222.

Paulin, Roger, *The Brief Compass: the Nineteenth-Century German Novelle* (Oxford: Clarendon Press, 1985).

Perez, Carmen Camero, 'Le Temps de la nouvelle', *La Licorne*, 21 (1991), 125-33.

Petit, Jacques, *Essais de lecture des 'Diaboliques' de Barbey d'Aurevilly* (Paris: Minard, 1974).

Polanyi, Livia, 'What stories tell us about their teller's world', *Poetics Today*, 2 (1981), 97-119.

____, 'The Nature of meaning in stories in conversation', *Studies in Twentieth-Century Literature*, 6 (1981-1982), 51-65.

____, 'Literary complexity in everyday storytelling', in *Spoken and Written Language: Exploring Orality and Literacy*, edited by Deborah Tanner (Norwood, New Jersey: Ablex, 1986), 155-70.

Pratt, Mary Louise, *Towards a Speech Act Theory of Literary Discourse* (Bloomington: Indiana University Press, 1997).

____, 'The Short Story: the long and the short of it', *Poetics*, 10 (1981), 175-94.

Raim, Anne Marmot, *La Communication non-verbale chez Maupassant* (Paris: Nizet, 1986).

Raitt, A.W., *Prosper Mérimée* (London: Eyre and Spottiswoode, 1970).

____, 'Flaubert and the art of the short story', *Essays by Divers Hands*, N.S., 38 (1975), 112-26.

____, *The Life of Villiers de l'Isle-Adam* (Oxford: Clarendon Press, 1981).

____, *Flaubert: 'Trois Contes'* (London: Grant & Cutler, 1991).

Raymond, Marcel, 'Histoire et poétique de la nouvelle', in *Vérité et poésie* (Neuchâtel, La Baconnière, 1964), 131-74.

Reid, Ian, *The Short Story*, The Critical Idiom, 37 (London: Methuen, 1977).
Rieger, Dietmar, 'Le *Rideau Cramoisi* von Barbey d'Aurevilly: Versuch einer tiefenpsychologischen Interpretation', *Germanisch-Romanische Monatsschrift*, 22 (1972), 176-92.
Robert, Guy, *'La Terre' d'Emile Zola* (Paris: Belles Lettres, 1952).
Rodina, Herta, 'Textual Harassment: Barbey d'Aurevilly's *Les Diaboliques*', *Nineteenth-Century French Studies*, 24 (1995-1996), 144-53.
Rogers, B.G., *The Novels and Tales of Barbey d'Aurevilly* (Geneva: Droz, 1967).
Rousset, Jean, *Le Lecteur intime* (Paris: Corti, 1986).
Ryave, Alan R., 'On the achievement of a series of stories', *Studies in the Organization of Conversational Interaction*, edited by Jim Schenkein (New York: Academic Press, 1978), 113-32.
Sachs, Murray, 'The Emergence of a Poetics', in *The French Short Story*, edited by Philip Crant. French Literature Series, II (Columbia: University of South Carolina, 1975), 139-51.
Sacks, Harvey, *Lectures on Conversation*, edited by Gail Jefferson. 2 vols (Oxford: Blackwell, 1992).
Sartre, J.-P., *Qu'est-ce que la littérature?* Idées (Paris: Gallimard, 1964).
Schapira, Charlotte, 'Maupassant et le fait divers', *Hebrew University Studies in Literature and the Arts*, 14 (1987), 23-32.
_____, 'L'Elaboration de l'histoire dans un conte de Maupassant: "Monsieur Parent"', *Studi Francesi*, 34 (1990), 43-59.
Schapira, Marie-Claude, *Le Regard de Narcisse: romans et nouvelles de Théophile Gautier* (Presses Universitaires de Lyon, 1984).
Shryock, Richard, *Tales of Story-telling: embedded narrative in modern French fiction* (New York: Lang, 1993).
Sivert, Eileen, 'Text, body and reader in Barbey d'Aurevilly's *Les Diaboliques*', *Symposium*, 31 (177), 151-64.
Schopenhauer, *Pensées et fragments*, trans. by Jean Bruneau (Geneva: Slatkine, 1979).
Smith, Barbara Herrnstein, *On the Margins of Discourse: the Relation of Literature to Language* (University of Chicago Press, 1978).
_____, 'Narrative versions, narrative theories', *Critical Inquiry*, 7 (1980-1981), 212-36.

Spoerri, Theophil, 'Mérimée and the Short Story', *Yale French Studies*, 4 (1949), 3-11.
Stanzel, F.K., *A Theory of Narrative*, trans. by Charlotte Goedsche (Cambridge University Press, 1986).
Soubias, Pierre, 'La Place de l'Afrique dans l'imaginaire de Maupassant: une lecture des Nouvelles Africaines', in *Maupassant multiple* (Toulouse: Presses Universitaires du Mirail, 1995), 29-39.
Stephens, Sonya, 'Boundaries, limits and limitations: Baudelaire's *poèmes-boutades*', *French Studies*, 52 (1998), 28-41.
Sullivan, Edward D., *Maupassant: the Short Stories* (London: Arnold, 1962).
Tedlock, Dennis, *The Spoken Word and the Work of Interpretation* (Philadelphia: University of Pennsylvania Press, 1983).
Todorov, Tzvetan, *Grammaire du Décaméron* (The Hague and Paris: Mouton, 1969).
_____, *Introduction à la littérature fantastique* (Paris: Seuil, 1970).
_____, *Poétique de la prose* (Paris: Seuil, 1971).
Todorova, Lorina, 'Observations sur la composition et le style de la nouvelle "La Partie de trictrac" de Prosper Mérimée', *Philologia*, 4 (1978), 56-61.
Trahard, Pierre, *La Jeunesse de Prosper Mérimée (1803-1834)*, 2 vols (Paris: Champion, 1925).
_____, *Prosper Mérimée et l'art de la nouvelle* (Paris: Presses Universitaires de France, 1952).
Unwin, Timothy, 'Barbey d'Aurevilly conteur: discours et narration dans *Les Diaboliques*', *Neophilologus*, 72 (1988), 353-65.
Vax, Louis, *La Séduction de l'étrange: étude sur la littérature fantastique* (Paris: Presses Universitaires de France, 1965).
Véron, Dr Louis, *Mémoires d'un bourgeois de Paris*, 6 vols (Paris: Gonet, 1853-1855).
Vial, André, *Guy de Maupassant et l'art du roman* (Paris: Nizet, 1954).
Vibert, Bertrand, *Villiers l'inquiéteur* (Toulouse: Presses Universitaires du Mirail, 1995).
Voisin, Marcel, *Le Soleil et la nuit: l'imaginaire de Théophile Gautier* (Université de Bruxelles, 1981).
Whyte, Peter, 'Gautier, Nerval et la hantise du double', *Bulletin de la Société Théophile Gautier*, 10 (1988), 17-31.

―――, *Théophile Gautier, conteur fantastique et merveilleux* (Durham, DMLS, 1996).

Williams, Roger L., *The Horror of Life* (Chicago University Press, 1980).

Ziegler, Robert, 'Escaping the mortal web of time in Marcel Schwob's "Arachné"', *Nineteenth-Century French Studies*, 24 (1995-1996), 440-446.

Index of Main Stories Discussed

Stories to which brief mention is made are not listed

Balzac
　Grande Bretèche, La, 162–6.

Barbey d'Aurevilly
　A un dîner d'athées, 167–71, 174, 175.
　Rideau cramoisi, Le, 68–72, 79, 167.
　Vengeance d'une femme, La, 87–96.

Flaubert
　Hérodias, 159–60.
　Légende de Saint Julien l'Hospitalier, La, 160.
　Un cœur simple, 160.

Gautier
　Avatar, 131–6, 145–6.
　Jettatura, 136–46.
　Roi Candaule, Le, 126–31, 142–3, 144–6.

Maupassant
　Au printemps, 150.
　Aveu, L', 148–9.
　Bécasses, Les, 24–27, 48–49.
　Boule de Suif, 55–56, 152–3, 183.
　Bûche, La, 58–59.
　Enragée? 59–60.
　Garde, Le, 13–19, 156.
　Héritage, L', 57.
　Horla, Le, 123–4, 156.
　Marroca, 99–104, 105–6.
　Moiron, 151–2.
　Mouche, 148.
　Moyen de Roger, Le, 75.
　Parure, La, 99.

Promenade, 108-11.
Remplaçant, Le, 60-62.
Retour, Le, 149.
Serre, La, 57-58.
Signe, Le, 154-59.
Un cas de divorce, 62-67.
Un duel, 153-4.
Un fils, 154.
Une partie de campagne, 152-3.

Mérimée
Ames du Purgatoire, Les, 82.
Arsène Guillot, 82.
Carmen, 28-40, 48-50.
Djoûmane, 115-19.
Partie de trictrac, Le, 80-87, 94-96.
Vase étrusque, Le, 77-78.
Vicolo di Madame Lucrezia, Il, 30-31.

Schwob
Arachné, 112-14.

Villiers de l'Isle-Adam
A s'y méprendre! 164-5.
Brigands, Les, 104-5.
Convive des dernières fêtes, Le, 172, 179-83.
Intersigne, L' 175-6.
Sombre récit, conteur plus sombre, 40-50.
Vox Populi, 107.

Lightning Source UK Ltd.
Milton Keynes UK
UKOW040201201012

200878UK00002B/8/P